THE
MEANING
OF SERVICE

THE MEANING OF SERVICE

HARRY EMERSON FOSDICK

ABINGDON PRESS
NASHVILLE

THE MEANING OF SERVICE
A Festival Book

Copyright © 1920 by
the International Committee
of Young Men's Christian Associations

All rights reserved.

Festival edition published by Abingdon Press, February 1983.

ISBN 0-687-23961-3

Special acknowledgment is gladly made to the following: to E. P. Dutton & Company for permission to use prayers from *A Chain of Prayer Across the Ages;* to the Rev. Samuel McComb and the publishers for permission to quote from *Prayers for Today,* Copyright, 1918, Harper & Brothers; to the Pilgrim Press for permission to make selections from *Prayers of the Social Awakening* by Walter Rauschenbusch and *The Original Plymouth Pulpit* by Henry Ward Beecher; to Little, Brown & Company for permission to quote one prayer from *Prayers, Ancient and Modern* by Mary W. Tilestone; to George H. Doran Company for permission to use one prayer from *Pulpit Prayers* by Alexander Maclaren; to Jarrolds (London) Ltd. for permission to make quotations from *The Communion of Prayer* by William Boyd Carpenter, Bishop of Ripon; and to Longmans, Green & Company for permission to quote from *Prayers for the City of God,* by Gilbert Clive Binyon.

The Bible Text used in this volume is taken from the American Standard Edition of the Revised Bible, copyright, 1901, by Thomas Nelson & Sons, and is used by permission.

To
FRANK SHELDON FOSDICK
My Father

who for nearly
half a century, as an
educator of youth, has illustrated
in his life the meaning
of service.

PREFACE

This little book completes a trilogy which it has long been my hope to write. *The Meaning of Prayer* is a study in the Christian's inward experience of fellowship with God; *The Meaning of Faith* is a study in the reasonable ideas on which the Christian life is based; and now *The Meaning of Service* is a study in the practical overflow of the Christian life in useful ministry.

This last book has been written at a time when its theme is most congenial with the crucial need of the world and the dominant mood of thoughtful folk. The overturn of human society in the Great War has inevitably brought to the top those elements of Christian life and thought which center about service. The task to be accomplished on earth is so immense, the cheap optimisms which once contented us are so impossible, the enemies against whom the Christian program must win its way are so formidable, and the need of unselfishness, public-mindedness, and sacrificial love is so urgent, that anyone who thinks at all about humanity's condition must think about service, its meaning, motives, and aims. I have not tried to keep these immediate and pressing conditions of our time from showing themselves in this book. One can write more timelessly about prayer and faith than he can about service. Yet I trust that I have not altogether lost the accent of those universal Christian truths and principles which make service, in any age, the indispensable expression of discipleship to the Master.

To many books and many friends, beyond the possibility of individual acknowledgment, I am indebted for the inspiration of these studies. In particular I am once more under heavy obligation to my friend and colleague, Professor George Albert Coe, Ph.D., for his careful reading of the manuscript, and to my publishers for their unfailing kindness and painstaking care in preparing it for the press.

November 1, 1920.   H.E.F.

CONTENTS

CHAPTER I

SERVICE
AND CHRISTIANITY

Daily Readings

One of the most inveterate and ruinous ideas in the history of human thought is that neither service to man nor any moral rightness whatsoever is essential to religion. In wide areas of religious life, to satisfy God has been one thing, to live in righteous and helpful human relations has been another. As Professor Rauschenbusch put it: "Religion in the past has always spent a large proportion of its force on doings that were apart from the real business of life, on sacrificing, on endless prayers, on traveling to Mecca, Jerusalem, or Rome, on kissing sacred stones, bathing in sacred rivers, climbing sacred stairs, and a thousand things that had at best only an indirect bearing on the practical social relations between men and their fellows."

The conviction that a man who is not living in just and helpful relations with his fellows by no means whatever can be on right terms with God, is one of man's greatest spiritual illuminations, the understanding of which cost long centuries of slow and painful progress out of darkness into light. Note in the daily readings some old, pre-Christian attitudes toward this matter. They are still in evidence, for even yet we have on the one side appalling human need, and on the other an immense amount of religious motive power and zeal, which are not harnessed to the problems of human welfare. *Even yet one of mankind's most insistent needs is the interpretation of religion in terms of service and the attachment of religion's enormous driving power to the tasks of service.*

11

First Week, First Day

How much of the latent moral energy of religious faith is wasted *because many people, even yet, have only a partially righteous God!* We still need to go back for instruction to a Hebrew prophet like Micah.

Wherewith shall I come before Jehovah, and bow myself before the high God? shall I come before him with burnt-offerings, with calves a year old? will Jehovah be pleased with thousands of rams, or with ten thousands of rivers of oil? shall I give my first-born for my transgression, the fruit of my body for the sin of my soul? He hath showed thee, O man, what is good; and what doth Jehovah require of thee, but to do justly, and to love kindness, and to walk humbly with thy God?—Mic. 6:6-8.

Translate that into modern terms: Wherewith shall I come before the Father of Jesus, and bow myself before the God who is love? Shall I come before him with gorgeous ceremonies, with elaborate rituals? Will the Father of all mercies be pleased with thousands of repeated credos or with ten thousands of eloquent sermons? Shall I give the bending of the knee for my transgression, the offering of my purse for the sin of my soul? He hath shewed thee, O man, what is good; and what doth the Father require of thee, but to do justly, and to love kindness, and to walk humbly with thy God? How many of us need such instruction yet in the utterly righteous character of God, and his demands on men! Raymond Lull, who, after a life of splendid usefulness, was stoned to death by Muhammadans in North Africa in 1315, urging his "sweet and reasonable appeal" for Christ, put a primary truth into worthy words: "He who would find Thee, O Lord, let him go forth to seek Thee in love, loyalty, devotion, faith, hope, justice, mercy, and truth; for in every place where these are, there art Thou."

O Father of Light and God of all Truth, purge the world from all errors, abuses, corruptions, and sins. Beat down the standard of Satan, and set up everywhere the standard of Christ. Abolish the reign of sin, and establish the kingdom of grace in all hearts; let humility triumph over pride and ambition; charity over hatred, envy, and malice; purity and temperance over lust and excess; meekness over passion; disinterestedness and poverty of spirit over covetousness and the love of this perishable world. Let the Gospel of

Christ in faith and practice prevail throughout the world.—French
Coronation Order.

First Week, Second Day

Another reason why so much of religion's driving power is
unharnessed to the tasks of service is *man's curious ability to keep
divine relationships in one compartment of life and human
relationships in another*. Are we yet beyond the reach of Isaiah's
swift and terrible indictment?

**What unto me is the multitude of your sacrifices? saith
Jehovah: I have had enough of the burnt-offerings of rams, and
the fat of fed beasts; and I delight not in the blood of bullocks, or
of lambs, or of he-goats. When ye come to appear before me, who
hath required this at your hand, to trample my courts? Bring no
more vain oblations; incense is an abomination unto me; new
moon and sabbath, the calling of assemblies,—I cannot away
with iniquity and the solemn meeting. Your new moons and your
appointed feasts my soul hateth; they are a trouble unto me; I am
weary of bearing them. And when ye spread forth your hands I
will hide mine eyes from you; yea when ye make many prayers, I
will not hear: your hands are full of blood. Wash you, make you
clean; put away the evil; learn to do well; seek justice, relieve the
oppressed, judge the fatherless, plead for the widow.—Isa.
1:11-17.**

Here are people who are religious, but their piety does not
involve goodness, nor their faith justice, nor their worship
humaneness. Their life with God has no connection with their
daily relationships; it does not make them better home-folk,
friends, neighbors, or citizens. Are not plenty of such cases in the
Christian churches? How many folk believe in God's good purpose
for mankind with the religious side of their minds, but never order
their practical ambitions as though there were such a purpose in
the world! Or with the religious part of their nature they believe
that God loves all men, while with the practical side they
themselves neglect, mistreat, and contemn men. We still need the
advice which was given to David Livingstone by an aged
Scotsman: "Now, lad, make religion the everyday business of your
life, and not a thing of fits and starts."

Lord! Our Light and our Salvation, help us, we beseech Thee, to enter into, and abide in, the secret place of the Most High; and may the shadow of the Almighty be our covering defense. Help each of us to set his love upon Thee, to bring thoughts and affections and purposes to Thyself, to think as Thou dost teach us, to love as Thou hast loved us, to do and will as Thou dost command us. So may we live in union with Thyself, and our word-worship in this place be in harmony with our consecration of life in our daily work.—Alexander Maclaren.

First Week, Third Day

Unmoral religion such as we are considering is often caused by *a preoccupying interest in the subordinate and trivial corollaries of religion*, its external expressions, its accidental accompaniments. Still the thunder of Amos is needed to clear our air!

I hate, I despise your feasts, and I will take no delight in your solemn assemblies. Yea, though ye offer me your burnt-offerings and meal-offerings, I will not accept them; neither will I regard the peace-offerings of your fat beasts. Take thou away from me the noise of thy songs; for I will not hear the melody of thy viols. But let justice roll down as waters, and righteousness as a mighty stream.—Amos 5:21-24.

How impatiently the prophet contrasts the etiquette of religious ritual with the importance of human justice! Many a man needs so to take his religion out of doors from the suffocating narrowness of small rubrics and petty rules, and to see it in terms not of "mint and anise and cummin," but of "justice and mercy and faith." Quintin Hogg poured out his life in Christian service for the poor boys of London. In a letter to one of the reclaimed lads, he wrote: "I do not care a rush what denomination you belong to, I do not very much care what special creed you profess, but I do care beyond all expression that the result of that creed in your daily life should be to make you a power for good amongst your fellowmen. . . . We hear much talk about creeds, professions of faith and the like; but I want you to remember that when God started to write a creed for us, He did it, not in words that might change their meaning, but He set before us a life, as though to teach us that whereas theology was a science which could be argued about, religion was a life and could only be lived."

Guide me, teach me, strengthen me, till I become such a person as Thou wouldst have me be; pure and gentle, truthful and high-minded, brave and able, courteous and generous, dutiful and useful.—Charles Kingsley.

First Week, Fourth Day

Still another familiar source of a religious life divorced from practical goodness and daily usefulness is the *segregation of the Church,* setting it apart from life, as though God dwelt in a temple instead of living in the struggles of humanity. So, of old time, Hosea cried:

O Ephraim, what shall I do unto thee? O Judah, what shall I do unto thee? for your goodness is as a morning cloud, and as the dew that goeth early away. Therefore have I hewed them by the prophets; I have slain them by the words of my mouth: and thy judgments are as the light that goeth forth. For I desire goodness, and not sacrifice; and the knowledge of God more than burnt-offerings.—Hos. 6:4-6.

When the Master, for service's sake, ate with the ceremonially unclean (Matt. 9:13) and again when for human helpfulness he transgressed the Sabbath rules (Matt. 12:7), and in both cases was denounced as an enemy of God, he fell back upon this passage from Hosea: "Go ye and learn what this meaneth, I desire mercy and not sacrifice." He felt as General Booth did, of whom it was said that, in comparison with the importance of helping men, "Every canon of society appeared in his eyes as the trivial and pitiful etiquette of a child's doll's house." The Master could not patiently see his Father treated as old fire-worshipers might have treated their sacred fire, keeping it aloof in their shrine and refusing it to the people to warm their houses, cook their food, and illumine their darkness. For, in Jesus' eyes, God was not primarily in church; God was in the midst of needy, sinning, aspiring, failing humanity. And religion was not professional piety. As Henry Ward Beecher said: "Religion means work. Religion means work in a dirty world. Religion means peril; blows given, but blows taken as well. Religion means transformation. The world is to be cleaned by somebody and you are not called of God if you are ashamed to scour and scrub."

Almighty God, Fountain of Life and Light, who didst raise up prophets in ancient times to warn and instruct, and whose Son Jesus Christ did send abroad into the world apostles, evangelists, pastors, and teachers, we beseech Thee to raise up in these days an increasing number of wise and faithful men, filled with the old prophetic fire and apostolic zeal, by whose labours Thy Church may be greatly blessed, and Thy Kingdom come and Thy Will be done on earth as it is in heaven.—John Hunter.

First Week, Fifth Day

Still another reason for the great quantity of religious motive power not yet belted into human service is *defective ideas of what is morally right*. Religious zeal does not necessarily argue ethical enlightenment. We are shocked to read of an ancient temple in Mexico, surrounded by 136,000 human skulls symmetrically piled; we wince at the thought of serving God, as some cults do, by murder and prostitution. But one need only read the prophets to see what a struggle it cost to be rid of such abominations in our own religious heritage. Are we yet rid of the heavy incubus of ethical blindness on religious life? Is "zeal without knowledge" a past problem? Rather Jeremiah might still hurl his invective at Christendom:

Thus saith Jehovah of hosts, the God of Israel, Amend your ways and your doings, and I will cause you to dwell in this place. Trust ye not in lying words, saying, The temple of Jehovah, the temple of Jehovah, the temple of Jehovah are these. For if ye thoroughly execute justice between a man and his neighbor; if ye oppress not the sojourner, the fatherless, and the widow, and shed not innocent blood in this place, neither walk after other gods to your own hurt: then will I cause you to dwell in this place, in the land that I gave to your fathers, from of old even for evermore.

Behold, ye trust in lying words, that cannot profit. Will ye steal, murder, and commit adultery, and swear falsely, and burn incense unto Baal, and walk after other gods that ye have not known, and come and stand before me in this house, which is called by my name, and say, We are delivered; and that he may do all these abominations? Is this house, which is called by my name, become a den of robbers in your eyes? Behold, I, even I, have seen it, saith Jehovah.—Jer. 7:3-11.

Here were people who were zealous in their religious life. Feel the ardent intensity with which they cry up "the Temple." But they had not learned that simple lesson which Dr. Wilfred Grenfell, from his practical service on the Labrador Coast, has put into wholesome words: "Whether we, our neighbor, or God is the judge, absolutely the only value of our 'religious' life to ourselves or to anyone is what it fits us for and enables us to do."

My Father and My God . . . let the fire of Thy love consume the false shows wherewith my weaker self has deceived me. Make me real as Thou art real. Inspire me with a passion for righteousness and likeness to the Man of Nazareth, that I may love as He loved, and find joy as He found His joy in being and doing good. Dwell Thou within me to give me His courage, His tenderness, His simplicity, to transform my own poor shadow-self into the likeness of His truth and strength. Amen.—Samuel McComb.

First Week, Sixth Day

And as for thee, son of man, the children of thy people talk of thee by the walls and in the doors of the houses, and speak one to another, every one to his brother, saying, Come, I pray you, and hear what is the word that cometh forth from Jehovah. And they come unto thee as the people cometh, and they sit before thee as my people, and they hear thy words, but do them not; for with their mouth they show much love, but their heart goeth after their gain. And lo, thou art unto them as a very lovely son of one that hath a pleasant voice, and can play well on an instrument; for they hear thy words, but they do them not.—Ezek. 33:30-32.

Ezekiel here has run upon unmoral religion in a common form. See how amiable the spirit of these people was, how ingratiating their manners, how ready their responsiveness! They loved to *hear about* God's will, but they did not *do* it. So aspen leaves, tremulous, sensitive, quivering, sway with agitated responsiveness in every breath of wind. Endlessly stirring, the night finds them just where they were in the morning. They move continuously but they move nowhere. Many a man's religion is *emotional responsiveness without practical issue.* He substitutes delight in hearing the Gospel for diligence in living it. He does not see that religion is "action, not diction."

17

From infirmity of purpose, from want of earnest care and interest, from the sluggishness of indolence, and the slackness of indifference, and from all spiritual deadness of heart, save us and help us, we humbly beseech Thee, O Lord.

From dullness of conscience, from feeble sense of duty, from thoughtless disregard of others, from a low ideal of the obligations of our position, and from all half-heartedness in our work, save us and help us, we humbly beseech Thee, O Lord.—Bishop Ridding.

First Week, Seventh Day

Woe unto you, scribes and Pharisees, hypocrites! for ye compass sea and land to make one proselyte; and when he is become so, ye make him twofold more a son of hell than yourselves.

Woe unto you, ye blind guides, that say, Whosoever shall swear by the temple, it is nothing; but whosoever shall swear by the gold of the temple, he is a debtor. Ye fools and blind: for which is greater, the gold, or the temple that hath sanctified the gold? And, Whosoever shall swear by the altar, it is nothing; but whosoever shall swear by the gift that is upon it, he is a debtor. Ye blind: for which is greater, the gift, or the altar that sanctifieth the gift? . . .

Woe unto you, scribes and Pharisees, hypocrites! for ye tithe mint and anise and cummin, and have left undone the weightier matters of the law, justice, and mercy, and faith: but these ye ought to have done, and not to have left the other undone. Ye blind guides, that strain out the gnat, and swallow the camel!—Matt. 23:15-19, 23, 24.

The greatest single contribution of the Hebrew prophets to human thought was their vision of the righteous nature of God and of his demands on men. Their supreme abhorrence was unmoral religion. In all our study we shall see the Master sharing their conviction, elevating it to heights they never dreamed, stating it in terms that flash and pierce and burn as theirs could not. The Master, too, hated unmoral religion. He pilloried the Pharisees in everlasting scorn. Their pettiness, their quibbling, their false emphases, their bigotry, their uncharitableness, their lack of forthright honesty, aroused his indignation. Their religion made them worse, not better; one feels that they would have been improved without it; their religion was the most unlovely thing about them. What should have made them large had made them little; what should have made them generous had made them mean. But to the Master religion meant graciousness and magnanimity, self-forgetfulness and self-denial, high purpose and deep joy in ministry, boundless brotherhood and a love balked by no ingratitude or sin. The heights of his faith in God conspired to send service pouring down to men in inexhaustible good will. He was sure that the good God can be content with nothing less than goodness in his children, and that the crown of goodness is a positive life of outgoing service to all mankind.

O Lord, grant to me so to love Thee, with all my heart, with all my mind, and with all my soul, and my neighbor for Thy sake, that the grace of charity and brotherly love may dwell in me, and all envy, harshness, and ill will may die in me; and fill my heart with feelings of love, kindness, and compassion, so that, by constantly rejoicing in the happiness and good success of others, by sympathizing with them in their sorrows, and putting away all harsh judgments and envious thoughts, I may follow Thee, who art Thyself the true and perfect Love. Amen.

COMMENT FOR THE WEEK

I

No one can doubt the central place which service held in the life and teaching of the Master. Consider the parable of the good Samaritan (Luke 10:30-37), or that other more solemn utterance, where the standing of the dead before the throne of God depended on whether they had fed the hungry, clothed the naked, given drink to the thirsty, and visited the imprisoned and sick (Matt. 25:31-46). Consider the sayings, sparks from the anvil where he hammered out the purpose of his life: "The Son of man came not to be ministered unto, but to minister, and to give his life a ransom for many" (Matt. 20:28); "He that is greatest among you shall be your servant" (Matt. 23:11); "I am in the midst of you as he that serveth" (Luke 22:27). Consider even more his life itself. In devoted love to individuals, so that, with the whole Kingdom of God upon his heart, he yet poured out his care on a blind Bartimeus, or a discouraged prodigal, or an evilly entreated widow crying for her rights; in the revealing of great truths that bless and redeem human life; in the starting of a movement that with all its faults has flowed like a river down from Nazareth to revive man's character; in the possession of a radiant spirit that throws out light on every side as naturally as the sun shines, so that his very personality has been man's greatest benediction; in that ultimate test of service, vicarious sacrifice, that gives up life itself for the sake of others; everywhere one sees that the characteristic expression of the Master's spirit was ministry. Nor was this ministry expended first upon the amiable and the great. Who can read Rabindranath Tagore's lines and not think of Jesus?

Here is thy footstool and there rest thy feet where live the poorest and lowliest and lost.

When I try to bow to thee, my obeisance cannot reach down to the depth where thy feet rest among the poorest and lowliest and lost.

Pride can never approach to where thou walkest in the clothes of the humble among the poorest and lowliest and lost.

My heart can never find its way to where thou keepest company with the companionless among the poorest, the lowliest, and the lost.

Surely there is little use in any man's calling himself the disciple of such a Master if he does not possess the spirit and know the meaning of service.

It is evident, however, that plenty of professed Christians have not interpreted their religion in such terms as these. Consider those social evils—war, poverty, disease, ignorance, vice—the endless tragedy of which is the commonplace of the modern world! One sees that, with one third of the population of the globe nominally Christian, there must have been some misunderstanding as to what Christianity is all about to allow so many professed disciples of Jesus to live side by side for so long a time with such dire need. Christianity has been content, in wide areas of its life, with some other interpretation of its own meaning than that which at first kindled the passion for service in the hearts of its disciples and sent them out from the shadow of the Cross, the spirit of the Cross within them. "I promise you," cried Hugh Latimer, preaching in Cambridge in 1529, "if you build one hundred churches, give as much as you can make to gilding of saints and honouring of the Church; and if thou go on as many pilgrimages as thy body can well suffer and offer as great candles as oaks; if thou leave the works of mercy and the commandments undone, these works shall nothing avail thee. . . . If you list to gild and paint Christ in your churches and honour Him in vestments, see that before your eyes the poor people die not for lack of meat, drink, and clothing." One catches there the authentic accent of the Christian spirit. Surely our world would be a far more decent and fraternal place if such an interpretation of the will of Christ in terms of practical service had been deeply apprehended and faithfully obeyed by the great body of his professed disciples.

At the beginning of our study, therefore, we well may examine some of the partial and perverted ways in which we Christians are tempted to misconceive our faith and so to mistake the message of the Master.

II

For one thing, Christianity to many people who profess it is no more than a formality. It is one of life's descent conventions. They were taught it in youth; they have never doubted its theoretical validity; they perceive that its profession is a mark of respectability; and they would no more be thought atheists than anarchists. But Christ's love for all sorts and conditions of men has never become the daily motive of their lives, and Christ's sacrificial faith in the possibility of a redeemed earth has never captured their imagination and their purpose.

The story of the religious experience of too many folk runs like this: they take the heavy lumber of their lives and build the secular dwelling in which habitually they abide; there they live and move and have their being in family and social life, in business and politics and sports; but because religion is a part of every conventionally well-furnished life they build as well, with what lumber may remain, an appended shrine, and there at times they slip away and pay their respects to the Almighty. Their religion is an isolated and uninfluential afterthought. Especially on Sundays when the banks are shut, the shops are closed, the rush of life is still, and finer forces stir within them, they go in company with their fellows to the church for formal worship. And when it is over they close the door on that experience and go back to their ordinary life again. So Bliss Carman sings:

They're praising God on Sunday.
They'll be all right on Monday.
It's just a little habit they've acquired.

When, in the midst of their customary lives, this isolated religious experience rises in their memory, it seems vague, unreal, like a sonata of Beethoven heard long ago or a poem once listened to and half remembered. They recall it as one thinks of his summer home beside the sea, when in the galloping turmoil of the city a chance recollection strays to it. It is a long way off in another kind of world.

So flying fish live in the sea; that is their native and habitual realm, but once in a while they make a brief excursion into the upper air and glisten for an instant in the sun—only to fall back into the sea again. To how many people is religion such a brief, occasional experience! And yet they call themselves disciples of him whose heart beat with an unintermittent passion to help people, whose God was love, whose worship was daily service, whose hope was the Kingdom, whose instrument was the Cross. They are not really Christians. They are flying fish. For true discipleship to Jesus is the opposite of spasmodic conventionality. We are even wrong when we call our public worship on Sunday "church service." Church service really begins on Monday morning at seven o'clock and lasts all the week. Church service is helpfulness to people; public worship is preparation for it. For the church service which the Master illustratd and approved is a life of ministry amid the dust and din of daily business in a sacrificial conflict to a Christian world.

III

The obscuring of practical service as the indispensable expression of the Christian Gospel is effected in many folk, not by thus making religion a listless and spasmodic formality but by *stressing, often with heated earnestness, all sorts of trivial accomplishments of religion that do not really matter.* So an English lord complained that the severest blow religion ever had received was the loss of the bishops' wigs!

Historic Christianity is like a river that carries with it not only its own pure water but all manner of debris as well, silt from its own bottom, logs from its banks, flotsam from its tributaries. At last these accumulations that came from the river block the river;

the rising water frets against the impediments that once expressed its life; and the river has to burst a new course through them and toss them impatiently aside. Such was the work of the Hebrew prophets amid the religious trivialities of their day and such the conflict of the Master with quibbling minds that tithed "mint and anise and cummin," and neglected "the weightier matters of the law."

Even yet when men say "Christianity" they often mean not so much the pure spirit of the heart of it as all the clutter collected on its way. But the wars through which we have lived have made multitudes discriminate. It is clear that some things in so-called Christianity matter very much and some things do not count at all. Too often Christianity becomes like a city's streets where all forms of traffic, big and little, jostle each other upon equal terms. The gutter-snipe and the merchant, the pushcart and the limousine, all have their rights, and in the fusion of them discrimination lapses and the streets are cluttered and confused. Then fire breaks out, and the whole street from end to end is cleared to let the engines by. When disaster comes the main business must be given gangway.

Such an effect war has had on men's thoughts of Christianity. They see that some things once deemed important are of small account. Denominational distinctions in Protestantism, for the most part, do not matter. A man who becomes excited about them in such a day as this is an anachronism. Old questions of biblical criticism that were once discussed as though men's very lives depended upon them, do not crucially matter. A man who becomes vexed and quarrelsome about such questions today is hopelessly belated. He has an ante-bellum mind. Many questions in theology that have vexed human hearts and have furnished basis for heresy trials do not matter. They may have a place upon the side streets of Christian thinking, but they ought to be kept from littering up the avenues. *For there is one thing that does matter.* There is nothing on earth that begins to matter so much. Can Jesus Christ, his faith and principles, be made regnant on this earth? Can we get men to believe vitally in him and in the truths he represents and to join the great crusade to make over this shattered world upon the basis of his ideals? Can lives now battered and broken by misfortune and by sin be reclaimed, and can our social life, its business, its statecraft, its international relationships be transformed by the renewing of men's minds until they be truly Christian? In comparison with that, nothing else matters.

In the presence of such a cause, for a man to have a sectarian mind, to ride theological hobbies, to be obsessed with favorite fashions in religious phylacteries, is to miss the main issue of the Gospel. One who, like General Booth, founder of the Salvation Army, knows thoroughly and feels deeply the physical, moral, and spiritual desolation of millions who live under the very shadow of our church spires, feels also with impatience the frivolous futility of much popular religion. "It is no better than a ghastly mockery," he says, "to call by the name of One, who came to seek and to save that which was lost, those churches which, in the midst of lost multitudes, either sleep in apathy or display a fitful interest in a chasuble. Why all this apparatus of temples, of meeting houses, to save men from perdition in a world which is to come, while never a helping hand is stretched out to save them from the inferno of their present life? Is it not time that, forgetting for a moment their wrangling about the infinitely little and the infinitely obscure, they should concentrate all their energies on a united effort to break this terrible perpetuity of perdition and to rescue some at least of those for whom they profess to believe their Founder came to die?"

IV

Of all the reasons why Christian people miss the indispensable fruit of real Christianity in service none is commoner than this: religion can itself become one of the most selfish influences in life. Men can accept religion, love it, cleave to it, not from any unselfish motives whatsoever but solely because of the inward peace, the quieted conscience, and the radiant hope which they themselves get from it. Religion becomes not a stimulus but a sedative; it is used not as an inspiration to service but as a substitute for it. Mystical experiences of spiritual delight; a peaceful sense of being pardoned by God and reconciled with him; an emotional share, sometimes soothing, sometimes ecstatic, in the fellowship of public praise; hope of a future heaven—these blessings and others like them men get from religion. And sometimes these are all that they get. Religion reaches them only on their receptive side. It is life's supreme appeal to their selfishness.

Indeed the very nature of the Christian message lays us open to this special form of failure. For Christianity has two sides. On one side Christianity is the best news to which human ears ever listened. The fatherhood of God, the saviorhood of Christ, the friendship of the Spirit, the victory of righteousness, the life eternal—no other message half so exhilarating and comfortable has ever stirred the hearts of men. It is good to hear and the New Testament bears abundant witness that from the beginning of the Gospel's proclamation a peril arose from this very fact. The Good News was so good to hear that even in the first century folk began the pleasant but hopeless endeavor to absorb it by hearing only, and the New Testament keeps ringing out a warning. Says Jesus: "Everyone that heareth these words of mine, and doeth them not, shall be likened unto a foolish man, who built his house upon the sand" (Matt. 7:26). Says Paul: "Not the hearers of the law are just before God but the doers of the law" (Rom.2:13). Says James: "Be ye doers of the word, and not hearers only, deluding your own selves (James 1:22).

This insistence of the New Testament on the peril of a facile and passive response to the Gospel is no accident. It springs warm and urgent from the New Testament's thought of what the Gospel is. It is good news to be heard, but it is something more; it presents a task to be achieved. It calls for devoted, sacrificial service. It has launched a movement which for breadth and depth of present influence and for latent power cannot be matched in history. It has meant a crusade to turn the world upside down. Christianity is not simply a message to be heard; it is a deed to be done.

All the profoundest experiences in human life are thus two-sided, and are complete only as reception and action are balanced. The love which makes a home has two aspects. On one side it is romance. The poets sing about it endlessly—the

> tender and extravagant delight,
> The first and secret kiss by twilight hedge,
> The insane farewell repeated o'er and o'er.

But on the other side a complete love involves unselfishness, willing sacrifice, mutual forbearance, absolute fidelity, boundless devotion. In one aspect love is all lure and witchery and enchantment; in the other it is loyalty and self-denial and fidelity "till death us do part." On one side it is responsivenss; on the other it is responsibility. Miserable bargain hunters in the realm of spirit are those who try to get one side without the other!

Christian history bears painful testimony to the absorbing

preference of multitudes of so-called Christians for the comfortable aspects of the Gospel. There never has been any lack of folk to listen with ready receptiveness to the consolations of the faith. Religion made impressive in architecture, beautiful in music, glorious in art, vocal in preaching, vivid in sacrament, has brought hope, cheer, and comfort to multitudes. But too often this elemental fact has been forgotten, that every Christian truth, gracious and comfortable, has a corresponding obligation, searching and sacrificial. Every doctrine has its associated duty, every truth its task. On a Sunday morning, for example, a congregation litens to a sermon on the central message of the Christian faith, God's love for every son of man. None is so small and so obscure, so lost to general observation and to private care, the preacher cries, that God does not think on him. He loves us every one as though he had no other sons to love. It is a glorious Gospel. And if the preacher be a master of gripping phrase and luscious paragraph, how surely with such a theme he will cast a witching spell over any audience! But such a spell, however delectable, may be an unwholesome experience. That Gospel, when the Master first proclaimed it, was not intended primarily for preaching; it was intended for action. Do we not see, as he did, the appalling sin, the haggard want, the infuriating oppression, which are befalling these folk, every one of whom God loves? If personality is as sacred as that teaching says, then there is urgent business afoot upon this earth to challenge the service of all who believe the teaching. For on every side ruin is befalling these countless men and women for whom Christ died because he thought that they were worth dying for.

One of the most remarkable sights in the high Rockies is "timber line." One mounts from the valleys where the forests are immense and bountiful and ever as he rises the trees grow dwarfed. At last he comes to "timber line." It is the final frontier of the trees, the last stand where they have been able to maintain themselves against the furious tempests of the upper heights. Far above stretch the snowclad summits, and here are such twisted, stunted, whipped, and beaten trees as one could not imagine without seeing them. Twenty-eight rings were counted in one courageous struggler there, two inches high. Twenty-eight years of bitterest fighting against impossible odds had brought two inches of misshapen growth!

What is this, however, in comparison with the human timber

line? Consider the terribly handicapped and beaten masses of mankind, whipped by poverty, sickness, ignorance, sin. The most beautiful religious poem of recent years, "The Hound of Heaven," was written by Francis Thompson. But Thompson, a few years before he wrote it, was a tatterdemalion figure on the streets of London, holding the heads of strangers' horses to make a few pence for opium to drug himself. The tragedy there was pitiful: Francis Thompson so outwardly circumscribed and inwardly cowed that he could not *be* Francis Thompson at all. In ways dramatic or obscure how common that story is! Personality with rich possibilities in it is everywhere nipped and stunted, its flowers unopened, its fruit unborne.

Only recently a young man sailed from New York City for Liberia. See what amazing contrasts that young man's experience presents! When first he comes upon our view, he is a naked savage nine years old, discovered by a missionary in the jungle of Africa. His father is a worshiper of demons, obsessed by witchcraft; his mother is a native of the forest; his tribe is sunk in the depths of barbarism. He borrows a bit of calico from his mother for a loin cloth and leaves his home for a Wesleyan school. Yet only yesterday that young man, now in his twenty-ninth year, a graduate of Harvard University with high honors, a Christian of beautiful spirit, whose presentation of the cause of Liberia in Washington, so competent authorities report, was worthy of the finest traditions of British and American statesmanship, sailed back to Liberia to help his people. One rejoices in that single experience of personality released from crippling handicaps. But what a woeful waste in multitudes of other lives, also capable of fine expansion, who still are dwarfs of their real selves!

A sheer question of sincerity is raised, therefore, if one professes to believe that all these folk, battered and undone, are infinitely valuable in the sight of God. That is not chiefly a message to be enjoyed. That is chiefly a challenge to be answered with self-denying toil. The sacredness of personality is the most disturbing faith a man can hold. We are wretched bargain hunters in religion if we try to keep the comforts of the gospel and to avoid its sacrifices.

> No mystic voices from the heavens above
> Now satisfy the souls which Christ confess;
> Their heavenly vision is in works of love,

A new age summons to new saintliness.
Before th' uncloistered shrine of human needs
And all unconscious of the worth or price,
They lay their fragrant gifts of gracious deeds
Upon the altar of self-sacrifice.

V

This, then, is the conclusion of the matter: *the inevitable expression of real Christianity is a life of sacrificial service.* If by making religion a spasmodic formality, or by centering our thought upon its trivial corollaries, or by choosing its comfortable aspects and avoiding its self-denials, we refuse this characteristic expression of the Master's spirit, we cannot really have the Master's spirit at all. One law of the spiritual life from the operation of which no man can escape is that nothing can come into us unless it can get out of us. We commonly suppose that study is the road to learning. Upon the contrary, long-continued acquisitive study, absorbing information without expressing it is the surest way to paralyze the mind. He who would be a scholar must not study but teach, write, lecture, apply his knowledge to practical uses. Somehow he must give what he gets or soon he will get no more. As with a swamp, so with a mind, an inlet is useless without an outlet, since he who gets to keep can in the end get nothing good.

So a man who tries to assimilate Christianity by impression without expression can receive no real Christianity at all. If one stands perfectly insulated on a glass foundation he may handle live wires with impunity. Electricity may not come in where it cannot flow through. So the Christian Gospel demands outlet before it can find inlet. The failure of many Christians lies at the point of intake; they are estopped from real faith and prayer; they have no vital contact with divine realities. But the disaster of multitudes comes from a cluttered outlet. They do not know the meaning of service.

----

[1]Professor Francis G. Peabody.

CHAPTER II

THE PERIL
OF USELESSNESS

Daily Readings

Lord Melbourne is reported to have said: "If we are to have a religion, let us have one that is cool and indifferent; and such a one as we have got." Here is a candid desire for a faith which does not involve devoted service, but which makes possible a life insipidly neutral. Such a man is not outrageously cruel and inhuman, but he frankly accepts the ideal of negative harmlessness. Let us consider this week certain familiar attitudes which cause plenty of decent, not unamiable people, even though they may be religious, to accept for themselves such a colorless, useless life.

Second Week, First Day

And he came to Nazareth, where he had been brought up: and he entered, as his custom was, into the synagogue on the sabbath day, and stood up to read. And there was delivered unto him the book of the prophet Isaiah. And he opened the book, and found the place where it was written,
The Spirit of the Lord is upon me,
Because he anointed me to preach good tidings to the poor:
He hath sent me to proclaim release to the captives,
And recovering of sight to the blind,
To set at liberty them that are bruised,
To proclaim the acceptable year of the Lord.
And he closed the book, and gave it back to the attendant, and sat down: and the eyes of all in the synagogue were fastened on him. And he began to say unto them, To-day hath this scripture been fulfilled in your ears.—Luke 4:16-21.

When Jesus went to church he thought about service. Service was the crux of his whole spiritual experience; it was the great matter with which, in his eyes, public worship and all that it represents were concerned. When he worshiped his Father, he worshiped One, who was not willing "that one of these little ones should perish" (Matt. 18:14); when he prayed in solitude, he remembered friends like Peter, sorely tempted and needing help (Luke 22:31, 32); when he thought of immortality, he rejoiced that some, cruelly handicapped in this life, would have another chance (Luke 16:19-31); when he was transfigured he straightway harnessed his refreshed power to practical ministry (Matt. 17:9-18). His public worship, his faith in God, his private prayer, his eternal hope, and his transfigured hours all centered around and issued in a devoted life of helpfulness to people. The first reason why many folk are content with a "cool and indifferent religion" is that they have missed utterly the meaning of the Master's life. Whatever their religion may mean to them—correctness of formal belief, historic continuity of church establishments, exactness of ritual, respectable conventionality—it is not of that quality which causes them in the church to be thinking, as Jesus did, about the poor, the captive, the blind, and the bruised.

O Thou, who art the Light of the minds that know Thee, the Life of the souls that love Thee, and the Strength of the thoughts that seek Thee; help us so to know Thee, that we may truly love Thee, so to love Thee that we may fully serve Thee, whose service is perfect freedom; through Jesus Christ our Lord, Amen.—Gelasian Sacramentary (A.D. 494).

Second Week, Second Day

Another reason for that type of decent religion, which nevertheless is "cool and indifferent" to human service, is the strange idea that God, like some vain earthly potentate, enjoys being praised, and that, therefore, a due amount of adoration is highly gratifying to him and quite sufficient for us. But consider the clear teaching of the Master:

If therefore thou art offering thy gift at the altar, and there rememberest that thy brother hath aught against thee, leave there thy gift before the altar, and go thy way, first be reconciled to thy brother, and then come and offer thy gift.—Matt. 5:23, 24.

Religion is like patriotism in this respect: both of them at the beginning are emotions which we enjoy. We praise our country in patriotic oratory and resounding song, and we like it. But the days come when a man's country expects of him something more than praise. Patriotism lays its hands on all the active, outgoing, courageous elements in his life; it means sacrificial self-denial; it may even lead a man to vicarious death. So, says Jesus, does God ask something far more than worship. He asks self-sacrificing, brotherly relations between men. God is no fool to be pleased by flattery. What does he care for our songs, except as our lives are serving his other children? "Not every one that saith unto me, Lord, Lord," cried Jesus, "but he that doeth the will of my Father" (Matt. 7:21).

Almighty and most merciful Father, who has given us a new commandment that we should love one another; give us also grace that we may fulfill it. Make us gentle, courteous, and forbearing. Direct our lives, so that we may look each to the good of the other in word and deed. And hallow all our friendships by thy blessing of Thy Spirit; for His sake who loved us, and gave Himself for us, Jesus Christ our Lord. Amen.—Bishop Westcott (1825-1901).

Second Week, Third Day

Another reason for a neutral, useless life among amiable and decent people is *sheer lack of information about the needs of folk beyond the borders of our social circles.*

And they came to the other side of the sea, into the country of the Gerasenes. And when he was come out of the boat, straightway there met him out of the tombs a man with an unclean spirit, who had his dwelling in the tombs: and no man could any more bind him, no, not with a chain; because that he had been often bound with fetters and chains, and the chains had been rent asunder by him, and the fetters broken in pieces: and no man had strength to tame him. And always, night and day, in the tombs and in the mountains, he was crying out, and cutting himself with stones.—Mark 5:1-5.

How many of the people in the neighboring village of Gadara knew of this man, or had tried to help him? But Jesus, by an instinctive sympathy, never went into any neighborhood without finding at once the sick, the poor, the bedeviled. We live in our secluded social circles; we do not know even the maids in our kitchens, the workmen in our factories, the bootblacks and the newsboys who serve us. We deal with our fellows on a cash basis, not on a basis of human interest. And as for the conditions of life in the slums of our own communities, in the jails and asylums, among the sick, the vicious, the homeless, the unemployed, the mentally defective, how little too many of us know—or care! But imagine Jesus in one of our communities! He would not live in a social cocoon. He would soon know all the worst need of the town.

O Lord God, arise, for the spoiling of the poor, for the sighing of the needy; for Thou respectest not the persons of princes nor regardest the rich more than the poor. Give justice to the afflicted and destitute, rescue the weak, and may Thy Kingdom come on earth, through Jesus Christ our Lord.—Bishop Vernon Herford.

Second Week, Fourth Day

Jesus made answer and said, A certain man was going down from Jerusalem to Jericho; and he fell among robbers, who both stripped him and beat him, and departed, leaving him half dead. And by chance a certain priest was going down that way: and when he saw him, he passed by on the other side. But a certain Samaritan, as he journeyed, came where he was: and when he saw him, he was moved with compassion, and came to him, and bound up his wounds, pouring on them oil and wine; and he set him on his own beast, and brought him to an inn, and took care of him. And on the morrow he took out two shillings, and gave them to the host, and said, Take care of him: and whatsoever thou spendest more, I, when I come back again, will repay thee. Which of these three, thinkest thou, proved neighbor unto him that fell among the robbers? And he said, He that showed mercy on him. And Jesus said unto him, Go, and do thou likewise.—Luke 10:30-37.

The Master presents clearly here three familiar types. The robbers are aggressively destructive, cruel, inhuman. The Good Samaritan is aggressively unselfish. The priest and the Levite are neither one nor the other. They did not hurt the man; they did not help him. They refused to mix in the unpleasant affair at all. They stood aloof alike from robbery and service. Preoccupied about their own affairs, they did not wish to distract their thought, disarrange their schedule, or soil their hands with this sorry business of a wounded man. How like they are to many among us, who, *from mere dislike of having our ordinary, comfortable course of life disturbed, miss countless opportunities for usefulness!* Consider the intense indignation of the Master, which this parable reveals, against such a listless, apathetic attitude toward human need!

They that are ensnared and entangled in the extreme penury of things needful for the body, cannot set their mind upon Thee, O Lord, as they ought to do; but when they be disappointed of the things which they so mightily desire, their hearts are cast down and quail from excess of grief. Have pity upon them, therefore, O merciful Father, and relieve their misery from Thine incredible riches, that by Thy removing of their urgent necessity, they may rise up to Thee in mind. Thou, O Lord, providest enough for all men with Thy most liberal and bountiful hand; but whereas Thy gifts are, in respect of Thy goodness and free favour, made free unto all men, we (through our haughtiness and niggardship and distrust) do make them private and peculiar. Correct Thou the things which our iniquity hath put out of order; let Thy goodness supply that which our niggardliness hath plucked away. Give Thou meat to the hungry and drink to the thirsty; comfort Thou the sorrowful; cheer Thou the dismayed; strengthen Thou the weak; deliver Thou them that are prisoners; and give Thou hope and courage to them that are out of heart.—Queen Elizabeth's Prayer Book.

Second Week, Fifth Day

Still another reason for a listlessly useless life is that *folk content themselves with meditating on the fact that they are not doing any harm.*

Ye are the salt of the earth: but if the salt have lost its savor, wherewith shall it be salted? it is thenceforth good for nothing, but to be cast out and trodden under foot of men.—Matt. 5:13.
Salt is good: but if the salt have lost its saltness, wherewith will ye season it?—Mark 9:50.

In view of this familiar condemnation, consider what evil in denatured salt can so deserve the Master's disapproval. What harm does it do? It is not poison that one should dread it. It is a neutral, harmless thing, by which no ruin is brought on anyone. Yet to this homely example of savorless salt the Master turned for the picture of a kind of life which seemed to him intolerable. Poor Richard's Almanac contains this sentiment: "The noblest question in the world is, What good can I do in it?" That is a test on which the Master insisted. When therefore, any man contents himself with asking of his empty life, What harm do I do? he may expect the scathing rebuke of Jesus. Such self-satisfied negativeness, in his eyes, reduced the glorious possibilities of useful manhood to insipidity. He could no more endure denatured personality than denatured salt.

Eternal God, who committest to us the swift and solemn trust of life; since we know not what a day may bring forth, but only that the hour for serving Thee is always present, may we wake to the instant claims of Thy Holy Will; not waiting for tomorrow, but yielding today. Lay to rest, by the persuasion of Thy Spirit, the resistance of our passion, indolence, or fear. Consecrate with Thy presence the way our feet may go; and the humblest work will shine, and the roughest places be made plain. Lift us above unrighteous anger and mistrust into faith and hope and charity by a single and steadfast reliance on Thy sure will. In all things draw us to the mind of Christ, that Thy lost image may be traced again, and Thou mayest own us as at one with Him and Thee. Amen.—James Martineau.

Second Week, Sixth Day

But the unclean spirit, when he is gone out of the man, passeth through waterless places, seeking rest, and findeth it not. Then he saith, I will return into my house whence I came out; and when he is come, he findeth it empty, swept, and garnished. Then goeth he, and taketh with himself seven other spirits more evil than himself, and they enter in and dwell there: and the last state of that man becometh worse than the first.—Matt. 12:43-45.

The Master, illustrating a familiar experience, uses the popular ideas of his time with regard to the activity of demons. A man succeeds in expelling from his life some cruel temper, selfish passion, mean animosity; he rejoices in a heart "empty, swept, and garnished." What he rejoices in, however, the Master heartily condemns. *He cannot tolerate an empty life.* Many people suppose that to be a Christian is thus suppression of their instincts, a banishment of their impulses, a prohibition of their natural powers. Their whole ideal is negative. Consider, however, Henry Ward Beecher's description of Paul: "He was a man of immense conscience, immense pride, and immense combativeness. He was converted. His conscience did not diminish, his pride did not shrink, his combativeness did not flow out. All those great elements remained in him. Before he was converted, his conscience worked with malign feelings. Afterwards, his conscience worked with benevolent feelings. Before he was converted, his pride worked for selfishness. After he was converted, his pride worked for benevolence. Before he was converted, his combativeness worked for cruelty. After he was converted, it worked for zeal." A merely empty life always ends, as Jesus said, by being seven times more bedeviled than it was at first. But a thorough Christian is a man with all his active powers awake, well harnessed, and at work.

O Lord God of hosts, who maketh the frail children of men to be Thy glad soldiers in the conquest of sin and misery, breathe Thy Spirit, we pray Thee, into the students of this country and of all lands, that they may come together in faith and fellowship, and stand up an exceeding great army for the deliverance of the oppressed and for the triumph of Thy Kingdom; through Jesus Christ our Lord. Amen.—"A Book of Prayers for Students."

Second Week, Seventh Day

A life of negative uselessnss is also caused by *mere frivolity.*

Now the parable is this: The seed is the word of God. And those by the way side are they that have heard; then cometh the devil, and taketh away the word from their heart, that they may not believe and be saved. And those on the rock are they who, when they have heard, receive the word with joy; and these have no root, who for a while believe, and in time of temptation fall away. And that which fell among the thorns, these are they that have heard, and as they go on their way they are choked with cares and riches and plesures of this life, and bring no fruit to perfection. And that in the good ground, these are such as in an honest and good heart,

having heard the word, hold it fast, and bring forth fruit with patience.—Luke 8:11-15.

Consider the third kind of soil, where worldly cares, and love of gain, and delight of life's good times destroyed the fruit. Such a description does not involve conduct notoriously evil, but it does picture a style of living which lacks seriousness. Some of these folk were evidently light-headed, frivolous; they were preoccupied with pleasure, instead of being served by it. They may have been very gay and winsome, and not by any means unamiable, but, for all their engaging qualities, the fact remains that they flitted through life; frivoled their time and energy away; were tickled by many transient pleasures, tiring of which they sought for new; and their selfish and frittered lives "ended like a broom, in a multitude of small straws."

How familiar are these causes of useless living among descent folk! Some do not associate their churchgoing, as Jesus did, with service; some praise God indeed, but have never had their active powers captured by him; some do not know human life outside their little circles; some do not want their comfortable schedule of life disturbed; some are content with harmlessness; some define duty in terms of repression rather than expression; and some are absorbed in frivolity. Is there any one of us who is altogether free from such unserviceable faults?

Lord, let me not live to be useless!—John Wesley.

COMMENT FOR THE WEEK

I

Over against the virtues of a serviceable life stand in sharp contrast destructive qualities like cruelty, rapacity, and hatred. Against these and all their kin the Master loosed his wrath. *But he knew well that the majority of folk are not so much tempted to fall away from positive service into positive destructiveness, as they are tempted to fall between the two into negative uselessness.* It is worth our while, therefore, to note the intensity and persistency with which the Master bore down upon this deadly sin.

No outbreaking evil is reported of the pious travelers, the priest and the Levite, who in the parable of the good Samaritan left the robbed and wounded man untended in his trouble. One asks in vain what positive wrong they did. The Master's condemnation falls on them because they did nothing. They "went by on the other side." No oppressive wrongs are mentioned in the story of Dives who feasted sumptuously while Lazarus lay uncared for at his gate (Luke 16:19-31). The indictment concerns only what Dives did not do. He was useless. No destructive vices are reported of those who stand condemned in the great parable of the judgment (Matt. 25:31-46). The indictment against them is a comprehensive charge of uselessness: "I was hungry, and ye did not give me to eat; I was thirsty, and ye gave me no drink; I was a stranger, and ye took me not in; naked, and ye clothed me not; sick, and in prison, and ye visited me not."

Everywhere in the teaching of our Lord this central emphasis is found. Sometimes he illustrates his thought in terms of *business*. No positive dishonor is charged against the man of one talent who hid his entrustment in a napkin while his fellows profitably traded with their capital and multiplied it (Matt. 25:14-30). He is accused by the Master of doing nothing. But in the Master's eyes no charge is more terrific. He was "a good-for-nothing servant"; he must be cast into "outer darkness." Sometimes the Master illustrates his thought in terms of *agriculture*. Three kinds of ground stand heartily condemned in the parable of the sower (Mark 4:1-20). One was hard and would not take the seed; one was stony and gave the seed thin rootage; one was rich and grew choking weeds. But the gist of the final fault in every case lay here: the ground was useless. Sometimes the Master illustrates his thought in terms of *domestic life. A most amiable boy is pictured in the vineyard (Matt. 21:28-31). "I go, sir," said one, a winsome, well-intentioned, gracious lad. "But he went not,"* said Jesus. That negative is one of the most damning charges that can be brought against a human life. However well-intentioned, the boy was useless. The Master's praise goes rather to the other son, whose words were not gracious but who did the work.

When the Master speaks of the future life, it is with useless people that his most fearful apprehensions are concerned. The useless chaff will be consumed, he says (Matt. 3:12); the useless weeds must necessarily be burned (Matt. 13:30). The very word Gehenna, which we translate Hell, means Valley of Hinnom, the place of incineration outside Jerusalem where the rubbish of the city was consumed. Such a picturesque and flaming figure may be uncertain in its doctrinal implications, but it makes convincingly clear the principle on which the Master estimated men. Above all other things he hated uselessness. Recall his condemnation of savorless salt, harmless but insipidly good for nothing. Recall his rebuke of lives that like candles under the bed or covered by a vessel burn, but burn uselessly (Luke 8:16). And consider his incisive words in the parable of the fig tree: "A certain man had a fig tree planted in his vineyard; and he came seeking fruit thereon, and found none. And he said unto the vinedresser, Behold, these three years I come seeking fruit on this fig tree, and find none: cut it down; why doth it also cumber the ground?" (Luke 13:6-9).

II

This same standard of judgment the Master used concerning institutions as well as persons. *In his eyes the only solid claim on perpetuity for any organization must rest on usefulness,* and he did not hesitate to force this issue home with ruthless severity on the most venerable religious institutions of his day. Nothing, for example, was more sacred in his people's thought than the Sabbath. They said that God himself had rested on the Sabbath; that God with his own fingers had written the sabbath law on Sinai. The rabbis said that God had created the human race that he might have some one to keep the Sabbath. Then Jesus came, and even that sacred day he subjected to the ruthless test of usefulness. The rabbis had said that men were created to keep the Sabbath; he answered that "the sabbath was made for man and not man for the sabbath" (Mark 2:27). He said that with all its venerable history and sacred associations, that holiest of days would stand or fall by one test: usefulness to people. If by it human life grew richer, well! If not, no theory of divine institution could sustain it. And because the Sabbath became a burden and not a blessing, it is gone in Christendom and the Lord's Day takes its place.

As the Master tested the Sabbath, so he tested the temple. The House of God on Zion was the most sacred spot the Jews had ever known. During long centuries of passionate devotion they had loved it when possessed, longed for it in exile, rebuilt it when regained, and in spirit from the ends of the earth had revisited it continually with ardent prayer. The Master shared this loyalty. From the time when twelve years old he stood within his Father's house and questioned the doctors of the law, to the day when, ready to face the Cross, he swung around the brow of Olivet and, seeing the gleaming dome on Zion, burst into tears, he was a lover of the temple. But he saw also the inviolable law which even the temple could not escape. Priests using the sacred courts to squeeze ill-gotten gains from the people's piety; rabbis loving to be called rabbi, seeking the chief places at the feasts; Levites hurrying up the Jerusalem-Jericho road to be on time at the temple sacrifice, but careless of victims who had fallen among thieves; Pharisees wearing their broad phylacteries and loading on the people's conscience burdens grievous and not of service—all that he saw, and though it broke his heart to say it, he cried out that not one stone should be left upon another.

Many dubious problems concerning the Master's life and teaching baffle our inquiry, but one central fact stands clear: in his eyes uselessness was a deadly sin, and no permanence or greatness could belong to any person however eminent or to any institution however sacred unless it served the people.

III

All history is a running commentary on the truth of this principle of Jesus. Even in the sub-human world, before ethical meanings are evident, we can perceive that there is some relationship between permanence and usefulness. We cannot answer our children's simple questions about the animals they love without recourse to it. Why do squirrels have bushy tails? Because they are useful for balancing in the branches of trees. Why do cats and dogs have eyes in the front of their heads. Because they are hunters, and eyes in front are useful to spy the game they seek. Why do rabbits have eyes on the sides of their heads? Because they are not hunters but are hunted, and eyes at the side are useful to watch in every direction for approaching foes. From such homely facts to the most learned explanation of the evolution of species, this truth is evident: that a useful function is the best guaranty of permanence, and that outgrowing that useful function any living thing falls into peril of extinction. If it survives at all, it is crowded as a derelict into the shallows and back eddies, out of the main stream of life. So the sense of smell, the most useful safeguard of the animals, become less necessary among men, grows immeasurably less acute. As Huxley says, *"The sense of uselessness is the severest shock that any organism can sustain."*

When one turns from sub-human nature to human society, this

principle becomes even more evident. The history of man is strewn with the wrecks of social customs and political institutions that seemed great and permanent. Men thought them inextricably wrought into the fabric of life. A world without them was unimaginable. But they were not useful to the progress and enrichment of mankind, and they have vanished.

Consider so contemporary a matter as the prohibition of the liquor traffic in the United States! Convivial drinking goes back to the dawn of history. It is one of the immemorial traditions of the race. It has been enshrined in story, exalted in art, made fascinating in song, and countless customs of private friendship and public ceremonial have been entwined with it. Moreover, in our modern time billions of dollars have been invested in the traffic. It seemed absurd to propose its abolition. But one unescapable fact was more than a match for this enormous weight of power: the liquor traffic was not useful. All men who knew the facts saw that from the cavernous maw of the liquor traffic came an endless stream of wrecked homes and blasted lives, of unspeakable personal filth and public degradation, of economic inefficiency and unproductiveness. Whatever else the liquor traffic involved, it always involved this. Tradition, wealth, the ingrained habit of millions of men—not all these together could withstand that fact. The liquor traffic must go, for usefulness is the only assured basis of survival for any institution in society.

Countless social customs and organizations now fallen on ruin bear witness to this ruthless impatience of life with unserviceable things. Though they may long survive, they are at infinite disadvantage. Absolute monarchy, slavery, the duel, the ordeal, judicial torture, great empires built on conquest and by brute force maintained—how long is the list of proud, inveterate institutions, once boastfully sure of their reasonableness and perpetuity, that now are gone because they were not useful! Serviceableness is not a pleasant ideal, superimposed on life by ethical dreamers. Serviceableness is one of the most formidable demands of life, by the satisfaction of which alone can any institution hope finally to survive. For though men scoff at it, rebel and chafe against it, seek escape by subterfuge, or try to brush back the sea with a broom, the truth remains that no international policy, no economic system, no social custom, no ecclesiastical establishment, no personal eminence, has any sure tenure of permanence and power unless it serves the people.

IV

The importance of this principle to Christian folk is evident. The institutions and the people that call themselves by the name of Jesus are not exempt from the laws of Jesus. Only usefulness can assure their continued influence. Without that all successfully defended doctrines, all possession of regal station, of social prestige and wealth, all theories of divine ordination, all venerable associations accumulated through long centuries, are powerless to sustain their strength. With nothing more than such things to plead, our churches will disappear like a thousand other organizations, whose

> pomp of yesterday
> Is one with Nineveh and Tyre.

To pour out into the world a multitude of people who have caught the sacrificial spirit of the Master, and who, in his faith and purpose, give themselves to the service of mankind—that alone is the sustaining glory and hope of the Christian Gospel.

Indeed, this principle of Jesus, severe as it is and ruthless as its operation often seems, is full of hopeful prophecy. In the life of our churches today are many belated elements, from outgrown ideas to needless sectarian divisions, which are no longer useful. They serve no purpose in enriching the spiritual life of men and in spreading the Kingdom of God. If the Master in person were here, he would visit on them the same treatment which he visited on the Sabbath and on the temple. And for all men of forward-looking spirit it means courage to perceive that the universe itself conspires against these unserviceable things. When any custom once useful loses its function, the very stars in heaven fight with us against that Sisera.

Alike the spirit of the Master, therefore, and the special call of our times urge on Christians the aspect of the Gospel which we have set ourselves to study. The passing generations have their various needs, and under the urgency of changing circumstances, the manifold aspects of the Christian faith, one by one, are lifted to the front. Now this truth is specially demanded, now that duty must be specially enforced. In our day, for the sake of the integrity of Christian character, the progress of the Christian Church, and the salvation of the world, we need a new hatred of uselessness in institutions and persons, and a new baptism of the spirit of sacrificial and effective service.

V

In particular, as Christians and churchmen we well may give thought to the necessary extension of the idea of Christian service with which our times manifestly face us. *We are here not simply to save people out of the world but to save the world.* A lamentable feud exists between the partisans of personal and social Christianity. I believe in personal Christianity, says one. I believe in preaching the Gospel of Jesus to individuals. The sole business of the Church is to proclaim the evangel of divine forgiveness and regeneration until those who accept it are soundly saved and inwardly transformed. On the other side another cries: I believe in social Christianity. I seek the application of the principles of Jesus to our economic and international order. I am a patriot of the Kingdom of God upon the earth, and only as our social wrongs are righted does that Kingdom come. So do the devotees of personal and social Christianity confront each other.

The dilemma, however, on which they impale themselves is false. The full truth, as so often happens, flies like a bird with two wings, and maimed in either by our partial thinking it flutters a crippled creature on the ground. The partisans of individual Christianity are right in this: the Christian Gospel seeks the redemption of personality. Men and women are the infinitely valuable children of God. Christianity ardently desires to save them from every enemy that cripples and enslaves them, to unfold their possibilities, to lead them out into spiritual triumph and abundant life. And the partisans of social Christianity are right in this: that you cannot really be in earnest about saving personality and still neglect the social life from which personality springs and by which it is tremendously affected. Those who plead for the personal evangel against social reformation contradict themselves.

To say that we have Christian love for children, while we are careless of the conditions of child labor that deaden and damn the souls of children before they are old enough to know their hapless plight; to say that we long to save men from the power of lust, when we placidly allow city officials to grow rich on the gains of lust, commercially organized and publicly flaunted; to say that we desire personality redeemed, while we passively let disease and poverty beat men in body and in soul, and unstirred see families live in hovels where all reticence and modesty are made impossible and vice grows rank; to say we long to lead men into abundant life, while we hear unmoved of tens of thousands of men in one American corporation who work twelve hours a day, seven days a week; to say that we want Christ to triumph in the spirits of all men, while we let international relationships remain un-Christianized, with their inevitable issue in bitterness and hatred and all the ugly tempers that are the spawn of war—what is all this but sheer hypocrisy?

To be sure, some of the most thrilling stories of Christian victory concern folk touched to fine issues by Christ's Gospel, who came up out of the lowest conditions to spiritual triumph. So, though a plank thrown on the sward have but a single nail hole in it, some aspiring blade of grass will find it and come up from the obscurity and darkness underneath to rejoice in the splendor of the sun. But one who sees, with understanding eyes, that miracle of individual triumph, cannot be content. Consider all the dead and withered grass for which no way of escape was found! So blighting conditions lie across the lives of millions of folk today alike in heathendom and Christendom. Here and there some few break through to liberty. But the crushed multitudes—how can a disciple of Jesus think of them with equanimity? Men are not disembodied spirits. They are tremendously moved and molded by the environment in which they live. No one can hope to save the world without saving men; but neither can one hope to save men without saving the world. The two involve each other; they are one. The Church's best gift to mankind is redeemed personality; but redeemed personality's best gift to mankind is a better world, more fit to be a home for the family of God. He who is a partisan for either of these avenues of service against the other is a fair target for that newly discovered saying of our Lord: "Thou hearest with one ear, but the other thou hast closed."

Too long have many Christians been content with the ideal of negative unworldliness. The true antidote for worldliness is not unworldliness alone, but better-worldliness. Worldliness says, Indulge as you will in drink; unworldliness says, Be a teetotaler; better-worldliness says, The whole accursed liquor traffic can be stopped. Worldliness says, Salacious drama is a permissible delight; unworldliness says, The theater is utterly taboo;

better-worldliness says, The recreation of the people must be redeemed to decency and worth. Worldliness says, Play politics according to the current rules of the game; unworldliness says, Eschew politics altogether; better-worldliness says, The State can be as Christian as a man and Christian men must make it so. Worldliness says, Business is a selfish conflict for revenue only; unworldliness says, Seek not to be rich; better-worldliness says, Business is an indispensable service to mankind, and if it be organized and fairly run for man's sake and not for money only, it can be made as Christian as a church. Worldliness says, When war comes, fight; unworldliness says, No Christian must ever fight at all; better-worldliness says, International anarchy is a relic of barbarism and if Christian folk will seriously set themselves to organize the good will of the world, it can be stopped. In a word, worldliness says, Let the world be; unworldliness says, Come out from the world, better-worldliness says, In God's name, save the world!

The great days of the Church come when the full scope of service is accepted as the Christian task. When Carey gives the Bible in translation to millions of people; when Livingstone throws wide the doorways of a new continent to civilization; when Paton lays the foundation of a new social order in the Hebrides; when Hamlin drives the opening wedge of Christian civilization into Constantinople—then come the great days of the Church. When of William Wilberforce's fight against the slave traffic it can be said: "The clergy to a man are favorable to the cause" and "the people have taken up the matter in the view of duty and religion, and do not inquire what any man or set of men think of it," then come great days to the Church. For great days never can come to the Church, except as she shares the spirit of her Lord, and her Lord's demand was not simply new men in an old world but a new world to house new men.

CHAPTER III

THE STRONG AND
THE WEAK

Daily Readings

We are to consider this week the problem created by human inequality. Where some are by nature and privilege more highly endowed than others, Christianity at once insists on the use of the superior strength in service. In our daily readings we shall endeavor to see the dangers associated with the possession of superior strength, if this Christian principle is not observed.

Third Week, First Day

Paul from his prison writes to his friends at Philippi as follows:

But I rejoice in the Lord greatly, that now at length ye have revived your thought for me; wherein ye did indeed take thought, but ye lacked opportunity. Not that I speak in respect of want: for I have learned, in whatsoever state I am, therein to be content. I know how to be abased, and I know also how to abound: in everything and in all things have I learned the secret both to be filled and to be hungry, both to abound and to be in want. I can do all things in him that strengtheneth me.—Phil. 4:10-13.

One half of that passage is not at all surprising. I know how to be abased; I know how to be hungry; I know how to be in want—how familiar that testimony is, from those who have learned from Christ faith, steadiness, and overcoming power in times of hardship! But the other half of the passage is decidedly unusual. "I know how to abound"; Paul writes as though *that* were a difficult affair. "I know how to be filled," he says, "I can do all things in him that strengtheneth me." Paul evidently feels that dealing with abundance is quite as difficult as dealing with abasement. It is as though he said: I am now an old man. In my experience I have swept the gamut of human life. I have experienced proud eminence and contemptuous ostracism. I have had culture, education, money; and I have been tossed about the earth a poor tentmaker, apostle of a persecuted faith. At the end I bear witness that Jesus Christ enables a man to stand anything that can happen to him. I could even stand success. I know how to abound.

How often have we so considered our privileges as a difficult problem to be spiritually mastered?

O most liberal Distributer of Thy gifts, who givest us all kinds of good things to use, grant to us Thy grace, that we misuse not these Thy gracious gifts given to our use and profit. Grant us to be conversant amongst Thy gifts, soberly, purely, temperately, holily, because Thou art such a one; so shall not we turn that to poison of our souls, which Thou has given for the medicine of our bodies, but using Thy benefits thankfully, we shall find them profitable both to soul and body. Amen.—"Christian Prayers," 1566.

Third Week, Second Day

Now there was a certain rich man, and he was clothed in purple and fine linen, faring sumptuously every day: and a certain beggar named Lazarus was laid at his gate, full of sores, and desiring to be fed with the crumbs that fell from the rich man's table; yea, even the dogs came and licked his sores. And it came to pass, that the beggar died, and that he was carried away by the angels into Abraham's bosom: and the rich man also died, and was buried. And in Hades he lifted up his eyes, being in torments, and seeth Abraham afar off, and Lazarus in his bosom. And he cried and said, Father Abraham, have mercy on me, and send Lazarus, that he may dip the tip of his finger in water, and cool my tongue; for I am in anguish in this flame. But Abraham said, Son, remember that thou in thy lifetime receivedst thy good things, and Lazarus in like manner evil things: but now here he is comforted, and thou art in anguish. And besides all this, between us and you there is a great gulf fixed, that they that would pass from hence to you may not be able, and that none may cross over from thence to us.—Luke 16:19-26.

The minds of the Pharisees who heard Jesus were already furnished with the popular, lurid picture of future punishment which Jesus uses here. What is new to them is not the background of flaming condemnation, but the character of the person who is condemned. Jesus takes a familiar setting and puts into it an unfamiliar personnel. For what the Master says is this: *The condemned character is a man who having superior privileges proves himself unfit to have them.* How much we need that lesson! In our eyes, success is in itself an estate most to be desired; we forget that success is a fine art, of all arts most difficult to handle. We clamor for power—fortune, wealth, prestige. How can I succeed? is our question. We do not ask, Am I *fit* to succeed? Yet the second question is more important. It is one thing to be in a happy and fortunate estate; it is another to be fit to be there. It is one thing to be well fed; it is another to be worth feeding. Is is one thing, like Dives, to have money and influence and social position, and it is another to be the kind of man who is fit to have them. And the Master insists that fitness to possess any privilege can be proved only by service to the unprivileged. There is no hope for Dives until he learns to pray like this:

Blessed Lord, who for our sakes wast content to bear sorrow and want and death; Grant unto us such a measure of Thy Spirit that we may follow Thee in all self-denial and tenderness of soul. Help us by Thy great love, to succour the afflicted, to relieve the needy and destitute, to share the burdens of the heavy-laden, and ever to see thee in all that are poor and desolate. Amen.—Bishop Wescott (1825-1901).

Third Week, Third Day

And he spake a parable unto them, saying, The ground of a certain rich man brought forth plentifully: and he reasoned within himself, saying, What shall I do, because I have not where to bestow my fruits? And he said, This will I do: I will pull down my barns, and build greater; and there will I bestow all my grain and my goods. And I will say to my soul, Soul, thou hast much goods laid up for many years; take thine ease, eat, drink, be merry. But God said unto him, Thou foolish one, this night is thy soul required of thee; and the things which thou hast prepared, whose shall they be? So is he that layeth up treasure for himself, and is not rich toward God.—Luke 12:16-21.

Let us imagine this colossal failure in his youth. He may have been able, steady, energetic, ambitious. He wished to succeed and he was willing to pay the price. He gave himself efficiently to his labor; he lived a clean, hard-working life; he made no fool of himself with debauchery. So long as he had success to gain he was a good man. But when he had gained it—there the Master's record of his utter ruin begins! For it is often easier to gain success than to use it well. Some men are ruined by adversity. But alas! for the many who do not fail, who climb high and higher yet before the applauding eyes of their fellows, until they fall over the precipice of their own prosperity! It is not easy to abound. With what appreciation do we read Erasmus's description of his powerful friend, Sir Thomas More: "Elevation has not elated him or made him forgetful of his humble friends. He is always kind, always generous. Some he helps with money, some with influence. When he can give nothing else he gives advice. He is Patron-General to all poor devils."

For those who in their plenty live delicately, contemn the poor, and forget God; for all people whose hearts are so perished within them that pity has departed; Shew them Thy ways. Amen.—"A Book of Prayers for Students."

Third Week, Fourth Day

Charge them that are rich in this present world, that they be not highminded, nor have their hope set on the uncertainty of riches, but on God, who giveth us richly all things to enjoy; that they do good, that they be rich in good works, that they be ready to distribute, willing to communicate; laying up in store for themselves a good foundation against the time to come, that they may lay hold on the life which is life indeed.—I Tim. 6:17-19.

Why is such an injunction so apt in every generation? Is it not in part because the possession of power in any form, whether political prestige, social station, popularity, or wealth, always begets the thirst for more? Success for its own sake becomes an absorbing passion. If a man have none of it, he may solace himself without it. But if a man gain even a little of it, like strong drink it may soon become indispensable to him. He must have more and more of it. At last he joins the multitude whose portrait the New Testament so exactly sketches: "They that are minded to be rich fall into a temptation and a snare" (I Tim. 6:9). Paul does not say, "They that are rich"; he says, "They that *are minded to be rich.*" The thirst is on them. At all costs they propose for themselves to be rich. Whether with one kind of wealth and power or another, in some degree we are all endowed; and the only attitude that can make possible a Christian character is revealed in such a prayer as this:

O my God, make me a good man! O my Father, come what may, make me a simple-minded, honest, humble, and brave Christian! Let me seek no favour but Thine, and give my heart to no labour but in Thee and for Thee! With God my Saviour as my help and guide may I, ere I die, be a blessing to the city in which I dwell, especially to the poor and miserable in it, for whom my heart bleeds. Amen.—Norman Macleod.

Third Week, Fifth Day

Consider the Master's description of the scribes and Pharisees:

But all their works they do to be seen of men: for they make broad their phylacteries, and enlarge the borders of their garments, and love the chief place at feasts, and the chief seats in the synagogues, and the salutations in the marketplaces, and to be called of men, Rabbi. But be not ye called rabbi: for one is your teacher, and all ye are brethren. And call no man your father on the earth: for one is your Father, even he who is in heaven. Neither be ye called masters: for one is your master, even the Christ. But he that is greatest among you shall be your servant. And whosoever shall exalt himself shall be humbled; and whosoever shall humble himself shall be exalted.—Matt. 23:5-12.

The scribes and Pharisees were the privileged classes of their day. They had social rank, education, culture, public influence. And the issue of such possessions the Master saw there, as he can see it in any generation: pride, exclusiveness, unbrotherliness. For one peril that is always associated with any kind of success or power is that it will kill humility, beget pride, and break brotherhood. Wrote the Duchess of Buckingham to Lady Huntingdon about the early Methodists: "Their doctrines are most repulsive, and strongly tinctured with impertinence and disrespect to their superiors. It is monstrous to be told that you have a heart as sinful as the common wretches that crawl the earth. This is highly insulting, and I wonder that your Ladyship should relish any sentiment as much at variance with high rank and good breeding."

Let us pray!

Thou, O God, who givest Grace to the Humble, do something also for the Proud Man: Make me Humble and Obedient; take from me the Spirit of Pride and Haughtiness, Ambition and Self-Flattery, Confidence and Gayety; Teach me to think well, and to expound all things fairly of my Brother, to love his worthiness, to delight in his Praises, to excuse his Errors, to give Thee thanks for his graces, to rejoice in all the good that he receives, and ever to believe and speak better things of him than of myself.

O teach me to love to be concealed and little esteem'd, let me be truly humbled and heartily ashamed of my Sin and Folly. Teach me to bear Reproaches evenly, for I have deserv'd them; to refuse all Honours done unto me, because I have not deserv'd them; to return all to Thee, for it is Thine alone; to suffer Reproach thankfully; to amend my faults speedily, and when I have humbly, patiently, charitably, and diligently served Thee, change this Habit into the shining Garment of Immortality, my Confusion into glory, my Folly into perfect Knowledge, my Weakness and Dishonours into the Strength and Beauties of the Sons of God. Amen.—Thomas á Kempis (1379-1471).

Third Week, Sixth Day

And Jesus looked round about, and saith unto his disciples, How hardly shall they that have riches enter into the kingdom of God! And the disciples were amazed at his words. But Jesus answered again, and saith unto them, Children, how hard is it for them that trust in riches to enter into the kingdom of God! It is easier for a camel to go through a needle's eye, than for a rich man to enter into the kingdom of God. And they were astonished exceedingly, saying unto him, Then who can be saved? Jesus looking upon them saith, With men it is impossible, but not with God: for all things are possible with God.—Mark 10:23-27.

We marvel at men who, heavily handicapped by *adversity*, succeed in achieving victorious lives. The Master marveled at men who, heavily handicapped by *prosperity,* were able to rise above it. It seemed to him a superhuman task to get the spiritual mastery of success. Abraham Lincoln and William Ewart Gladstone were born in the same year. One was born in a cabin, and the other in a castle. One was so poor that he says the first day he earned a dollar was the proudest day of his life; and the other was so rich that from his birth to his death he never had to give an anxious thought to his ample fortune. One was so bereft of opportunity that all his books he borrowed and read by a pine knot on the hearth; the other had everything the schools of England could afford and Christ Church College, Oxford, could furnish. The one was so homely that a member of his Cabinet called him a gorilla, and the other was one of the handsomest men in Europe. One started with nothing; the other started with everything. Put yourself in the place of each, and consider: if a humble, brotherly, serviceable Christian life were your ideal, under which set of circumstances do you think that you would meet the greater obstacles?

Take from us, O God, all pride and vanity, boasting and forwardness; and give us the true courage that shows itself by gentleness; the true wisdom that shows iself by simplicity; and the true power that shows itself by modesty.—Charles Kinsley.

Third Week, Seventh Day

And he spake also this parable unto certain who trusted in themselves that they were righteous, and set all others at nought; Two men went up into the temple to pray; the one a Pharisee, and the other a publican. The Pharisee stood and prayed thus with himself, God, I thank thee, that I am not as the rest of men, extortioners, unjust, adulterers, or even as this publican. I fast twice in the week; I give tithes of all that I get. But the publican, standing afar off, would not lift up so much as his eyes unto heaven, but smote his breast, saying, God, be thou merciful to me a sinner. I say unto you, This man went down to his house justified rather than the other: for every one that exalteth himself shall be humbled; but he that humbleth himself shall be exalted.—Luke 18:9-14.

Here is the final consequence of a successful, prosperous life: this Pharisee in his pride and self-content loses any genuine sense of

51

the need of God. How often indeed do we ourselves secretly feel that religion is for the wicked and the weak! It comforts people when they are sad; it steadies them when they are sick; it offers forgiveness when they are condemned; it gives them hope when they come to die. Religion is medicine for feebleness. If one has health, fortune, and reputation, he needs it little. As one calls in a nurse when he is ill, so folk when fortune fails them turn to religious faith. It is narcotic; it soothes them.

Over against this familiar idea, set what we have been saying this week. Not adversity but prosperity is for many men the greater strain upon their characters. Multitudes of folk in each generation collapse into uselessness, not because they were weak, but because they could not master the strength entrusted to them. The fact is that we never need a deep, convincing, and powerful spiritual life more than when all things are going well with us. Let us hold this in mind as we turn to study the obligation which the strong, if they are to be Christian, must discharge to the weak.

O God, who knowest us to be set in the midst of so many and great dangers, that, by reason of the frailty of our nature, we cannot always stand upright; grant to us such strength and protection as may support us in all dangers and carry us through all temptations; through Jesus Christ our Lord. Amen.—Book of Common Prayer, 1662.

COMMENT FOR THE WEEK

I

One fact which plunges us at once into the heart of the problem of service is inequality. Popular interpretations of the Declaration of Independence to the contrary notwithstanding, men are not born equal. All men by right of birth should have an equal chance to become all that they are capable of being, but this principle is yet a long way from producing actual equality. *On some terms the strong and the weak must live together.*

Men are not equal in *practical ability*. Under any easily predictable economic system, if riches were to fall like snow upon a windless day, making dead level everywhere, upon that scene of financial equality the wind of unequal ability would blow and some fields would be drifted high and some fields blown quite bare. Men are not equal in *intellectual capacity*. How shall we explain a family where eight children come, none destined to any eminence, but where the ninth, Daniel Webster, grows to a personal impressiveness that used to make the houses on Beacon Street look smaller when he walked by, and to a mental power that in debate was irresistible? We get no answer to our curious inquiry. Only we know that some men put the pressure on their brains and find them there, alert and eager; and others turn on the current of their intellectual ambition with no better consequence than burning out the fuse. Men are not equal in *spiritual capacity*. All men have in them the power to open up their lives to the influence of the Divine Spirit, and by Him to be transformed, but some are thimbles in comparative capacity, and others are oceans with tides and gulf streams and commerce-bearing depths. Whatever may be the possibilities in the far reaches of eternal life, we see upon the earth small souls in all degrees growing alongside the capacious spirits through whom supremely God reveals himself.

What is true of individuals is true of groups of men. Races are not equal. We know why no more than we can tell why one son in a family may be a genius and his twin a dunce. Only the fact is clear that some races, put anywhere on earth, will at once construct a stable government and live by law. But others, after unimpeded tenure of a continent for ages, cannot unaided establish a settled government at all. Whatever the solution of this puzzling problem, the fact is clear. The strong and the weak, in individuals and races, must somehow live together on the earth. Moreover, we all are involved in this complication. None is so weak as not to bear, in some aspect of his life, the relationship of strength to some one weaker still. Consider the children, the tendrils of whose slender vines reach up for the sustenance of our maturer lives. Recall our friends, who in giving us their trust give us enormous power over their welfare and their happiness.

This relationship of the strong to the weak claims our special attention because it has been the fruitful mother of the cruelest tragedies of human life. How has God stood it through the ages, watching the strong squeeze the weak like grape clusters into their chalices that they might drink blood like wine! One cannot easily open his Bible without running upon some outburst of indignation over this tragic sin. Moses rips his dignities and titles off that he may not even indirectly share in Pharaoh's oppression of his helpless countrymen. Nathan falls like lightning upon David because, being very rich in sheep, he has robbed his neighbor of his one ewe lamb. Isaiah cries: "What mean ye that ye crush my people and grind the face of the poor?" (Isa. 3:15). Amos cries: "Ye kine of Bashan . . . that oppress the poor, that crush the needy" (Amos 4:1). And when the Master comes, with what overflowing wrath does he denounce strong men who rob widows' houses and cover their crime with the pretense of prayer!

II

If one asks, then, what Christianity proposes as the solution of this difficult relationship, Paul tersely sums up the spirit of the whole New Testament: "We that are strong ought to bear the infirmities of the weak and not to please ourselves" (Rom. 15:1). *The strong bearing the burdens of the weak*—was ever a more revolutionary principle announced? The weak, the undefended, the immature, have always been the prey of the strong. They have been ruthlessly cut up, strewn in, and plowed under to make a richer soil for the strong to grow in. The saddest chapters in history recount the story of the strong, wringing the weak dry of their toil and flinging them heedlessly aside, or displaying their power in shameless cruelties, as when a Roman patron crucified two thousand slaves beside a highway to satisfy his whim.

Indeed, this right of the strong over the weak has been in our day asserted as the true teaching of science and philosophy. "The struggle for existence" and "the survival of the fittest" have been interpreted to suit the strong and have been erected into a theory of conduct for all life. So far from seeing any law of usefulness running through creation, men have seen only a law of grasping selfishness and bitter war. The tall tree in the forest does not solicitously serve the sapling at its base. It stamps the sapling out, steals its sustenance, blots out its sun, rots it back into the forest mold, that the strong tree may be stronger yet. The horticulturist when he finds a few blooms upon his rosebush and many stunted ones, does not pinch back the finer flowers that the nipped and feeble ones may have a chance. He amputates the weak. He is no democrat seeking the welfare of all the people. He is an aristocrat sacrificing the common run to the finest specimens. He does not plead for humanity; he seeks the superman. Such a philosophy of life, alike in the theory and practice, has in recent years been tragically influential, and its consequences are written in lines of fire across the world. So Nietzsche reviles the Gospel for the very reason that makes us praise it: "Christianity is the one great curse, the one great spiritual corruption." And Nietzsche can truly claim that large areas of human life, personal, economic, and political, are founded upon principles the very opposite of Christian. Empires for conquest, industrial systems for exploitation, individual ambition rising on stepping stones of fallen folk—how much of life is based upon the pagan principle that the weak must bear the burdens of the strong and must not please themselves!

The scientific answer to this heathen doctrine is being written by the experts. In Kropotkin's *Mutual Aid,* in the works of Novikov, we see Greek meet Greek in the scientific field. The fact is that even a forest represents cooperation quite as much as it represents conflict, and the story of animal life shows clearly that capacity for mutual aid, far more than brute strength, has made species fit to survive. The bees have lasted; the ichthyosaurus is gone. Conflict and carnage are in nature, but the development of altruism is an integral part of the story from the beginning and the higher the scale of existence rises, the less does brute force count and the more life's progress depends upon cooperation. A few facts in the origin of life may seem to favor the exploitation of the weak by the strong. The whole course of evolving life, which has lifted spiritual powers into preeminence and has made life's continuance and worth depend upon good will and mutual aid, is overwhelmingly against it.

The Christian Gospel, however, did not wait for the battledore and shuttlecock of scientific argument. It leaped at once by the insight of love to the heart of the matter. Many things in so-called Christianity can be dispensed with—dogmas, institutions, rituals, of which when they are gone the world will cry, "Good riddance!" But the principle that the highest strength should be put at the service of the lowliest weakness is a central pillar of the Gospel, around which if any blind Samson ever winds antagonistic arms and breaks it down, all the Gospel will come clattering into ruin. "Though he was rich, yet for your sakes he became poor that ye through his poverty might become rich"—no truer summary of the Master's spirit does the New Testament contain. And wherever that spirit has come to its proper utterance in his followers, this ministry of strength to weakness is its characteristic expression. To be sure, the *prevention* of weakness, perpetuating itself through evil heredity and circumstance, is primary, but the weak who are already here are not, in the Christian program, to be left to hopelessness. Father Damien going out to serve the lepers; John Howard visiting the vilest prisons in Christendom, passionate for the redemption of the criminals; Mackay laying his life upon Uganda and breathing a new spirit into depraved and barbarous folk; William Booth plunging into "Darkest England" and seeking a way out for squalid millions—these are the proper fruits of the Christian Gospel. And so far has this principle at least ceased to be a paradox and become a principle of sane government that, as Lord Askwith has said: "The test of every civilization is the point below which the weakest and most unfortunate are allowed to fall."

III

We may well consider, therefore, some of the facts which make this central principle of Christian conduct seem convincing. For one thing, if we regard huma history in the large it is clear that, *strong and weak alike, we all are coming up together from the same primitive conditions, and that we who in any sense are strong are simply those who are a little way ahead.* Our strength does not belong to us in free simple to possess and to use as we will. We are the custodians of the gains of the whole race for the sake of all mankind.

An English-speaking Christian may be tempted to look down upon a cannibal as a hopeless specimen of a degenerate race. Why spend strength upon such a wretch? Our condescension might be chastened by these words of Jerome, the Christian scholar of the fourth century: "When I was a boy living in Gaul, I saw the Scottish people in Britain eating human flesh and though they had plenty of cattle and sheep at their disposal, yet they would prefer a ham of the herdsman or a slice of the female breast as a luxury." Is it any special merit of ours that we, whose ancestors were also cannibals, have now a little ahead of our brethren climbed out of that horrible morass?

Or a modern man, heir to the scientific labors of these last few generations, reads with horror a missionary's story like *Mary Slessor of Calabar*. The blasting superstitions of witchcraft and demon worship fall with such tragic incidence upon the African tribes where Miss Slessor toiled, that one wonders whether such expenditure of consecrated strength on such degraded feebleness can be worth while. But a pause is given to our doubt when as late as the sixteenth century in our own racial history, we read the words of Montaigne: "The day will never come when the common ruck of men will cease to believe in witchcraft. If the lawyers and judges of our modern sixteenth century France, men trained to sift evidence and learned in science, can be so far deceived as to send thousands of victims to their death for impossible crimes, how can we ever hope that the common man will avoid these errors?" Is supercilious pride paticularly befitting us, who so recently have escaped slavery to a superstition which still shackles thousands of God's children upon the earth?

There is no end to such comparisons. All races, however superior they now may seem, are but the advance guard of an emerging humanity. If we are tempted to think meanly of ignorance because we are educated, let us read again a couplet from our own literature only a few centuries behind us:

> There was a wight who such a scholar was
> That he the letters in a book could read.

If we shudder at the sacrifice of children by their parents in heathen cults, let us recall that our fathers in Britain used to put young girls in wicker baskets and run swords through them, that they might tell from the way the blood flowed what the will of the gods was. One principle is given us in Scripture so simple and so human that no fair-minded man can escape its grip: we are bound to show mercy to folk who still struggle in difficulties where we ourselves have been: "Love ye therefore the sojourner; for ye were sojourners in the land of Egypt" (Deut. 10:19).

If in a family of two children grew up together, could their relations be regulated on any other principle than that which Christianity suggests? One of the children comes first to the age of poise, self-mastery, and power. The other still is infantile. If the older should use his superiority to mistreat the younger, with what indignant admonition would the father speak! "You two are growing together in the same home," so he would say, "and *you* are a little way ahead. That is not greatly to your credit; you had the first start. This maturity of growth was not given you for self-inflation, but for service. You hold it in trust for the whole family's sake."

No good home could be run on any other principle. Nor can God run his world otherwise. Strength ought to be put at the service of weakness, for in all possession of privilege and power we are trustees of the advance gains of the race for the sake of the whole human family.

IV

A second reason has always undergirded this Christian principle of putting the best strength at the service of the lowliest weakness. *The weak are worth serving.* The Master's life is based upon this faith and is aglow with its meaning. If at an auction of musical instruments a battered violin with dusty body and sagging strings had been bid for in cents as a worthless article; if some one should pick up the instrument, dust it look at the maker's name, bid it up into the hundreds of dollars, and when pressed bid higher still; if word went round that the man was Kreisler, that Fritz Kreisler wanted the violin, no matter what it cost; how the estimate of the instrument's worth would rise! So Jesus put new value into despised men. Boys in a far country, rotten with harlotry and sunk to low estate among the swine—all the world called them lost and good for nothing. But the Master bid his life for them. Let the cost be the crown of thorns, the spear, the Cross; the Master counted personality, however ruined, worth it all. Wherever the Gospel has gone, its characteristic fruitage has been service for all sorts of men in the faith that all sorts of men are worth serving.

This Christian confidence in the worth and latent possibility of all mankind is not a faith neatly to be proved in theory, but in practice it has been justified upon a scale that only the most optimistic could have dreamed. *The spread of civilization* justifies it. The Greeks despised the barbarians as an inferior breed, until Alexander the Great conquered the barbarians and brought Greek and non-Greek culture into vital contact. Then it was discovered that the barbarians could learn anything that the Greeks had to teach, and within a few centuries the center of the world's culture had shifted from Athens to Alexandria. So within our own time great nations and races long despised have awakened out of sleep and have displayed an aptitude for progress, a capacity for learning all that the most advanced races know and for pushing farther still the boundaries of enterprise, that ought to humble any racial pride. *The spread of democracy* justifies it. Democracy means not only political copartnership; it means the right of all men everywhere to all the privileges the race has won. It means popular access to education, leisure, economic self-control. It means copartnership rather than autocracy in industry as well as in government. But all this has underneath it an amazing venture of faith in human nature and in the power of whole classes of the population long despised to achieve intelligence, self-mastery, and the cooperative spirit. Wherever democracy succeeds in any realm, the triumph of Christian faith in the capacities of lowly folk is seen.

Perhaps most of all *the missionary movement* has justified the Christian faith in the worth of the weak. When Charles Darwin sent his subscription to the Christian orphanage on Tierra del Fuego, he wrote: "The success of the Tierra del Fuego Mission is most wonderful and shames me, as I always prophesied utter failure. . . . I certainly should not have predicted that all the missionaries in the world could have done what has been done." As glass is made of sand, so repeatedly out of the dull, opaque material of low castes and degraded races the Christian Gospel has made the most transparent sainthood. Into the office of the dean of one of the greatest American universities walked recently a man from one of the South Sea Islands, whose cheeks were scarred with the mutilations of primitive savage rites. He was eight years old before he had seen a white man. He was asking now for a course in advanced Semitics that he might translate the Old Testament from its original sources into his own tongue. He had passed in a single lifetime from the lowest pit of barbarism to the highest intellectual privileges of the modern world. When the Master announced the direction of his ministry "unto the least of these my brethren," who could have foreseen the wide areas of human life in which that revolutionary principle would be justified? For this is the Christian conviction which underlies the greatest practical venture of social faith in the race's history: that the outcast, downtrodden, and despised are worth saving, that every son of man, however ignorant and bestial, is not beyond redemption to sanity and virtue; that there is no personal or social inferiority that need be final; and that, therefore, the weak by their potential capacity to become strong have a right to the service of strength.

V

Another fact underlies this Christian principle. *Any strength that does not serve weakness is itself doomed.* Why should Midas in his palace care for Tom-all-alone in his cellar? asks Dickens; and he answers: "There is not an atom of Tom's slime, not a cubic inch of any degradation about him but shall work its retribution." We read the story of strength's oppression of weakness with pity for the weak. But no cruelty of the mighty toward the feeble ever worked agony for the feeble any more certainly than it worked ruin for the strong. "For the oppression of the poor, for the sighing of the needy, now will I arise, saith the Lord"—such is the habitual accent of the Scripture. That judgment of Scripture is everywhere carried out in history. No retributions surpass the penalties for misused strength. "Who reckless rules right soon may hope to rue." After Louis XVI come Robspierre; after the Czar comes Lenin; after industrial despotism comes revolution. The slave trade, from its sources in Africa to its consummation in Christendom, was as cruel and apparently as safe an exploitation of the weak by the strong as history knows. But all the agony of the enslaved was matched by the punishment of the enslavers, and Lincoln's words have application far beyond the immediate circumstances that gave them birth: "Yet, if God wills that . . . every drop of blood drawn with the lash shall be paid by another drawn with the sword, as was said three thousand years ago, so still it must be said, 'The judgments of the Lord are true and righteous altogether.' "

Nor is this inevitable incidence of penalty upon the strong for any wrong they do the weak an arbitrary matter. The reason for it is wrought deeply into the texture of human life. We are all bound up together, rich and poor, learned and ignorant, sick and well, good and bad, in one bundle of life. No harm can fall on any which does not in the end affect all. No isolating walls can keep the ill of the weak from reaching the strong. Carlyle tells us of an Irish widow who in Edinburgh with three helpless children sought help in vain, fell ill of typhus, and, infecting seventeen others, died. "The forlorn Irish widow," cries Carlyle grimly, "applies to her fellow creatures, 'Behold I am sinking bare of help. I am your sister; one God made us. You must help me.' They answer, 'No, impossible: thou art no sister of ours!' But she proves her sisterhood; her typhus kills *them;* they actually were her brothers though denying it."

This inevitable sharing of the strong in the ills of the weakest and most helpless people with whom they deal has now been stretched to take in all mankind, and everyday the intermeshing relationships grow more intimate and unesapable. The laying of the first Atlantic cable was heralded everywhere as opening a new era in man's life; it was one of the most stirring bits of news that Stanley told Livingstone in the heart of Africa; it woke Whittier to rhapsody:

> For lo, the fall of Ocean's wall,
>   Space mocked and time outrun;
> And round the world the thought of all
>   Is as the thought of one.

But the relationship of all races, advanced and backward, Christianity and non-Christian, high and low, which the laying of the cable thus foretokened is more than a welcome gain. It is a portentous fact. All ignorance everywhere, all sin, superstition, ill will, disease, and blasting poverty are now a peril everywhere. No one is safe till all are safe. No privilege is secure till all possess it. No blessing is really owned until it universally is shared. That service to "one of the least of these my brethen," so far from being a superfluous ideal, is an ineradicable law of life, is indicated by this basic fact: in the last analysis self-preservation depends upon it. For whenever the strong neglect or oppress the weak, they must face that same principle at the heart of the Eternal which found impressive utterance on the lips of Caliph Omar: "By God! he that is weakest among you shall be in my sight the strongest until I have vindicated from him his rights; but him that is strongest will I treat as the weakest until he complies with the laws."

VI

Because strong and weak emerge together toward the light and the strong for the sake of all have been trusted with the lead; because the weak are potentially strong and the release of their life from weakness into strength is their right; because no ill can rest upon the weak that does not also smite the strong; for such reasons the strong should bear the burdens of the weak. But not all these reasons together plumb the depth of the Christian motive. *The strong should bear the burdens of the weak, because they, too, are weak.* At first we said that none is so weak as not to bear the relationship of strength to some one weaker still; it is equally true that none is so strong as not to bear the relationship of weakness to some one stronger yet.

We have called Paul's principle paradoxical; but in one institution it always has been the fundamental law. Who is king of the home? Not the father, however strong, nor the mother, however important. The baby is king of the home. He is feebleness incarnate, yet if he cries all are attent; if he is ill no science is too skilled to serve him, no sacrifice of comfort too prolonged to meet his needs. At home the mother's thoughts, in business the father's ambitions center in the cradle. In this basic institution of human life we that are strong *do* bear the burdens of the weak and do not please ourselves. Each of us had that done for him. It were a shame if we could not live for others on a principle without which we ourselves never could live at all.

Nor have we escaped dependence upon superior strength because we now are grown to adult years. Strong in some respects, how weak we are in others! A thousand human ministries from family and friends support us in our frailties. Without such constant sustenance of superior strength we could not live for a day in worthiness, happiness, and peace. Moreover, when we think of standing in the presence of the Living God all conceit of independent strength vanishes utterly. The world looks up to a man and cries, "Strong!" But when he looks at himself he knows that he is dependent upon a mercy for which he cannot pay and on a power that he must receive with thankfulness, not earn with pride. He goes out to serve the immature, the handicapped, the backward, the oppressed, with no condescending superiority. He feels himself in a fellowship of mutual dependence upon a strength greater than his own. He is too heavily indebted to One who lavished the highest gifts upon the lowliest needs to find condescension possible. He signs all his service as our fathers signed their letters, "I am, sir, your most obliged and humble servant."

CHAPTER IV

THE ABUNDANT LIFE

Daily Readings

That the love of pleasure is one of the chief enemies of an unselfish life is a commonplace of experience. We all wish to be happy, and we are not wrong in wishing it. "A happy man or woman," says Robert Louis Stevenson, "is a better thing to find than a five pound note. He or she is a radiating focus of good will; and their entrance into a room is as though another candle had been lighted." But what makes life really happy? Let us consider a few of the elements, distinctly *not* selfish, which we at once recognize as necessary to abiding happiness.

Fourth Week, First Day

This is my commandment, that ye love one another, even as I have loved you. Greater love hath no man than this, that a man lay down his life for his friends. Ye are my friends, if ye do the things which I command you. No longer do I call you servants; for the servant knoweth not what his lord doeth: but I have called you friends; for all things that I heard from my Father I have made known unto you.—John 15:12-15.

Friends are necessary to a happy life. When friendship deserts us we are as lonely and helpless as a ship, left by the tide high upon the shore; when friendship returns to us, it is as though the tide came back, gave us buoyancy and freedom, and opened to us the wide places of the world. Proteus in *Two Gentlemen of Verona* says: "I to myself am dearer than a friend." How clearly such a man has blocked from his life one of the great avenues of happiness! But

63

friendship is essentially unselfish; its proper voice is heard in such words as Jesus spoke to his disciples that last night at the Table. To be sure, friendship can be perverted and caricatured, but even in its low forms some self-forgetfulness creeps in, and in its high ranges, where it brings the richest joy, it is nearest to pure unselfishness. Evidently a happy life cannot be all self-seeking.

O Lord of Love, in whom alone I live, kindle in my soul Thy fire of love; give me to lay myself aside, and to think of others as I kneel to Thee. For those whom Thou hast given me, dear to me as my own soul, Thy best gift on earth, I ask Thy blessing. If they are now far away, so that I cannot say loving words to them today, yet be Thou near them, give them of Thy joy, order their ways, keep them from sickness, from sorrow, and from sin, and let all things bring them closer to Thee. If they are near me, give us wisdom and grace to be true helpers of one another, serving in love's service all day long. Let nothing come between us to cloud our perfect trust, but help each to love more truly, more steadfastly, more unselfishly. Amen.
—Samuel McComb.

Fourth Week, Second Day

For yourselves know how ye ought to imitate us: for we behaved not ourselves disorderly among you; neither did we eat bread for nought at any man's hand, but in labor and travail, working night and day, that we might not burden any of you: not because we have not the right, but to make ourselves an ensample unto you, that ye should imitate us. For even when we were with you, this we commanded you, If any will not work, neither let him eat. For we hear of some that walk among you disorderly, that work not at all, but are busybodies. Now them that are such we command and exhort in the Lord Jesus Christ, that with quietness they work, and eat their own bread. But ye, brethren, be not weary in well-doing. II Thess. 3:7-13.

One of Paul's most engaging qualities was his sturdy self-respect, his love of economic independence, his pride in his handicraft. *Honest and useful work* in self-support, with something left over with which to help others, was necessary to his happiness. "Let him that stole steal no more," he wrote to the Ephesians, "but rather let him labor, working with his hands the

thing which is good, that he may have to give to him that needeth."
Any normal man understands Paul's feeling in this respect.
Idleness is the most deadly boredom that life can know, and hard
work, honestly done, with just pride in efficiency and skill, is life's
fundamental blessing. Deprive us of it for many months and we are
as restless, unsatisfied, and unhappy as a homesick boy away from
his own household. But good work is self-expenditure; it is the
forthputting of personality in creative labor. Manifestly, happiness has in it requirements of self-investment as well as of
self-regard.

*Accept the work of this day, O Lord, as we lay it at Thy feet. Thou
knowest its imperfections, and we know. Of the brave purposes of the
morning only a few have found their fulfillment. We bless Thee that
Thou art no hard taskmaster, watching grimly the stint of work we
bring, but the Father and Teacher of men who rejoices with us as we
learn to work. We have naught to boast before Thee, but we do not
fear Thy face. Thou knowest all things and Thou art love. Accept
every right intention, however brokenly fulßled, but grant that ere
our life is done we may under Thy tuition become true master
workmen, who know the art of a just and valiant life. Amen.—*
Walter Rauschenbusch.

Fourth Week, Third Day

First, I thank my God through Jesus Christ for you all, that
your faith is proclaimed throughout the whole world. For God is
my witness, whom I serve in my spirit in the gospel of his Son, how
unceasingly I make mention of you, always in my prayers making
request, if by any means now at length I may be prospered by the
will of God to come unto you. For I long to see you, that I may
impart unto you some spiritual gift, to the end ye may be
established; that is, that I with you may be comforted in you, each
of us by the other's faith, both yours and mine.—Rom. 1:8-12.

Of course Paul wished to see Rome. Paul was an imperial man
and Rome was the imperial city. Paul's happiness consisted in part
in this very fact, that he had *large interests,* and was not shut up to
provincial enthusiasms. Wherever good and evil met in combat,
wherever great business was afoot, wherever Christ was building
up his Church, Paul's heart was engaged. How much of happiness

depends upon such breadth of interest! Joy is the tingling sense of being fully alive, and that cannot come to narrow minds, absorbed by selfish concerns. They are pent, cooped up, suffocated; they lack the expansion of life which comes with large interests and generous enthusiasms. But an expanded life is of the very essence of unselfishness. How much of the throbbing joy which runs through the whole New Testament is due to the fact that Christ had taken many narrow, provincial spirits and had widened them to great hopes, liberal interests, and large devotions!

I am weary of my island life, O Spirit; it is absence from Thee. I am weary of the pleasures spent upon myself, weary of that dividing sea which makes me alone.

I look out upon the monotonous waves that roll between me and my brother, and I begin to be in want; I long for the time when there shall be no more sea.

Lift me on to the mainland, Thou Spirit of humanity, unite my heart to the brotherhood of human souls. Set my feet "in a large room"—in a space where many congregate. Place me on the continent of human sympathy where I can find my brother by night and by day—where storms divide not, where waves intervene not, where depths of downward distance drown not love.

Then shall the food of the far country be swine husks; then shall the riot and the revel be eclipsed by a new joy—the music and dancing of the city of God. Amen.—George Matheson.

Fourth Week, Fourth Day

These things have I spoken unto you, while yet abiding with you. But the Comforter, even the Holy Spirit, whom the Father will send in my name, he shall teach you all things, and bring to your remembrance all that I said unto you. Peace I leave with you; my peace I give unto you: not as the world giveth, give I unto you. Let not your heart be troubled, neither let it be fearful.—John 14:25-27.

Even as the Father hath loved me, I also have loved you: abide ye in my love. If ye keep my commandments, ye shall abide in my love; even as I have kept my Father's commandments, and abide in his love. These things have I spoken unto you, that my joy may be in you, and that your joy may be made full.—John 15:9-11.

Read these verses to observe one thing: the Master's earnest desire to share with his disciples the best blessings he had. His peace, his love, his joy—he did not wish to keep them to himself. And undoubtedly the more he shared, the more he possessed, for spiritual goods always multiply by division. Are we not facing here a basic truth in our lives? *Before we can fully enjoy anything we must share it.* Even a good book, good music, beautiful scenery—anything is enjoyed the more when we divide with others the experience. But this prerequisite for full happiness is distinctly unselfish. No man can achieve this special brand of abiding satisfaction by any manipulating of self-regard alone.

> All who joy would win
> Must share it. Happiness was born a twin.

Everlasting Father, I beseech Thee to enable me to love Thee with all my heart and soul and strength and mind, and my neighbor as myself.

Help me to be meek and lowly in heart. Sweeten my temper and dispose me to be kind and helpful to all men. Make me kind in thought, gentle in speech, generous in action. Teach me that it is more blessed to give than to receive; that it is better to minister than to be ministered unto; better to forget myself than to put myself forward.

Deliver me from anger and from envy; from all harsh thoughts and unlovely manners. Make me of some use in this world; may I more and more forget myself and work the work of Him who sent me here; through Jesus Christ our Lord. Amen.—W. Angus Knight.

Fourth Week, Fifth Day

For this cause I bow my knees unto the Father, from whom every family in heaven and on earth is named, that he would grant you, according to the riches of his glory, that ye may be strengthened with power through his Spirit in the inward man; that Christ may dwell in your hearts through faith; to the end that ye, being rooted and grounded in love, may be strong to apprehend with all the saints what is the breadth and length and height and depth, and to know the love of Christ which passeth knowledge, that ye may be filled unto all the fulness of God.—Eph. 3:14-19.

Here surely was a source of happiness in Paul's life, without which he would have been utterly bereft: he had *spiritual resources* within him on which even in his Roman prison he could fall back for re-creation and refreshment. Sooner or later all men come to the need of such inner wells of living water. Trouble falls upon us and by it we are driven in upon ourselves. The days arrive when happiness cannot spring from outward circumstance; we must discover it within, and carry it with us amid forbidding conditions. But a selfish man never can find such sources of joy within himself. Pascal was right: "The man who lives only for himself hates nothing so much as being alone with himself." A life inwardly rich and resourceful must be, as Paul prayed, "rooted and grounded in love." Alas! for a man, thrown back by fickle fortune on himself, who discovers in his own narrow cupboard nothing to live on except the resentments, the exaggerated self-regard, the disappointed ambitions of a selfish heart!

O God of patience and consolation, give us such good will, we beseech Thee, that with free hearts we may love and serve Thee and our brethren; and, having thus the mind of Christ, may begin heaven on earth, and exercise ourselves therein till that day when heaven where love abideth shall seem no strange habitation to us. For Jesus Christ's sake. Amen.—Christina Rossetti.

Fourth Week, Sixth Day

For I am already being offered, and the time of my departure is come. I have fought a good fight, I have finished the course, I have kept the faith: henceforth there is laid up for me the crown of righteousness, which the Lord, the righteous judge, shall give to me at that day; and not to me only, but also to all them that have loved his appearing.—II Tim. 4:6-8.

In these farewell words of Paul there is the unmistakable accent of a victorious and joyful spirit. And this is the secret of his joy: *he has lived his life for a cause that is worth living and dying for.* The deep satisfactions of a purposeful existence, dedicated to a worthy end, remain with him to the death. His final note is that of a happy warrior: "I have fought the good fight." Compare with this the retrospect of a self-centered, frittered life! The selfish man may have been carnal, deserving Carlyle's terrific comment on the eighteenth century, "Soul extinct; stomach well alive!" He may have been cruel, like Milton's "sons of Belial, flown with insolence and wine." Or he may have been only a languid, pulseless, self-centered man. But in any case he has missed the supreme satisfaction of life. "This is now to be said," wrote Alfred the Great, "that whilst I live I wish to live nobly, and after life to leave to the men who come after me a memory of good works."

Help us, O Lord, to live out on the open sea of Thine all-reaching love, and to move with the currents of Thy power; to fill life's sails with the fresh winds of spiritual truth and freedom; to sail up and down time's glorious coast, carrying a heaven-scented cargo of better life to men; to be conscious less of effort and more of power; to see the needy men on the shore and bring them the bread of life; trusting always that when the sails grow gray and the spars and planks begin to groan in the gale, Heaven's safe harbor may welcome in peace the Captain of the Abundant Life. Amen.—George A. Miller.

Fourth Week, Seventh Day

Is it not plain from this week's study that he who seeks for happiness without unselfishness has missed his road? Friends, useful work, expanded interests, the delights of shared experience, inward spiritual resources, and a worthy purpose at life's center—such unselfish things as these are of the very substance of a joyful and abundant life.

All wise men in all ages have perceived that love and life thus belong together, and all of us do indulge in more or less unselfishness. But our service is fluctuating and unsteady. When the Master takes possession of us, straightway the principle of service begins to flower out. It widens its horizons to take in all the world; it deepens its vision to take in the most unlovely and the lost; it enlarges its scope to include even our enemies; it surrounds itself with majestic motives in the love of God, and at last a real Christian stands unfolded, with the spirit of service grown to a "lordly great compass" within. Such a development is not unhappy; it is the very blossom and fruitage of joy. So the Master said:

I am the door; by me if any man enter in, he shall be saved, and shall go in and go out, and shall find pasture. The thief cometh not, but that he may steal, and kill, and destroy: I came that they may have life, and may have it abundantly.—John 10:9, 10.

O God, Author of the world's joy, Bearer of the world's pain, make us glad that we are men and that we have inherited the world's burden; deliver us from the luxury of cheap melancholy; and, at the heart of all our trouble and sorrow, let unconquerable gladness dwell; through our Lord and Saviour Jesus Christ. Amen.—Henry S. Nash.

COMMENT FOR THE WEEK

I

Such a dedicated use of strength in service as we have been considering plainly involves self-sacrifice. George Eliot in "Romola" says of Tito: "He was to be depended on to make any sacrifice that was not unpleasant." Such a costless amiability is common, but seriously to put service for all sorts of folk at the center of one's purpose involves readiness for self-renunciation which hurts. We run at once, therefore, upon that stumbling block which more than any other trips people up who start to be of use. We want *happiness* for ourselves; we want for ourselves a full, rich, vibrant life; and this clamorous self-regard seems desperately at war with self-sacrifice.

Of all arresting words of Jesus, none is stranger than his declaration on this seeming conflict between self-regard and self-renunciation. So significant is it that oftener than any other single thing he said it is referred to in the gospels: "Whosoever would save his life shall lose it: and whosoever shall lose his life for my sake shall find it." (Matt. 16:25. cf. Matt. 10:39; Mark 8:34, 35; Luke 9:23, 24; Luke 17:33; John 12:25.) He too, then, is in love with happiness; he too is seeking for his followers a tingling, copious, satisfying life. The fourth gospel expressly states his purpose: "I have come that they may have life and have it to the full." And the New Testament is radiant with the consciousness of having found the secret of abundant living. But whether in the Master himself or in those who closely followed him, one everywhere finds a strange prescription for their overflowing joy. If you wish blessedness, head for service; if you wish the crown of joy, take up the cross of sacrifice; if life is to be yours, lose your life in other lives and in causes that have won your love. *So far from seeing abundant living and sacrificial service as mutually exclusive, they see one as the road to the other.*

However reluctant we may be to base our daily conduct upon this principle, however the subtle suspicion may intrude that the paradox is not quite true, there are times when its truth is evident. Crises come, sudden, unforeseen, that shake men down into the deeper levels of experience, where there is no keeping life except through life's surrender. "If I save my life, I lose it," is the motto engraved upon a statue of Sir Galahad in Ottawa. These are the last words of a youth, in whose memory the statue stands, who, seeing two skaters fall through the ice, plunged in and was drowned in rescuing them. Any such crisis makes evident to a courageous spirit as it did to this youth, the truth of the Master's words. During the Great War who has not wonderingly watched men and women finding their joy and glory in self-renouncing devotion to a cause? Multitudes of folk faced selfish ease and terrific sacrifice, and chose sacrifice. Not for all the world in such an hour of need would they have chosen anything besides.

> Though love repine and reason chafe,
> There came a voice without reply,
> 'Tis man's perdition to be safe
> If for the truth he ought to die.

Nevertheless, while this principle of Jesus is thus written in sympathetic ink upon the hearts of men so that the acid of a world catastrophe does bring it out where all can read, it pales again in common days. Men find it easier to die for a cause in a crisis than to live for it in ordinary hours. They do not really believe that self-realization through self-surrender is a universal law of life. But the Master saw this principle not as an occasional motive in a tragic hour, but as the common property of all hours. He saw that as surely as a seed must give itself up or else fail of increase, so only in sacrificial service can men find the secret of abundant life (John 12:24).

II

When we seek thus to understand, as the Master did, the relationship between self-realization and self-scrifice, we need first of all to consider what the *self* is of which we speak. Children in the nursery play with a fascinating toy, which superficially seen appears to be a single box, but which on investigation reveals box within box, and ever more boxes still, each drawn from the interior of another until the floor is littered with them. so multiple and complicated a thing is the human self. When, therefore, one cries, I must care for myself, the answer comes, Which self? This smallest, meanest self, that last of all comes up from the interior of your life? This infinitesimal creature of narrow, clamorous, egoistic needs? To live for that self is to lose real life utterly. For all the while there is the larger possible self, that may inclose and glorify the smaller, compounded of family love, of friendship, of devotion to neighborhood and country, of loyalty to human kind, and to good causes on which man's weal depends. To live for that larger self is to live the abundant life.

Consider how true it is that our personalities are thus *a telescoping series of larger and smaller selves!* A young girl begins her life petted, pampered, spoiled. Her innermost and narrowest self is the only one she knows. Then love draws her out. She lives not quite so much within that narrow self as in the larger area of another's life, which to her has become dearer than her own. Then children come to increase the acreage of her spirit. Some day in that home toddling feet go down to the edge of the valley of the shadow. Her own life is in the balance then. Not something outside her stands hesitating there upon the valley's brink; it is part of her very being; and when her child's feet come clambering up the slippery slope again it is her own life that has come back to her. Expanded thus by experience she looks with increasing sympathy and understanding eyes upon humanity. She sees, as Chaucer sang:

> Infinite been the sorwes and the teres
> Of oldé folk and folk of tendre yeres.

In her awakened womanhood she spends herself in unselfish service that this earth may be a more decent place for the family of God. Philanthropy, good government, the Christian cause—these things become part of herself. When she prays, "Thy Kingdom come" she means it. She can understand now what Milton felt: "I conceive myself to be not as mine own person, but as a member incorporate into that truth whereof I am persuaded." If now some friend who knew her coddled youth should say, "See! you have lost your old self!" would she not answer? "Thank God, I have lost it! I have lost my life and found it."

The paradoxical principle of Jesus, therefore, that self-surrender is necessary to self-realization is true in everyday experience. We all have this series of possible selves, from the meanest egoism that like a fledgling bird yammers with open mouth for the world to feed it, to that great self that can embrace within its sympathy and incorporate into its life the welfare of the world. The fundamental question is, Which self shall be subjugated to the other? Washington could have saved his self, his Virginia planter self, in ease and comfort, but so he would have lost his real self, Father of the Nation. The Master could have saved his self, his carpenter of Nazareth self, redeeming words unspoken, but so he would have lost his real self, Savior of the World. We can save ourselves, our infinitesimal and futile selves, in unsacrificial ease. But what we have really done is to throw away the greatness of our lives.

Self-sacrifice is not, therefore, a bitter amputation of our personalities. *It is the enlargement of our personalities to comprehend the interests of others*. It is finding life, disguised as losing it. We overpass the boundary that separates *I* from *You;* we learn to think and live in terms of *We* and *Our,* and lo! we have found our greater selves. Sometimes the preacher pleads for self-regard. Care for yourselves, he says. Your personality is the most sacred entrustment God has given you. "What shall it profit a man if he gain the whole world and lose his own self?" And sometimes the preacher pleads for self-denial. You must sacrifice yourselves, he says. What is self that it should stand athwart the progress of God's good causes in the world? No one has learned the rudiments of Christian living who has not learned to deny, abnegate, crucify self. So do self-regard and self-denial appear in conflict. Nor is there any solution of this dilemma, except as we learn to incorporate our life by love into the life of others, until we live in them and they in us. Then self-sacrifice and self-relization flow together. What has become of the conflict between self-regard and self-denial in a great friendship, where two persons blend? When I care for myself, I am caring for my friend, and when I think of my friend, I am thinking of myself. We live in each other's lives. So Mrs. Browning sings of her husband:

> The widest land
> Doom takes to part us, leaves thy heart in mine
> With pulses that beat double. What I do
> And what I dream include thee, as the wine
> Must taste of its own grapes.

Indeed, let any generous man ask himself where his *self* is, and how surprising is the answer! It is not alone where his body is. It is where his children dwell. What strikes them strikes him. It is where his friends are. What befalls them befalls him. It is where with difficulty causes forge ahead, on which his heart is set. Every large-hearted man is scattered over all creation. Where was David when, safe in the watchtower, he cried, "O my son, Absalom! would God I had died for thee, O Absalom, my son"? Where was Livingstone, when he cried of Africa, "All I can add in my loneliness is, may Heaven's rich blessing come down on every one—American, English, Turk—who will help to heal the open sore of the world"? Personality is marvelously extensible. Like an alarm system with a central registering bell and many sensitive wires stretching every whither, so is a human person. We are not narrowly delimited things; we are spiritual beings, capable of infinite expansion, able to live ourselves out in other people and in causes that have claimed our love. No man is complete in himself; all that he cares for is part of him. The glory of the Master is that he so lived out his life in the lives of all mankind that he could say and mean it, "Inasmuch as ye did it unto one of these my brethren, even these last, ye did it unto me." This is self-sacrifice; but it is also self-realization. It is the effulgence of life into its full size and glory, even though it be true that

> He who lives more lives than one
> More deaths than one must die.

III

In spite of the acknowledged truth just presented, one may be tempted still to plead the case in favor of self-regard. The necessity and duty of caring for our individual selves, however narrow one may call them, are imperative. A solid and important truth lies in Shakespeare's words in *Henry V*, "Self-love, my liege, is not so vile a sin as self-neglecting." To till a field for wheat that one selfishly may eat it all, while starving neighbors look on unhelped, is bad enough. But to let a good field run to weeds untilled for any purpose, is still worse. A man's first responsibility is his own individual life, to till it, to enrich it, to make it bear all that it will yield. The summary of the law and the prophets tells us to love ourselves well and then to love others just as much (Luke 10:27).

Because this is a Christian's primary responsibility, as it is any other man's, a charge of insincerity is sometimes lodged against the preacher and his congregation when self-sacrifice is exalted in the church. "See!" cries the scoffer, "All your words about self-renouncing service are hypocrisy. You and all your parishioners, like everybody else, want good things for yourselves. Homes, food, clothes, books, music, leisure, the elemental creature comforts and the luxuries that minister to fullness of life—you want all these, and you propose to have them if you can. In what, then, do you differ from any other men?"

To such an objection this parable may be an answer: The Sea of Galilee and the Dead Sea are made of the same water. It flows down, clear and cool, from the heights of Hermon and the roots of the cedars of Lebanon. The Sea of Galilee makes beauty of it, for the Sea of Galilee has an outlet. *It gets to give.* It gathers in its riches that it may pour them out again to fertilize the Jordan plain. But the Dead Sea with the same water makes horror. For the Dead Sea has no outlet. *It gets to keep.* That is the radical difference between selfish and unselfish men. We all do want life's enriching blessings; we ought to; they are divine benedictions. But some men get to give, and they are like Galilee; while some men get to keep and they are like the brackish water that covers Sodom and Gomorrah. "We Florentines," says one of George Eliot's characters, "live scrupulously that we may spend splendidly."

The Master's principle, then, that only by self-surrender can we win through to self-fulfilment, does not mean that the individual self is unimportant. It means that the individual self is but a fragment of the whole personality, and if it is to come to its fullness, must expand to take in its brethren. "Love to one's neighbor," says Professor Todd, "does not mean the annihilation of one's self, but simply the recognition that self and neighbor are fundmentally one."

One corollary of this truth is clear. *The selfish man is not a complete man; he is not whole, normal, healthy.* He is a truncated section of himself. He may think himself a natural, sensible, hard-headed, practical person. The truth is that he is sick.

Indeed, our insistence that unselfishness and abundant life involve each other and to be meanly selfish is to renounce the glory of living, is illustrated by the fact that the symptoms of invalidism and the symptoms of selfishness are the same. No one suffers long with a debilitating, nagging illness without being tempted to think wholly of his narrowest self. His mind tends to wind inward with circular, moody thoughts about himself. He is absorbed in his own needs. Querulous, touchy, waspish, wanting attention, impatient when he does not receive it, discontented when he does—unless it be spiritually conquered, such is the mood of illness.

Consider then the road by which a man moves out from this lamentable state toward health again! He begins to worry less and less about himself. He gains some surplus energy of thought to spend on some one besides himself. He feels in time a dawning capacity to be happy in the happiness of others. At length he eats and sleeps again with relish and delight, and sheds his returning radiance on all around. Rising within him like a tossing mill race, he feels returning vigor, fretting to be let loose upon some mill wheel. He wants to do something for somebody. At last, his sickness gone, happily objective, not moodily subjective, thinking of others, not worrying about himself, spending abroad his surplus vigor, not hoarding it greedily for his depleted strength, he goes out into life, a dynamic man come back to health again. By as much as he extends himself, giving more than he gets, making his contributions offered greater than his contributions levied, he shows the marks of a well man. For selfishness is sickness, and overflowing usefulness is spiritual health and abounding life.

IV

The necessary relationship between self-surrender and self-fulfilment is seen clearly in one more basic fact. Existence is given to us all to start with; our problem is somehow out of existence to make life. Existence is an entrustment; life is an achievement. Now all human experience is unanimous that real life can come only when *a worthy purpose runs down through the center of existence, to give it meaning.* This is plain when one tests its truth by the lives of the greatest men. As on raised letters, so on the outstanding characters of history even blind folk can read the truth that a worthy purpose is essential to abundant life. Amid infinite variety in details one attribute is always present when a great man comes: he has centered his existence around some aim concerning which he feels like Paul, "This one thing I do." The one intolerable life from which all high-minded men must shrink, as Matthew Arnold says his father shrank from it, is a frittered existence:

> Not without aim to go round
> In an eddy of purposeless dust,
> Effort unmeaning and vain.

Nor is this attitude the peculiarity of the most capacious souls alone. We all may have it. The Mississippi River makes the central plains of the United States a rich and fruitful place. From the Rockies to the Gulf, calling in tributaries from every side, it has organized the life of a continent. What, then, has made the beauty and productiveness of some small valley, whose woods and farms, though quite unheralded, are a benediction to the few who know them? There, too, a stream with tributary rivulets has organized and fructified the valley's life. So a central, serviceable purpose is the secret of abundant living, whether in continental men or in obscure and lowly folk. No man lives at all until he lives for something great.

To many, such a purposeful and dedicated life seems stern, forbidding. We want pleasure: "the loose beads with no straight string running through." We cannot wake and sleep and spend the hours between, we say, concentered on a serious aim. But a serviceable purpose does not thus somberly becloud life and exclude its free-hearted happiness. It rather is the one element in life that can put foundation under happiness. When one goes from New York to San Francisco he does not tensely sit through the week, saying with deliberate insistence, I must go to San Francisco. His purpose to reach his destination does not exhaust his thought. He thinks of a thousand other things; his delight in friendship and scenery upon the way is unaffected and spontaneous; no single happy or interesting experience need he miss. But all the same his major purpose controls his action; nothing is allowed to keep him from going on to San Francisco; and when he reaches his destination all that has happened on the way—the pleasant fellowships, the gorgeous scenery—has been but incidental to his dominant desire which brought him to his journey's end.

So whatever may be his special calling, through a real Christian's life runs a controlling purpose to be of use. It does not substitute itself for other things; it permeates everything. Its subtle secret influence flows through all the rest. It shuts out no wholesome, happy experience of good report. Rather it includes them all, and irradiates them with significance and worth. Such a man alone is truly happy, for pleasure never lasts when it is made the main business of life. It has abiding quality only when it is founded upon a worthy purpose. As a life that is all vacation knows no vacation, since the very essence of a holiday lies in having hard work upon all sides of it, so a life that is all pleasure-seeking knows no pleasure. For the essence of all abiding pleasure is to be mainly busy about some serviceable task.

Too long have the pallid and tubercular figures of saints in medieval cathedrals symbolized the meaning of Christian life! Consider rather a man like Henry Drummond. Few men have been more mastered by a central purpose. He lived to bring men into fellowship with Jesus Christ. The influence of his preaching and his personal interviews upon the student life of Scotland abides long after he has gone. His biographer says that writing the story of his life is "like writing the record of a fragrance." Yet as to the glow and buoyancy of his daily life, let a friend testify:

He fished, he shot, he skated as few can, he played cricket; he would go any distance to see a fire or a football match. He had a new story, a new puzzle, or a new joke every time he met you. Was it on the street? He drew you to watch two message boys meet, grin, knock each other's hats off, lay down their baskets and enjoy a friendly chaffer of marbles. Was it on the train? He had dredged from the bookstall every paper and magazine that was new to him. . . . If it was a rainy afternoon in a country house, he described a new game, and in five minutes everybody was playing it. If it was a children's party, they clamored for his sleight of hand. . . . The name he went by among younger men was The Prince.

As a brook flows down from the high hills sparkling in the sunlight, gathering itself in friendly pools, playing among the shallows near the shore, or running out into deep places where all is cool and still, so spirits like Drummond's flow among men. But whether they seem serious or happy they are mastered by one thing: the gravitation from the high hills whence they came. Their flow is all one way: a testimony to the fullness and beauty of Christian life and to the sufficiency of the Master from whom it comes.

Once more, therefore, losing the smaller self in a larger self, organized around a serious desire to serve mankind, is self-renunciation indeed, but it is self-fulfillment, too. The man who achieves it possesses an expansive personality which is the secret of abiding joy. Even when disasters fall, he is not undone as selfish men must be, for his smallest self is not the whole of himself, and what happens to his smallest self leaves still the larger areas of his life untouched. Like soldiers who fall wounded upon the battlefield, he himself may suffer, but still rejoice exceedingly to see his cause advanced.

Paradoxical as it may seem, therefore, the Master was speaking from a rich and real experience of fact when he said, "Whosoever will be great among you, let him be your minister, and whosoever will be chief among you let him be your servant." To be sure, the natural grain of the human wood runs another way altogether. Whosoever would be great among you, let him conquer or rule or gain wealth; let him *be served* by multitudes of slaves, by millions of subjects, by the labor of the poor—such is the idea which underlies the larger part of human history. The Master turned topsy-turvy this inveterate conviction that a man's glory consists in service received. He substituted in its place the amazing proposition that man's glory consists in the extent and quality and unselfishness of service rendered. And none who ever dared to live upon the Master's principle has denied its truth. The way of the Cross is the way of overflowing life. "He that will take that crabbit tree, and will carry it cannily," said Samuel Rutherford, "will yet find it to be such a burden as wings are to a bird and sails to a boat."

CHAPTER V

SELF-DENIAL

Daily Readings

Our study during the last week centered about the Master's principle that in the expenditure of life lies the saving of it. There are times, however, when this truth is anything but obvious. A mountain's summit may glisten in the sunlight, while its lower altitudes are all beclouded. So this ideal of finding life through losing it may shine in its loftiest exhibitions, as in the character of Christ, while, on our common levels, it is obscure and difficult of access. Self-denial at times seems not to be glorious and life-giving at all. We shall try, this week, to deal with the meaning of such self-denial. Let us in our daily readings deal with the fact of it.

Fifth Week, First Day

And if thy right eye causeth thee to stumble, pluck it out, and cast it from thee: for it is profitable for thee that one of thy members should perish, and not thy whole body be cast into hell. And if thy right hand causeth thee to stumble, cut it off, and cast it from thee: for it is profitable for thee that one of thy members should perish, and not thy whole body go into hell—Matt. 5:29, 30.

One elemental form of self-denial, demanded by a life of Christian service, is the *resolute rejection of positive evils* that mar character and therefore hurt usefulness. "There never was a bad man," said Edmund Burke, "that had ability for good service." How much this kind of self-denial costs, anyone who has ever seriously tried it knows. We must continually resist the down-drag of popular habits, to the practice of which the majority of folk consent. For the majority, however we must commit to it the arbitrament of political affairs, is almost sure to be wrong about any matter that requires fine discrimination. Put to popular vote the preference between ragtime and Chopin's nocturnes, the cinema and Shakespeare, cheap love-stories and the English classics, and is there any question what the majority would decide? So to be a good Christian is an achievement, won only by resistance to the pull of popular tastes and common practices. It costs to be among those whose characters lift up against the gravitation of commonly accepted evil. "The world is upheld," said Emerson, "by the veracity of good men: they make the earth wholesome."

My Father, may the world not mould me today, but may I be so strong as to help to mould the world! Amen.—John Henry Jowett.

Fifth Week, Second Day

The kingdom of heaven is like unto a treasure hidden in the field; which a man found, and hid; and in his joy he goeth and selleth all that he hath, and buyeth that field.

Again, the kingdom of heaven is like unto a man that is a merchant seeking goodly pearls: and having found one pearl of great price, he went and sold all that he had, and bought it.—Matt. 13:44-46.

Christian service plainly demands this second form of self-denial: *the abandonment of scattered loyalty for a life of dominant interest in the Kingdom of God on earth.* To be a Christian is not negative absence of outbreaking sin, as some seem to suppose. "I have known men," said Henry Ward Beecher, "who thought the object of conversion was to clean them, as a garment is cleaned, and that when they were converted they were to be hung up in the Lord's wardrobe the door of which was to be shut so that no dust could get at them. A coat that is not used the moths eat; and a Christian who is hung up so that he shall not be tempted—the moths eat him; and they have poor food at that." Rather, a Christian life is one of positive, single-hearted devotion to the welfare of man, to the service of the lowliest and lost, to the support of all good causes, to the hope of the Kingdom. But a life so centrally dedicated costs its price. Sometimes a man, as Jesus said, must give up for it all that he has. Under any circumstances, a life that cares, suffers. So when the Fugitive Slave Law was passed, a great New Englander wrote: "There is infamy in the air. I have a new experience. I wake in the morning with a painful sensation, which I carry about all day, and which, when traced home, is the odious remembrance of the ignominy which has fallen on Massachusetts, which robs the landscape of beauty and takes the sunshine out of every hour." Do you care for any good cause as much as that?

O Lord, fill us with the simplicity of a divine purpose, that we may be inwardly at one with Thy holy will, and lifted above vain wishes of our own. Set free from every detaining desire or reluctance, may we heartily surrender all our powers to the work which Thou hast given us to do; rejoicing in any toil, and fainting under no hardness that may befall us, as good soldiers of Jesus Christ, and counting it as our crown of blessing, if we may join the company of the faithful who have kept Thy Name, and witnessed to Thy kingdom in every age. Amen.—James Martineau.

Fifth Week, Third Day

And he looked up, and saw the rich men and that were casting their gifts into the treasury. And he saw a certain poor widow casting in thither two mites. And he said, Of a truth I say unto you, This poor widow cast in more than they all: for all these did of their superfluity cast in unto the gifts; but she of her want did cast in all the living that she had.—Luke 21:1-4.

Christian service plainly demands *self-denial in money.* Extravagant expenditure while millions of people are in want, needless luxury, while good causes fail for funds—there is no use in claiming the Christian name if one indulges in such obviously unchristian conduct. Some have said that even luxurious expenditure is useful because it furnishes work for the laborer, but what it really does is to call both work and money away from necessary tasks to unproductive and needless investments. How justly does this satire fall on Dives!

> Now Dives daily feasted
> And was gorgeously arrayed;
> Not at all because he liked it,
> But because 'twas good for trade.
> That the poor might have more calico,

He clothed himself with silk;
And surfeited himself on cream
That they might have more milk.
And e'en to show his sympathy
For the deserving poor
He did no useful work himself
That they might do the more.

Compare such a character with the woman of the parable. She was taking her religion in earnest; and she gave good proof of it in her use of money. For the use of money can be made a touchstone of sincerity. If a man say that he loves his family, but, being able, makes no provision for their financial security, spending his income rather in his present pleasure, something is seriously the matter with his love. If a man say that he loves God and his fellows, but does not give till it hurts for their service, his professed love is not likely to be more than a theatrical gesture.

O Lord, who though Thou wast rich, yet for our sakes didst become poor, and hast promised in Thy Gospel that whatsoever is done unto the least of Thy brethren, Thou wilt receive as done unto Thee; give us grace, we humbly beseech Thee, to be ever willing and ready to minister, as thou enablest us, to the necessities of our fellow-creatures, and to extend the blessings of Thy kingdom over all the world, to Thy praise and glory, who art God over all, blessed for ever. Amen.—St. Augustine (354-430).

Fifth Week, Fourth Day

And Zacchaeus stood, and said unto the Lord, Behold, Lord, the half of my goods I give to the poor; and if I have wrongfully exacted aught of any man, I restore fourfold. And Jesus said unto him, To-day is salvation come to this house, forasmuch as he also is a son of Abraham. For the Son of man came to seek and to save that which was lost.—Luke 19:8-10.

Christian service demands not only self-denial in giving money, but *self-denial in making it.* Zacchaeus had pressed the opportunities of his position to the limit; he had charged all that the traffic would bear; he had narrowly looked at all chances for gain—honest, half-honest, or dishonest—and had squeezed them as dry as he could. The invasion of his life by Jesus meant an economic revolution. He was forced to review the sources of his income and to plan a radical change. One of the acutest self-denials demanded by Christianity and too often disregarded, is such a renunciation of profits. Needlessly high prices, needlessly low wages, needlessly unwholesome conditions of labor make dividends poisonous. No true Christian can ever knowingly coin the suffering and degradation of his fellows into cash for his own pocket. The problem presented by this fact, under conditions of modern industry, is enormously difficult for the individual to handle. As Professor Rauschenbusch wrote: "Stockholders are scattered absentee owners. A corporation might be composed of retired missionaries, peace advocates, and dear old ladies, but their philanthropy would cause no vibrations in the business end of the concern." The solution of the problem can come only with general alterations in public ideals of business and with economic changes to give such better ideals expression; but this does not excuse any man from an earnest, sacrificial endeavor to purge the sources of his income from unchristian elements.

Deliver us, we beseech Thee, O Lord, from all kinds of stealing, extortion, fraud in trade and contracts; from all making haste to be rich, and from taking advantage of the ignorance or necessity of the persons we deal with.—Bishop Ken.

Fifth Week, Fifth Day

And Jesus said unto Simon, Fear not: from henceforth thou shalt catch men. And when they had brought their boats to land, they left all, and followed him. . . . And after these things he went forth, and beheld a publican, named Levi, sitting at the place of toll, and he said unto him, Follow me. And he forsook all, and rose up and followed him.—Luke 5:10, 11; 27, 28.

Not everybody was thus called on to leave the ordinary business of life. Sometimes Jesus called men to stay where they were. So to the healed Gadarene demoniac, who wanted to join the traveling company of the apostles, the Master said, "Go to thy house and unto thy friends" (Mark 5:19). *But some men and women are called out for special work.* The comfort and security of home life and a settled business are denied them. They are missionaries; they toil in the slums of the cities; they undertake ventures in philanthropy; they pioneer fresh fields of truth and bear the brunt of the attacks that always fall on unaccustomed enterprises; they are the unusual folk, the martyrs in whom the sacrifice of Jesus is fulfilled, "He saved others, himself he cannot save" (Mark 15:31). Christian character involves the willingness to answer such a call as this. The self-denial involved in it is sharply obvious. Only the loftiest motives can sustain men in such self-sacrifice. So St. Bernard put it: "The faithful soldier does not feel his own wounds when he looks with love on those of his King."

O God, the God of all goodness and of all grace, who art worthy of a greater love than we can either give or understand; fill our hearts, we beseech Thee, with such love toward Thee, that nothing may seem too hard for us to do or to suffer in obedience to Thy will; and grant that thus loving Thee, we may become daily more like unto Thee, and finally obtain the crown of life which Thou hast promised to those that love Thee; through Jesus Christ our Lord. Amen.—"A Book of Prayers for Students."

Fifth Week, Sixth Day

Recall today the familiar scene where Naomi bids farewell to her daughters-in-law, and turns her face from Moab toward her home country:

And they lifted up their voice, and wept again: and Orpah kissed her mother-in-law; but Ruth clave unto her.
And she said, Behold, thy sister-in-law is gone back unto her people, and unto her god: return thou after thy sister-in-law. And Ruth said, Entreat me not to leave thee, and to return from following after thee; for whither thou goest, I will go; and where thou lodgest, I will lodge; thy people shall be my people, and thy God my god; where thou diest, will I die, and there will I be buried; Jehovah do so to me, and more also, if aught but death part thee and me. And when she saw that she was stedfastly minded to go with her, she left off speaking unto her.—Ruth 1:14-18.

Of how much self-denial in family relationships is this a type! *To be a real Christian in a home often means costly self-renunciation.* Controlled temper, decent demeanor no matter how you feel, a radiant spirit even under irritating circumstances—even such simple elements of Christian home life are not easy. Carlyle did not master that much self-denial in his relationships with his wife.

"Ah! if I only had five minutes with her," he said after her death, "if only to assure her that I loved her through all that." And often the demands of self-renunciation in a home go deeper. When poverty must be faced together, when sickness falls, the tragedy of which all share, when children are sent to college by parents who cannot afford it, when sin wrecks lives which nevertheless love will not give up—how intimate, exacting, and continuous are the gracious self-bestowals of a true home! Here live the modest martyrs of service whose names are written in heaven. For Ruth is one of an innumerable company who have found their sphere of self-renouncing love in the home and whose reward, like Ruth's, lies here, that she bore Obed, and "he is the father of Jesse, the father of David."

O Heavenly Father, shed forth Thy blessed Spirit richly on all the members of this household. Make each one of us an instrument in thy hands for good. Purify our hearts, strengthen our minds and bodies, fill us with mutual love. Let no pride, no self-conceit, no rivalry, no dispute ever spring up among us. Make us earnest and true, wise and prudent, giving no just cause for offense; and may Thy holy peace rest upon us this day and every day, sweetening our trials, cheering us in our work, and keeping us faithful to the end; through Jesus Christ our Lord. Amen.—Church Guild.

Fifth Week, Seventh Day

Such are the familiar self-denials which a Christian life involves: the withstanding of popular sins; the refusal of loose and scattered loyalty; the conquest of niggardliness; the renunciation of tainted income; the sacrifice of comfort, home, country, and life itself, if need be, to fulfil a special vocation; and, if that be not demanded, the daily self-renunciation without which home, neighborhood, and friendship are impossible. Such a program of self-denial the Master demanded without diminution or apology.

From that time began Jesus to show unto his disciples, that he must go unto Jerusalem, and suffer many things of the elders and chief priests and scribes, and be killed, and the third day be raised up. And Peter took him, and began to rebuke him, saying, Be it far from thee, Lord: this shall never be unto thee. But he turned, and said unto Peter, Get thee behind me, Satan: thou art a stumbling-block unto me: for thou mindest not the things of God,

but the things of men. Then said Jesus unto his disciples, If any man would come after me, let him deny himself, and take up his cross, and follow me. For whosoever would save his life shall lose it: and whosoever shall lose his life for my sake shall find it.—Matt. 16:21-25.

St. Francis Xavier, who knew from experience to what extremes Christian self-sacrifice could go, wrote once about this closing verse:

"It may be easy to understand the Latin, and the general meaning of this saying of the Lord, but when dangers arise, where the life about which you wish to decide will probaby be lost, and when, in order to prepare yourself to decide to lose your life for God's sake that you may find it in Him, you get down to details, everything else, even this clear Latin, begins to get hazy. And in such a case, however learned you may be, you can understand nothing, unless God, in His infinite mercy, makes your particular case plain."

Surely we may take it for certain, that if we have no idea what Xavier means, if we never have been hard put to it to bring ourselves to the point of a decisive and costly self-denial, we have not been following very closely in the footsteps of the Master.

Yea, O my God, we lay hold of Thy cross, as of a staff that can stand unshaken, when the floods run high. The tale told us is no fairy story of some far-away land: it is this world, and not another—this world with all its miseries and its slaughter and its ruin—that Thou hast entered to redeem, by Thine Agony and bloody Sweat.—H. Scott Holland.

COMMENT FOR THE WEEK

I

All that we have said about self-sacrifice as the road to self-fulfilment may be true, but it will take a fairer and more gracious world than ours to make it constantly seem true. There are persons with whom it is easy for ourlives to blend, until in losing self in them we find our selves returned to us, enlarged and glorified. So Paul said, "He that loveth his own wife loveth himself." (Eph. 5:28). There ar causes in the service of which our interest runs high, so that, giving ourselves to them, we find an expanded and satisfying life. But the spending of self in service is not always so obviously associated with rich return. There are times when self-sacrifice and self-fulfilment do not beautifully blend. Tennyson put the truth of our last chapter into poetry:

"Love took up the harp of Life, and smote on all the cords with might;
Smote the chord of Self, that, trembling, pass'd in music out of sight."

But often our individual selves, with all their clamourous rights and needs, are not so easily disposed of. They do not pass out of sight "in music," but in agony and rebellion. They chafe against the piercing self-denials that often are involved when we do our serviceable duty.

Some people it is a delight to serve. They are obviously worth it. Their response in gratitude, their alert capacity to avail themselves of proffered aid, their swift recovery from need to independence, visit any service rendered them with immediate reward. But one who sets himself, in the spirit of the Master, to lead a serviceable life, does not float day after day through such idyllic experiences. He sends boys through college and they turn out to be thankless rascals; he endeavors to advance an able girl to a more responsible position and she grows heady and hopeless; he conceives a fine plan to redeem an unsanitary neighborhood and with chagrin discovers that the hopeless sufferers prefer it as it is; he ministers tirelessly through many years to the exacting demands of a querulous and selfish relative, only to wonder at the end whether such poignant self-denial was right.

Moreover, self-sacrificial service that ideally should expand the life, often in practice seems to narrow it. Helpfulness, alluring at first, lapses into drudgery. Living in a settlement, going as a missionary, championing a worthy cause, helping all sorts of folk, may appear romantic; in fact, it is extraordinarily hard work. So when Florence Nightingale and her first corps of nurses were sailing up the Bosphorus to deal with the nameless horrors in the Crimea, the glow of adventure still was exciting the young women's thoughts. They uttered ecstatic exclamations over the coming days of service. But Miss Nightingale silenced them. "Young women," she said, "the strongest will be wanted at the washtub."

Not only does a serviceable spirit find itself dealing thus with unresponsive folk and monotonous tasks, but, as well, the times come when self-sacrifice means self-sacrifice with a vengeance. The claims of others cut clean across the dearest interests of our own lives. Not any expansion of the sacrificing self is obvious, but rather the utter self-renunciation with which the sweetest, wholesomest, choicest joys are given up for others' sake. Times come when saving others means that we cannot save ourselves. So David Livingstone laid his wife away, dead of the jungle fever, and broken-hearted and alone turned his face toward his last terrific journey into the interior. In his diary we find his outburst of agony: "Oh, my Mary, my Mary! How often we have longed for a quiet home, since you and I were cast adrift at Kolobeng"!

II

Granting, therefore, that only in unselfish, service can any life find true enlargement and satisfaction, we need still to consider in terms of concrete experience the problem of costly self-denials. For one thing, when the Master says, "If any man would come after me let him deny himself and take up his cross and follow me," he is not in the least unique. *Every art, science, feat of skill, and enterprise on earth says the same thing.* So Paul at the Greek games saw men who could not have guided so unerringly their swerving chariots, so tirelessly have run their races and sustained their combats, if with unwearying self-denial they had not disciplined themselves. And the apostle in whose heart it well may be that a fight was on against some resurgent wish for ease and comfort, went back to his own self-denying life, with the figures of the athletes in his thought: "They do it to obtain a corruptible crown; but we an incorruptible" (I Cor. 9:25).

Consider, then, the self-denial of *acrobats*. To children they are like automata, nimble in action, marvelous in skill. But older folk must think of the discipline that lies behind the precision of their feats. They have guarded their bodies by self-restraint and hardened them by exercise; they have risked life to learn new exploits; they have let neither boredom nor weariness nor illness prevent their continual appearances. And "they do it to obtain a corruptible crown."

Consider the *musicians*. When a master violinst plays a great passage from Beethoven, flawless in technique, gorgeous in coloring, till eyes grow wet and nerves are taut with exquisite delight, like the strings of the violin on which he plays, who can compute the cost of such consummate skill? Self-denial is no special property of Christian service. It is an elemental law of life.

Consider the *explorers*. What rigor of the northern cold, what exile from the comforts of home, what sustained and perilous self-renunciation did Peary undergo that he might be the discoverer of the North Pole! Or when, amid his freezing comrades, Scott lay dying on the homeward march from the South Pole, what splendid capacity for sustained self-sacrifice is revealed in what he wrote: "We took risks; we knew we took them, and therefore we have no cause for complaint, but bow to the will of Providence, determined still to do our best to the last. Had we lived, I should have had a tale to tell of the hardihood, endurance, and courage of my companions, which would have stirred the heart of every Englishman."

Consider *men of business*. One who deliberately risks life for a philanthropic cause is widely heralded, but business men in multitudes break down their health each year or, seeking their fortunes at the ends of the earth, put life in jeopardy. Missionaries leave country, family, comfort, and cherished opportunities, to bury themselves in obscure and uninviting places, often among folk whom only the grace of God can make one love at first. But is there any place where men go for Christ's sake, where they do not go for money's sake? Is there any outpost so remote where men carry the Gospel, to which also men do not carry the products of our factories? So Livingstone cried: "Can the love of Christ not carry the missionary where the slave trade carries the slaver?"

Or if one would know the lengths to which self-denial commonly goes in human life, let him consider the *patriot*. If the Master had said to us, I have a cause that at all costs and hazards must be pushed to a victorious issue; within five years it will cost twenty million dead and such a lavish outpouring of treasure that all the race in half a century cannot repay it, what would we have done? But patriotism has said that and we have answered. How common in history is the spirit of Ricasoli: "I would have killed my daughter, who was my great affection on earth, if she had been an obstacle to achieving the great end toward which so many Italians were straining."

One who shrinks from costly self-denial for service's sake may well consider, first of all, that self-denial is common coin, rung on every counter in the world where men buy anything which in serious earnest they desire.

"They do it to obtain a corruptible crown."

III

Such an approach to the problem of self-denial reveals its true nature. It is not the negative, forbidding thing that often we shake our heads about. In one sense there is no such thing as self-denial, for what we call such is the necessary price we pay for things on which our hearts are set.

This truth stands clear in all concerns of moral character. Many a young man is warned against the evils of illicit love, as though he were being asked chiefly to give up pleasure. The emphasis is all upon the repression of an appetite. Purity is made to seem merely a negative denial of deep desire. In the young man's thought, dissipation is the positively alluring life, full of charm and music, while purity is life stripped, straitened, and set in the forbidding grasp of prohibitory laws. What wonder that so many turn to the warmth and color of a wayward life!

The truth, however, about the self-denial which purity involves is based upon this positive fact: *the most beautiful possession on this earth which man has ever imagined or achieved is a Christian home.* Who has one is rich, and who may have one and meanly misses it, has played the fool. But so priceless a possession does not come by accident. Men do not drift into it. They must pay a price. If a man would have the full beauty of a Christian home, there are some kinds of life that he must not live.

The gripping appeal for self-denying purity, therefore, is not negative. Young man, so it might run, the girl whom you are going to marry is now alive. You may never have met her, but somewhere she is walking down a path which in the providence of God some day will cross yours. Wherever she may be, she keeps herself for you, and in her imagination you are even now a prince whom some day she will gladly marry. Not for the wealth of the world would she be grossly untrue to you. How, then, are you living? You have no right to take to such a girl a life smirched and rotted with unchastity. If you do, there is a secret shame you never will outgrow, a pang that you will feel whenever your children clamber to your arms. To have a home free from all that, with memories high and beautiful, is worth anything that it may cost. Those who have such homes do not call the price of them self-denial. It is all clear gain. They have surrendered dust for diamonds. For this is the deepest truth about self-denial: that men

91

positively set their hearts upon some high possession which they greatly want, and, paying the price of it in self-restraint, they count themselves the happiest of men to possess their treasure. Self-denial is not negative repression, but the cost of positive achievement.

So inextricably indeed is the fact of self-denial wrought into life that by no devious dodging can one escape it. Let a man say, Not self-denial but self-indulgence is my choice; I set no high and costly aims ahead of me; I seek an unrestrained and uncostly life! Has he then escaped self-renunciation? *Rather he has plunged head foremost into the most terrific self-denial that human life can anyhow sustain.* For if we will not deny ouselves *for* a Christian home, we shall deny ourselves a *Christian home!* What more appalling self-renunciation can there be? If we will not deny ourselves a loose and unchaste life, then we shall deny ourselves self-respect and a conscience fit to live with. If we will not deny ourselves bad temper and a wagging tongue, then we shall deny ourselves friendship—God pity us! If we will not deny ourselvs those habits of thought and life that keep divine fellowship away from human hearts, then we shall deny ourselves God. In short, if we will not give up evil for good, we shall surely give up good for evil. Where there is a will there is a won't. Self-denial is unescapable. It is not the negative, forbidding amputation of self from which men often shrink. It is the price men pay when they have positively set their hearts upon some chosen goal. At its highest it is the privilege life offers us of buying the best at the sacrifice of something less desired.

IV

The difference between men, therefore, does not lie in the presence of self-denial in their experience. That comes inevitably into every life. *The difference lies in the ends for which men deny themselves.* Some men place their individual selves at the center of their lives, and sacrifice everything beside in the service of that little god. George Eliot describes an ancient silver mirror, on which, if one brought a candle near, the multitudinous fine lines, wrought by much polishing, arranged themselves in concentric circles around the light of the candle flame. So to a mean man the large interests of human kind center about his self. *Self-centered* is the exact description of his life. The costly gains of civilization, the securities of government, the hard-won opportunities of trade, ties of family and friendship—all these in his eyes exist for his special benefit. They are to be dressed in livery, if he can manage it, and made to serve his interests. As in Joseph's dream, the sun, the moon, and the eleven stars all bow in obeisance before him. Does such a life escape self-denial? Rather to any man of spiritual vision such a man is practicing self-denial in its most extreme form.

He is denying himself that *generous outlook upon life* which alone can open human eyes to the worth and beauty of God's world. Moffatt gives the true translation of the Master's words: "If your Eye is generous, the whole of your body will be illuminated, but if your Eye is selfish, the whole of your body will be darkened" (Matt. 6:23). Look on mankind with self-forgetful, benevolent, magnanimous eyes, and life is radiant; look on mankind with churlish, avaricious, greedy eyes, and life, as Hobbes the philosopher of selfishness called it, "is solitary, poor, nasty, brutish, and short." Wordsworth confesses that his first view of the Alps was spoiled for him by irritation over an unsatisfactory lunch. So does our clamorous self-regard, allowed to usurp the central place and to obsess our thought, bind our vision, though all life's splendor were unrolled before us. Whatever gracious, helpful, inspiring thing is to be seen on earth, only an eye unspoiled by self-centeredness can see it.

Moreover, the self-centered man denies himself *friendship*. The games of children are the playful replicas of manhood's serious pursuits. "Tag"—the heated chasing of things hard to catch; "I Spy"—the diligent searching for things hard to find; "Puss Wants a Corner"—the competitive struggle for positions too few in number to supply the demand—so do children's games represent adult life. But "Prisoner's Base," where, caught by the enemy, only the touch of a friend can set us free, goes deeper yet. Our friends are our deliverers. They call us out of our narrow selves; they believe in our possibilities which we cannot discern; they stand by us when else we would surrender hope; they shine upon us like the sun and rain in refreshing fellowship; and they bring to maturity within us all that is excellent and of good report. Cries Emerson: "I can do that by another which I cannot do alone. I can say to you what I cannot first say to myself." But friendship is reciprocal. Only the friendly spirit can keep friends. The self-centered man has denied himself the most inspiring relationship on earth.

He has also denied himself *the thrilling satisfaction of helping men.* "Are you not lonely out here?" asked a visitor of a lighthouse keeper on an isolated reef. "Not since I saved my first man," came the swift answer. To be of use to people, to see them redeemed from misery and sin, to know in one's own experience the truth which Clement of Alxandria spoke long centuries ago, "At all times God, the lover of men, clothes himself with man to the attainment of the salvation of men," is one of the most penetrating and abiding joys of life. General Booth in the slums of London, through long weeks of eager, unrelenting pursuit, sought the reclamation of one wayward man. At last the sustained, compassionate friendship of the General wore through the man's obstinate resistance. "Kindness and love!" the wretched fellow cried as he broke down, "Kindness and love! Then there is a God!" Can ordinary plummets fathom the depth of satisfaction that lies in such an experience of saviorhood? But the self-centered man has denied himself all that.

He has denied himself as well the enlarging and enriching experience which belongs to the *cooperative fellowships of men.* The worth of life lies not where we self-centeredly cry *My* but where we loyally cry *Our.* Our family, our friends, our church, our college, our country—in such centers of self-effacing and self-expanding loyalty life finds its satisfaction. One man alone is no man at all. Robinson Crusoe is a poor segment of a man, segregated from his human fellowships, and only when braided back into the common loyalties and patriotisms that make life fruitful can he be himself again. But the self-centered man has denied himself all that. He lives in spiritual isolation, with walls about him more impassable than the seas that surrounded Crusoe's island. He is a human derelict. His soul has been marooned.

The self-centered man has denied himself also the exhilaration of believing in and working for *the consummation of all human hopes, the Kingdom of God upon earth.* In troubled hours the progress of mankind indeed seems dubious. We pass through a catastrophic war, with high expectations that out of it may come a redeemed earth. But the war overpassed, we fall into more baffling problems still, bewildering to our hopes. So in the seventeenth century the central part of London burned down. Terrific suffering was involved, but one thought buoyed up the spirits of the people. They saw that the disaster might contribute to a lasting benefit. They would rebuild a new and better London. Sir Christopher Wren drew up the plan. St. Paul's Cathedral was to be its center. The city officials sanctioned the enterprise; the citizens were eager to achieve it. When they faced the practical details, however, so many folk insisted that as for them their houses must be placed exactly where they were before, that in the end a new and better

London was not built. They reared the city once again upon its old foundations. So after the war are we rebuilding the old world upon old bases, and disillusionment is rampant everywhere. Human life seems like a brook, that cascading down the mountain, grows weary of the rapids and waterfalls and eagerly anticipates the quiet pool at the cataract's bottom. But come now to the pool, so long anticipated, it stays there not an instant, but is straightway shot out again into new rapids and waterfalls more tumultuous by far, it may be, then those just left behind. So have we passed from war, through the days of armistice, into the problems of peace.

Now the self-centered man looks on all this with cynical eyes. It well accords with his philosophy. As one who in the midst of conflagration thinks first of loot which he may seize, so the self-centered man in this mad and scrambling world gets what he can for himself while getting is possible. He sees no vision of man's circuitous rise to possibilities of finer life. No hope of a better day emerging even from the chaos of a world in ferment stirs his heart. No voice cries in his ear the words of Jeremiah to his nephew centuries ago in another catastrophic time, "Seekest thou great things for thyself? Seek them not" (Jer. 45:5). No faith that by God's grace and man's endeavor this earth can be made the home of human society more fair and fruitful than we have yet dared to dream, allures his loyalty. He cares nothing for the world and has no hopes for it. He is a profiteer on other men's disasters. He is a slacker from man's most ennobling war against the inner sins and outer circumstances that cripple human life—

> Unconcerned,
> Tranquil almost, and careless as a flower
> Glassed in a greenhouse, or a parlour shrub
> That spreads its leaves in unmolested peace,
> While every bush and tree the country through
> Is shaking to the roots.

Last of all, the self-centered man has denied himself all *fellowship with God*. For selfishness is a *cul-de-sac*, and no man ever yet broke through it into the Divine Presence. There is no thoroughfare to the love of God except through the love of man. The stories of all true saints are illustrations of this truth. The warm and vital religious life of Whittier has voiced itself in poems which, read as meditations or sung as hymns, are familiar expressions of Christian piety. Many think of him as achieving his spirituality by the wise use of solitude alone. He is to us a mystic, a quietist. But even Whittier's central fight was against selfishness. "I am haunted," he said, "by an immedicable ambition—perhaps a very foolish desire of distinction, of applause, of fame, of what the world calls immortality." Even Whittier's victory came when he unselfishly threw himself into the campaign for the abolition of slavery. That crusade was the most forlorn of all unpopular causes when he espoused it. So far from living a quiet life he was for years a busy agitator; he lost many of his friends; he was bitterly maligned; once in Philadelphia he was forced in disguise to flee the assaulting mob.

> We may not climb the heav'nly steeps
> To bring the Lord Christ down;
> In vain we search the lowest deeps
> For Him no depths can drown. . . .
>
> But warm, sweet, tender even yet
> A present help is he;
> And faith has still its Olivet
> And love its Galilee.

How winsome and profound his fellowship with God was! But one of the deep secrets of it he himself revealed, when in his old age he said to a young man: "My lad, if thou wouldst win success, join thyself to some unpopular but noble cause!"

So Moses began with indignant pity for the suffering Israelites in Egypt and ended beside the burning bush in fellowship with the Eternal. So Elijah began wih righteous wrath against the tyranny of Ahab and ended on the mountain's side alone, listening to a "still small voice." So Dante began with a great passion for a united Italy and ended with Beatrice standing before the Great White Throne. So many a humble servant of his fellows has found that God is love, and that where love is there God is also.

No self-denial in a self-centered life! A self-centered man surrenders the spiritual insight which can perceive life's worth and beauty and the spirit of friendliness which alone can make friendship possible; he loses the thrill of saving men, the joys of cooperative fellowship, the ennobling influence of a conscious share in the coming Kingdom of Righteousness upon the earth; he surrenders the possibility of fellowship with God. In a word, he denies himself everything that makes life significant.

The wretch concentered all in self
Living shall forfeit fair renown,
And, doubly dying, shall go down
To the vile dust from whence he sprung,
Unwept, unhonoured, and unsung.

V

From such a miserable life all men of depth and insight instinctively have shrunk. As one traces to its source the difference between the self-centered men and these generous servants of mankind, he is led back to the inner chambers of the heart where dwell our dominant desires. The secret of a selfish man is that all his masterful, controlling wants concern himself. Nothing seems so desirable to him as that he himself should be safe and fortunate. The secret of a useful man is that his heart is set on the happiness of his family, the welfare of his friends, the progress of good causes in the world, the redemption of the victims of want and sin, the coming of the brotherhood of man. His thoughts, affections, ambitions, and desires are centered outside his narrow self. And because he so wants in serious earnest to see these great ends gained, he willingly will pay the price. Such men never count their wounds or call their labors self-denial. To give up their work—that would be the renunciation of their real selves. So Sir Wilfred Grenfell, loving the fisher folk of Labrador, remarks that he dislikes to speak of self-sacrifice, for he cannot recall that he ever has indulged in it. So Livingstone, passionately desiring the salvation of Africa, could write: "People talk of the sacrifice I have made in spending so much of my life in Africa. . . . It is emphatically no sacrifice. Say rather it is a privilege." So is it written of the Master: "Who for the joy that was set before him endured the cross, despising shame" (Heb. 12:2).

CHAPTER VI

JUSTICE

Daily Readings

We are to accept this week the challenge of those who appeal from self-denying love to justice, as a more possible and practical ideal of conduct. They are suspicious of so lofty a standard as self-sacrificing service for all sorts of folk, but they are willing to be *just* to everybody. Let us see in our daily readings some very searching principles which are involved in justice, however much one may endeavor to reduce it to simple terms.

Sixth Week, First Day

And as ye would that men should do to you, do ye also to them likewise.—Luke 6:31.

But the Pharisees, when they heard that he had put the Sadducees to silence, gathered themselves together. And one of them, a lawyer, asked him a question, trying him: Teacher, which is the great commandment in the law? And he said unto him, Thou shalt love the Lord thy God with all thy heart, and with all thy soul, and with all thy mind. This is the great and first commandment. And a second like unto it is this, Thou shalt love thy neighbor as thyself. On these two commandments the whole law hangeth, and the prophets.—Matt. 22:34-40.

Here stand Jesus' two summaries of justice: to do as one would be done by, and to love others as one loves one's self. In a word, simple justice involves the treatment of another's personality as, equally with one's own, an object of respect and consideration. A just man, therefore, must *refuse to claim for himself what he is unwilling to grant to others.* That is no easy principle of conduct, on so much lower a plane than Christian love that with relief a man can fall back upon it. Picture children in a home being thus perfectly fair with one another; imagine men in business always treating others as though they themselves were in the others' places; conceive nations never claiming for themselves what they would be unwilling to grant to others; and how marvelously changed would be our home life, business life, and international relationships! If we mean by love affectionate good will, it is often far easier to feel that for individual people who come in contact with us closely enough to claim it, than it is to be scrupulously and impersonally just to people whom we do not know. "Because," says Professor George Herbert Palmer, "justice seeks to benefit all, but all alike. It knows no persons, or rather it knows everyone as a person and insures each his share in the common good. All the altruism of love is here, but without love's arbitrary selection and limited interest. . . . In this extended and superpersonal love altruism attains its fullest and steadiest expression."

O Almighty God, who hast entrusted this earth unto the children of men, and through Thy Son Jesus Christ callest us unto a heavenly citizenship; grant us, we humbly beseech Thee, such shame and repentance for the disorder and injustice and cruelty that is in our midst, that fleeing unto Thee for pardon and for grace we may henceforth set ourselves to establish that city which has justice for its foundation and love for its law, whereof Thou art the Architect and Maker; through the same Jesus Christ, Thy Son, our Saviour.—"Prayers for the City of God."

Sixth Week, Second Day

And the scribes and the Pharisees bring a woman taken in adultery; and having set her in the midst, they say unto him, Teacher, this woman hath been taken in adultery, in the very act. Now in the law Moses commanded us to stone such: what then sayest thou of her? And this they said, trying him, that they might have whereof to accuse him. But Jesus stooped down, and with his finger wrote on the ground. But when they continued asking him, he lifted up himself, and said unto them, He that is without sin among you, let him first cast a stone at her. And again he stooped down, and with his finger wrote on the ground. And they, when they heard it, went out one by one, beginning from the eldest, even unto the least: and Jesus was left alone, and the woman, where she was, in the midst. And Jesus lifted up himself, and said unto her, Woman, where are they? did no man condemn thee? And she said, No man, Lord. And Jesus said, Neither do I condemn thee: go thy way; from henceforth sin no more.—John 8:3-11.

This narrative is often used as an exhibition of the Master's superlative charity. But what is it in the woman's accusers that arouses his indignation? They are not *just*. They are visiting on another judgment which they are unwilling to have visited on themselves. They are neglecting the basic principle, not only of mercy but of law: "He who cometh into court must have clean hands." It is perfectly clear that if they had put themselves in the woman's place before they judged her case, they would have had some contribution to make beside flinging stones. *To be just in our judgments of others,* weighing fairly the circumstances which explain their conduct, letting no gusty excess of resentment distort our estimate, and willing that with what measure we mete it should be measured to us again—what a searching requirement is that! Yet that is simple fairness. "Judge not that ye be not judged. For with what judgment ye judge ye shall be judged" (Matt. 7:1, 2).

O God, we pray that Thou wilt bless the outcast, the poor, the ignorant, the wanderers—those that do not know better than to live in hatreds, in strifes, in every evil passion. Grant that we may not turn inhumanly away from them, as if they were not of us; as if they did not belong to our households; as if they were not men like ourselves; as if they were not parts of the great family to which we belong. Grant that those who go forth especially to seek them, to preach to them, to relieve them, and to succor them, may themselves be filled with the Spirit of the Master. May none turn back from well doing because they find among the poor and needy ingratitude, intractableness, indocility, and all manner of evil requitings. May they too, bear men's sins and carry their sorrows as Christ bore our sins and carried our sorrows. And so may they learn to follow Christ through good report, and through evil report, and exalt the conception of a Christian manhood in the eyes of men. Amen.—Henry Ward Beecher.

Sixth Week, Third Day

Ye have heard that it was said to them of old time, Thou shalt not kill; and whosoever shall kill shall be in danger of the judgment; but I say unto you, that every one who is angry with his brother shall be in danger of the judgment; and whosoever shall say to his brother, Raca, shall be in danger of the council; and whosoever shall say, Thou fool, shall be in danger of the hell of fire.—Matt. 5:21, 22.

Justice, in Jesus' eyes, involves abstinence not only from deliberately unfair judgment but from all *hasty, contemptuous treatment of our fellows*. Who can measure the harm done daily in the world by spoken scorn? How it withers the fine spirit of men, and rouses rancor and bitterness! It discourages hope, blights confidence, breaks friendship, and leaves everywhere a trail of disheartened, resentful lives. The Psalmist is right: to walk in the counsel of the ungodly is bad enough, to stand in the way of sinners is worse still, but to sit in the seat of the scornful is worst of all. No good thing is safe from an unjust tongue. Even King Arthur's Round Table goes to pieces before Vivien's contemptuous speech. She

> let her tongue
> Rage like a fire among the noblest names,
> Polluting, and imputing her whole self,
> Defaming and defacing, till she left
> Not even Launcelot brave, nor Galahad clean.

To be just in speech, never saying of another what we would resent if said about ourselves, to love our neighbor's reputation with our tongue as much as we love our own—is that an easy standard to attain?

If from all Thy good gifts, O Lord, I may ask but one, let that one be the spirit of kindness!

Let others have fame and fortune and jewels and palaces, if I may but have the kindly spirit! Give greatness and power to those that want them, but give to me Brotherly Kindness! Make somebody else to be comely of visage, if only I may wear a kindly countenance.

May I never wound the heart of any faltering child of Thine! Make me to do the little unremembered acts that quietly help without intending it. Grant me to bear about the unconscious radiance of a life that knows no grudge, but loves all men because they are children of my Father Who loved them enough to send His Son to save them. Amen.—George A. Miller.

Sixth Week, Fourth Day

And Jesus entered into the temple of God, and cast out all them that sold and bought in the temple, and overthrew the tables of the money-changers, and the seats of them that sold the doves; and he saith unto them, It is written, My house shall be called a house of prayer: but ye make it a den of robbers.—Matt. 21:12, 13.

Jerusalem was odinarily a city of about 50,000 inhabitants. But at the time of the great feasts, pilgrims to the number of 1,000,000 sometimes thronged the city. What an opportunity for loot! To victimize these pious pilgrims, to squeeze them dry of their money by ingenious profiteering schemes, became a lucrative means of livelihood. Here the Master faces this system of exploitation, overflowing into the temple courts. He resents it, as he always resented the victimizing of people for private gain. Now, in any case of such exploitation, the man who is making gain at another's expense is not doing what he would like to have done to himself. He is not just. For justice rules out *taking unfair advantage of another's position,* trading on another's weakness, ignorance, or necessity, making gain for oneself by making a victim of another man. Is that an easy principle to live by? Upon the contrary, many a man will find it far simpler to practice self-denying love in home and neighborhood for a year, than to practice such ordinary justice for a single day in business.

Dig out of us, O Lord, the venomous roots of covetousness: or else so repress them with Thy grace, that we may be contented with Thy provision of necessaries, and not to labour, as we do, with all toil, sleight, guile, wrong, an oppression, to pamper ourselves with vain superfluities. Give us grace continually to read, hear, and meditate Thy purposes, judgments, promises, and precepts, not to the end we may curiously argue thereof, or arrogantly presume thereupon, but to frame our lives according to Thy will. Amen.—Archbishop E. Grindal (1519-1583).

Sixth Week, Fifth Day

And he called to him a little child, and set him in the midst of them, and said, Verily I say unto you, Except ye turn, and become as little children, ye shall in no wise enter into the kingdom of heaven. Whosoever therefore shall humble himself as this little child, the same is the greatest in the kingdom of heaven. And whoso shall receive one such little child in my name receiveth me: but whoso shall cause one of these little ones that believe on me to stumble, it is profitable for him that a great millstone would be hanged about his neck, and that he should be sunk in the depth of the sea.—Matt. 18:2-6.

The Master so often and so rightly is regarded as the exemplar of sacrificial love, that it is well to remind ourselves, as we are doing this week, how much of his teaching is an appeal for justice. To *wrong children*, to refuse them a fair chance to become all that they have it in them to be, to make them stumble, and above all to use up their slender strength for our selfish benefit is not first of all lack of charity; it is outrageous injustice, against which the Master's spirit flames in anger. No one would wish his own childhood to have been so treated. "Some think we shall be born again on this earth under conditions such as we have deserved," writes Professor Rauschenbusch. "It would certainly be a righteous judgment of God if he placed us amid the conditions we have created and allowed us to test in our own body the after-effects of our life. How would a man feel if he knew that the little daughter that died in his arms twelve years ago was born as the child of one of his mill hands and is spinning his cotton at this moment?" Is not that a plain, straightforward application of the Golden Rule? Evidently the appeal from love to justice is not an easy one to live up to.

O Thou great Father of the weak, lay Thy hand tenderly on all the little children on earth and bless them. Be good to all children who long in vain for human love, or for flowers and water, and the sweet breast of Nature. But bless with a sevenfold blessing the young lives whose slender shoulders are already bowed beneath the yoke of toil, and whose glad growth is being stunted forever. Suffer not their little bodies to be utterly sapped, and their minds to be given over to stupidity and the vices of an empty soul. We have all jointly deserved the millstone of Thy wrath for making these little ones to stumble and fall. Grant all employers of labor stout hearts to refuse enrichment at such a price. Grant to all the citizens and officers of states which now permit this wrong the grace of holy anger. Help us to realize that every child of our nation is in very truth our child, a member of our great family. By the Holy Child that nestled in Mary's bosom; by the memories of our own childhood joys and sorrows; by the sacred possibilities that slumber in every child, we beseech Thee to save us from killing the sweetness of young life by the greed of gain.—Walter Rauschenbusch.

Sixth Week, Sixth Day

See that ye despise not one of these little ones: for I say unto you, that in heaven their angels do always behold the face of my Father who is in heaven. How think ye? if any man have a hundred sheep, and one of them be gone astray, doth he not leave the ninety and nine, and go unto the mountains, and seek that which goeth astray? And if so be that he find it, verily I say unto you, he rejoiceth over it more than over the ninety and nine which have not gone astray. Even so it is not the will of your Father who is in heaven, that one of these little ones should perish.—Matt. 18:10-14.

Here is a characteristic expression of the Master's outreaching mercy toward the weak, the strayed, the lost. Surely such an attitude of positive saviorhood involves more than justice. Yet when one takes the Golden Rule seriously, and asks himself what he would wish done, were he in the place of the victim, will he not run straight into the necessity of outgoing love? A man lost in the Welsh mountains in a heavy fog gave himself up to the prospect of a miserable night; when suddenly, as though at his very elbow, he heard a voice: "I wonder if he could have come this way." He was being searched for! The consciousness that some one was looking for him and that therefore he could be found thrilled through him. In any such situation, would not we wish so to be cared about and sought? Then what does the Golden Rule mean, if not that *positive saviorhood is also the demand of justice?* After all, justice and love run very close together. "We can be just only to those we love."

We beseech of Thee, O Lord our God, that Thou wilt have compassion upon all those for whom we should pray; those that are thralled; those that are ensnared; those that have fallen into the pit; those that are in great darkness and trouble and gloom and despondency; those who are sick; those whose prosperity has been overturned as by the wind from the desert; those who are strangers in a strange land; those who are filled with bitterness and self-condemnation; those that taste remorse; those that are neglected and outcast; those who are in prison, and who are appointed unto death; all that are wandering in poverty and abandonment; all that are steeped in ignorance, in vice, and in crime.

O good Lord, what dost Thou do? Is this world dear to Thee? Dost Thou love man? Our souls shake within us, and we are full of anguish when we look upon the face of man, and see how men betray; how men hate and devour; how full of wretchedness and sin the world is, that goes on repeating itself from generation to generation; how the voice of time is a wail; how all things are most sad to behold. And dost Thou sit looking forevermore upon these things? O Lord, reveal the right hand of Thy power. Come; for this desolate earth doth wait for Thy coming, more than for the coming of summer. Amen.—Henry Ward Beecher.

Sixth Week, Seventh Day

Ye have heard that it was said, Thou shalt love thy neighbor, and hate thine enemy: but I say unto you, Love your enemies, and pray for them that persecute you; that ye may be sons of your Father who is in heaven: for he maketh his sun to rise on the evil and the good, and sendeth rain on the just and the unjust.—Matt. 5:43-45.

One would suppose that loving one's enemies and doing them good were practices which clearly overpassed justice. Yet the Master here distinctly appeals for them on the basis of that fine impartiality which we ourselves have profited by and which is of the very essence of a just and equitable life. Consider the impartial service which a lighthouse keeper renders to all the wayfarers of the sea! Good men and bad men pass in the night-going ships, but he shines on all. If his worst enemy were passing and he knew it, he would not dim his light. He is magnanimous. He allows no personal petulance, no selfish pique, to interfere with his steady beneficence. *Such an impartial spirit, unswayed by individual resentment, is of the very substance of justice.*

Justice does not include all that love does. Love goes deeper, is more intense, will sacrifice more, and carries in its heart a personal self-bestowal which justice alone does not know. But if the Golden Rule is its summary, justice is something far beyond the infliction of appropriate penalties. When a man does as he would be done by, he judges fairly, speaks kindly, refuses to exploit personality for private gain, protects the weak, rescues the fallen, and treats even his enemies as though they might some day become his friends.

O God, who has taught us in Thy holy Word that we must always do to others as we would they should do to us: give me grace to cleanse my heart and hands from all falsehood and wrong, that I may hurt nobody by word or deed, but be true and just in all my dealings and do my duty in that state of life into which it shall please Thee to call me, that so keeping innocency and taking heed to the thing that is right, I may obtain peace at the last for the sake of Jesus Christ, Thy Son, our Lord. Amen.—"A Book of Prayers for Students."

COMMENT FOR THE WEEK

I

Self-denying service, such as we have been considering, so far from being difficult and unnatural, is in some of our relationships happily spontaneous. For there are people whom we love with eager, self-forgetful affection. To argue with us that we should serve them is absurd. A true mother does not need argument that she should care for her child, nor a true lover that he should give himself in loyal service to the girl whom he adores. Nature herself plays upon our instincts to secure such self-bestowals as we lavishly pour out in family love and intimate friendship. Without the privilege of giving vent to love in ministry, we should be utterly bereft; the acutest agony we can imagine would be the stoppage of our power to help those whose hearts are ours.

Outside this inner area of intimate friendships, however, there are wide stretches of human relations where such tenderness of affection does not apply. Whatever may be the ideal, the fact is evident: there are vulgar people from whom we shrink, bestial people who are repellent to us, unfriendly people whose unkindness we resent. There are racial boundaries across which affectionate relationships do not easily pass; cultural boundaries where, in spite of ourselves, our theoretical brotherhood encounters practical difficulties. Moreover, there are criminally minded people, cruel and conscienceless, whose depredations on society must be hated and withstood. In a word, there are multitudes of people whom we do not like. To be told to love them seems a counsel of perfection, not to be taken seriously in daily life.

One attitude toward them, however, we all agree is both possible and right. We can be just. So at a football game one cannot easily imagine the coaches urging the opposing players to love one another. But one can easily imagine the coaches saying: Young men, you will play this game fairly; you will take for yourselves no advantage that you would deny to others; you will be just.

It is of the first importance, therefore, that we should see what is involved in the idea of justice. As there are masterpieces of literature, like Milton's *Paradise Lost,* which all agree to praise, but which few read, so there are virtues which all applaud but few examine. Justice is one of them. Men may differ about loving everyone, but they agree concerning the duty of being just to everyone. Yet the unappreciated depth and height and breadth of this applauded virtue is at once suggested by the fact that its most succinct, complete description is the Golden Rule. Consider what large matters are involved in that!

The keeping of the Golden Rule is quite impossible without the use of *generous and sympathetic imagination*. No man can do to another what he wishes another to do to him, unless he has the gracious power to put himself in another's place. Two boys in the depth of New York City were overheard in controversy: "I can write"; "I can, too"; "You can't"; "I can"; "Prove it." and the challenged lad took from his pocket a piece of chalk and scribbled on a brick wall the words "Keep off the grass." Can you who were brought up where grass was green and plentiful, and all the countryside was open to your wandering feet, put yourself into that boy's place? Yet if you *were* that boy, who could handle fairly the delicate scales of judgment save one who could see your problem from within?

A critic has said of Robert Browning that he was born with a passion for living in other people's experiences—"Rabbi be Ezra," "Fra Lippo Lippi," "Andrea del Sarto," "Bishop Blougrahm," the characters in "The Ring and the Book," and a host of others. He saw their points of view, he thought their thoughts, he said the things they had to say. What the master of verse did for art's sake, the Master of spiritual life did for the sake of service. He saw by sympathy the prodigal's problem from within, when all the Pharisees around were condemning him as lost. He saw from within the meaning of the widow's slender gift and the passionate outpouring of Mary's gratitude in costly oil. He saw from within the way life looked to Zacchaeus and from within he knew the secret sifting of Peter's soul by Satan. The woman taken in adultery, with the crowd of angry men around, their robes girt up, and stone in hand to slay her—even her problem he saw from within, and perceived in her what no one looking from without could possibly have guessed. Whoever kept to the full the Golden Rule except the Master? It is not easy to keep. No one is just who does not put himself in the place of those with whom he deals. And to do that one must see men as he does stained glass in a cathedral window, not from without in, but from within out.

John Wesley tells us of a man against whom year after year his choler rose. He thought of him contemptuously as covetous. One day when he gave to one of Wesley's favorite philanthropies a gift that seemed too small, Wesley's indignation burst all bounds, and he raked him fore and aft with scathing condemnation. Wesley tells us in his diary that the man quietly said: "I know a man who at the week's beginning goes to the market and buys a penny's worth of parsnips and takes them home to boil in water, and all that week he has the parsnips for his meat and the water for his drink; and meat and drink alike cost him a penny a week." "Who is the man?" said Wesley. "I am," was the reply. And Wesley adds, "This he constantly did, although he then had two hundred pounds a year, that he might pay the debts he had contracted before he knew God. And this was the man that I had thought to be covetous." We cannot be just to anyone whom we do not understand. If, then, we agree that across all boundaries of personal dislike and racial difference we should be just, we set for ourselves a task that will take all the insight and generosity we have.

II

Moreover, to do to others what we wish them to do to us involves not only sympathy, but *active good will*. Who of us has not been served with constant, sacrificial care, by family and friends; and lacking such attendant ministry would not have slipped and fallen on ruin, moral and practical, a hundred times? So Wendell Phillips might magnificently sway his hostile audiences, and seem the very incarnation of audacity, but those who know perceive behind him his wife, invalid in everything but spirit, who used to lay her hand upon his shoulder with a parting charge: "Wendell, don't you shilly-shally!" So George Matheson may claim the homage of the world for his brave victory over blindness, but those who know perceive the truth of his biographer's comment: "The chief factor, undoubtedly, in his harmonious, successful, and marvelously fruitful life, was his sister, Miss Matheson." To do for others what we desire to have done for us is not a negative ideal. Too often justice is pictured in terms of abstinence from rank injustice. Not to be cruel, not to oppress the poor or to crush the faces of the needy, that is to be just. But the Golden Rule cannot so negatively be kept. Justice is positive. It means the painstaking bestowal upon other lives of the same sort of constant, sacrificial ministry by which we ourselves have lived and without which we could not really live at all.

Consider so elemental a relationship as that between a father and his son. All that is best in the father's life came from the impact of friendly persons. Like a lake with two outlets far up in the Rockies, where a passing breeze sends the water to the east until it finds the Mississippi and the Gulf, or to the west until it flows to the Pacific, so was that father's life in boyhood. He might have flowed down either slope, and if he did flow aright, it was because some strong, radiant spirits blew persuasively upon him. The justice of a father to his son, therefore, is no negative refraining from ill treatment. It is a positive outpouring on the boy's life of that companionship, which, were he a boy again, the father would crave for himself. If, remembering what it costs a boy to grow up right amid the terrific lure of sin, the father had to live his youth again, he would wish *his* father to take time to know him very well; for all the pleasure of busy days to lay his life close alongside in fraternal comradeship; to be, when one desires not talk but help, a constant and unfailing friend; above all, to lift up a Christian character so winsome, strong, convincing, that in the fiercest storms that beat on life, the thought of it would hold as an anchor holds a ship.

Now justice does not cease making this demand for active good will when one moves out from the inner realm of affectionate relationships into the wider areas where personal affection does not instinctively extend. When in imagination anyone puts himself in the place of the disinherited, the forsaken, the outcast, however unlovely and degraded they may be, he at once is crying for help. Father Damien goes out to the lepers because he knows that if he were a leper he would not wish to be left in hapless, unbefriended isolation, unrelieved by any touch of human kindliness. Florence Nightingale goes out to the Crimea because she knows that if she were a wounded soldier brought in from the battlefield, she would not want to toss in pain unnursed by a woman's gentleness. Pioneers blaze the trail to medical missions, because they know that if means of healing were anywhere available, they would not wish to live in needless pain and see their loved ones die in agony amid the rattle of witch doctor's drums. If once the Golden Rule were seriously taken, if men in earnest put themselves in the place of all oppressed, benighted folk, unbefriended, and cheated of their share in civilization's gains, and if in earnest they set themselves to do for them what they themselves in similar case would need, there would come a world-wide transformation of social life.

The far-flung meanings of the Golden Rule are evident, when a man puts himself in the place of young men and women who have gone to the ends of the earth for Christian service. As during the War the most alert and venturesome spirits sought France, desiring the post of danger at the front, as many daring Christian spirits among our youth turn their faces toward the foreign field. If he were one of them, above all else a man would desire that the Christian people at home should support his work with instruments of service to make his toil effective. He offers up the most precious thing a man can give—his life. He passionately craves that his investment of life shall be effective. To do lamely what could be done well with decent instruments—that is desolating. To stand in a great city where the sick and dying gather about him, like the sick around Jesus in the streets of old Capernaum, to have for investment in that great need the best medical education that modern science can bestow, and yet to have no adequate hospital, few nurses, no associates, to be compelled to do feebly what could be done magnificently—that is crushing. When a man sees missions and philanthropy not in abstract terms but interpreted in concrete personalities, and imagines himself to be one of them, he sees how wide is the scope and how searching the requirement of justice in realms where affection does not apply.

Justice says: You are a white man. Then put yourself in the place of the Negro, whose father was freed when he was a youth, and whose great-great-great-grandfather was brought over against his will on a slave ship from Africa, and see from the inside, how the problem of that man's life must appear to him. You are an American. Put yourself in the place of Britain, and France, and Italy, and Japan, and China, and those who but lately were our enemies, to see how this tangled world's problem must appear to them. You are a laboring man. Put yourself in the place of the employer, and see from his angle the perplexing problem of our economic life. You are an employer. Then put yourself in the place of the laboring man, to see how his life must appear to him. Justice is not less exacting than emotional affection, but more. It applies in realms where affection does not move. It holds a man to understanding sympathy and generous good will toward people whom instinctively he may dislike. At last it leads him to attack the organized injustice of our social and economic order, not because he himself is hurt, but because others are oppressed, in whose place he has imagined himself to be.

III

This extension of the Golden Rule into areas of human relationship where our affections do not easily go meets its greatest difficulty when it deals with *positively unfriendly folk.* Sympathy and good will may justly be expended upon some people beyond the borders of our emotional tenderness, but can it be just to give one's self in generous ministry to enemies? Is not justice comprehended in the old law of Leviticus (24:20) "Breach for breach, eye for eye, tooth for tooth; as he hath caused a blemish in a man, so shall it be rendered unto him? Such strict retribution appears just, but the Master's command to love our enemies and do them good seems far to overpass the limits of fair play.

Yet the fact is that the Sermon on the Mount is not the denial but the fulfilment of the Levitical law. In an age of barbarous morals, when none disputed the right of vengeance, this old law was set up to restrain the extravagant wrath of angry men. Its message is not: you may return to a man whatever harm he has done to you. Its message is rather: you may not return to a man *more* harm than he has done to you. Eye for an eye, tooth for a tooth—so much revenge you may take, if you must; no more.

What youth has not known hours when he was goaded to ungovernable rage? He lost his hold upon the throttle of his temper. He assailed his enemy with a mad desire to satisfy the anger he could not control. All calculations of exact retribution were forgotten. There was no nice estimate of proposed damage to the foe. Ability was the limit of purpose. Consider in such a case the restraint imposed by the old law: exact retaliation, no more! The commandment in Leviticus was intended to set limits to the vindictiveness of angry men. The river of vengeance might flow on; the time had not yet come utterly to dry its springs; but the stream had banks. When therefore the Master *annulled* what Leviticus had *limited,* he was not destroying the law but was fulfilling it; he was carrying an ethical reform to its logical conclusion.

That this logical conclusion to the old law of retaliation is indispensable ought to be evident to even ordinary moral insight. For one thing, the principle of tit for tat *makes too small business for a real life to be preoccupied about.* Even in legal procedure the rule of an eye for an eye issues in absurdity. In the code of Henry I, one finds this law: if a boy standing under a tree is killed by another boy who falls upon him out of the tree, then the boy who fell and did the killing must in his turn stand under a tree and let another boy fall on him until he dies. The ridiculous pettiness of such a legal principle is obvious; yet to that pass is anyone led who take seriously the law of retaliation. To go through life slapping back each time one is slapped, is the cheapest form of wasting life.

After Appomattox, when Robert E. Lee was President of Washington College, a professor derided Grant harshly in his presence. In swift indignation Lee thundered: "Sir, if ever I hear you speak again in my presence disrespectfully of General Grant, either you or I will sever his connection with this institution." A man in earnest about serious tasks has no time for vindictiveness. The Master, with the salvation of the world upon his heart, praying "Thy Kingdom come" with passionate desire, could not be expected to content himself with the narrow vengefulness of the Levitical law. Retaliation is a rule of little men; retaliation makes little men. Large spirits always are magnanimous. They even "love their enemies and do them good."

Moreover, the law of an eye for an eye is inadequate because *it makes no provision for the betterment of evil men.* Even the stern business of criminal law is discovering this. As late as 1833, in England, we are informed that, "Sentence of death was passed on a child of nine who poked a stick through a pane of glass in a shop front and stole some pieces of paint worth two-pence. This was housebreaking and the penalty of housebreaking was death." Even though after delay that sentence was commuted, it illustrates the appalling course of legal cruelty in Christendom. And if little by little the torture chamber, the racks and thumbscrews, the public pillories and whipping posts, the barbarous executions on wayside gibbets, the loathsome dungeons, are vanishing like nightmares when the sun rises, and prisons increasingly are reformatory in their aim, it is not mawkish sentiment that motives the change, but the sound sense of the Master. Retaliation gets nowhere. It is not only barbarous but it is stupid. Think of going out to save manhood with this device upon our banners, "Tit for tat," and with this for our slogan, "When you are slapped, slap back!" The only aim worth seeking is better men in a more decent world and the law of an eye for an eye is a futile instrument for such an enterprise.

IV

Not only does retaliation turn out to be too petty for largeminded men and too feeble for serious purposes, but despite the first appearance, *it is not just*. No one of us dares to suggest that he himself be treated on the principle of tit for tat. The parable of Jesus, where a servant, pardoned a debt of twelve million dollars, goes out to choke a fellow-servant who owed him seventeen dollars, cuts deep into the truth about us all. Such churlishness was not fair play. The pardoned debtor was refusing to another the forgiveness which he had himself received. He was taking what he would not give. So are we all pensioners on mercy, human and divine, and long since would have been utterly undone if retaliation without mercy had been given us. With no more sustenance than the principle of tit for tat can furnish, all the most beautiful human relationships would starve and die. From mothers who love before love is appreciated and keep on loving when it is not appreciated, to the world's saints and martyrs, prophets and apostles, who love human weal and serve it through the gainsaying and persecution of the very men they seek to help, our lives are all upborn by mercies which we have not deserved and for which we can never pay. And when one lifts his thought to God's judgment of him, he sees that he would have no hope if the Great White Throne were marked all over with the motto, "Tit for tat." Let a man face the mercies he already has received from family and friends, the unearned benedictions he already has been given, bought by other blood than his and the toil of other hands, the forgiveness he has needed and will need again from sources human and divine, and then let him face the Golden Rule! He will see that the Lord's Prayer is urging him to simple justice: "Forgive us our trespasses as we forgive them who trespass against us."

The justice of the Golden Rule involves understanding sympathy, active good will, and far-flung service. Its kingdom is wider than the narrow realm where our intimate affections dwell. It takes in even enemies. Only by such justice does a man contribute to life what to make living rich and worthy he must take from life. Only so does he find in himself the answer to an old prayer of the sixteenth century—a Christian's plea for a just spirit:

"Open our hearts, O Lord, that we may be no less moved at the needs and griefs of our neighbors than if they were our own. O most mild and merciful Christ, breathe upon us the spirit of Thy meekness and Thy goodness that, as Thy pitying of us made Thee endure most bitter death and torment for our sake, so our pitying of our neighbors may lead us to succor them."

CHAPTER VII

SMALL ENEMIES OF USEFULNESS

Daily Readings

We have been speaking of the spirit and practice of service as the necessary and beautiful expression of a Christian life. But here as everywhere else, the perversion of the best is the worst. As Bunyan found a passage to hell from under the walls of the celestial city, so are there ways to unlovely uselessness that run out from the very desire and intention to be of use. Let us consider this week some of these perversions of service.

Seventh Week, First Day

For we hear of some that walk among you disorderly, that work not at all, but are busybodies. Now them that are such we command and exhort in the Lord Jesus Christ, that with quietness they work, and eat their own bread.—II Thess. 3:11, 12.

For let none of you suffer as a murderer, or a thief, or an evil-doer, or as a meddler in other men's matters: but if a man suffer as a Christian, let him not be ashamed; but let him glorify God in this name.—I Peter 4:15, 16.

One of the commonest caricatures of usefulness is *meddlesomeness*. Intent on helping folk, we become busybodies; we assume responsibility where we are not wanted; we intrude ourselves where we would have helped more by minding our own business; our overweening ambition to do something for somebody makes our very presence a vexation. How many such folk there are! Desiring to be useful, they become presumptuous, officious, and obtrusive. They lack reticence, humility, tact. Their desire to help is commendable, but its effect is spoiled by their own loudness, awkwardness, impertinence. They have generosity, but they lack discrimination. After all, no amount of zeal can make up for the want of modesty and good sense in service. Those who help most are often not those who try hardest, but those who, like a full-laden apple tree, are so rich in their own spiritual fruitage that no one can brush against a branch without bringing down something good to eat. Many a hurried, fuming, pushing, presumptuous worker for the help of others might well pause to consider another type of spirit:

> "An incidental greatness charactered
> Her unconsidered ways."

Lord, let me be never courteous and easie to be entreated; never let me fall into a peevish or contentious Spirit, but follow Peace with all Men, offering forgiveness, inviting them by Courtesies, ready to Confess my own Errors, apt to make amends and desirous to be reconcil'd. Let no Sickness or Cross Accident, no Imployment or Weariness make me angry or ungentle, and discontented or unthankful or uneasie. Give me the Spirit of a Christian, Charitable, Humble, Merciful, and Meek, Useful and Liberal, Complying with every Chance, Angry at nothing but my own Sins, and Grieving at the Sins of Others. That while my Passion obeys my Reason, and my Reason is Religious, and my Religion is pure and undefiled, managed with Humility, and adorn'd with Charity, I may dwell in Thy Love, and be Thy Son and Servant for ever, through Jesus Christ our Lord. Amen.—Thomas á Kempis (1379-1471).

Seventh Week, Second Day

If there is therefore any exhortation in Christ, if any consolation of love, if any fellowship of the Spirit, if any tender mercies and compassions, make full my joy, that ye be of the same mind; doing nothing through faction or through vainglory, but in lowliness of mind each counting other better than himself; not looking each of you to his own things, but each of you also to the things of others.—Phil. 2:1-4.

Paul takes for granted here that the Philippian Christians will practice mutual helpfulness, but he is concerned about the spirit in which their service for each other will be bathed. That they should be modest, whole-hearted, without vainglory or condenscending pride, "humbly considering each other the better man," is, in his eyes, essential to Christian usefulness. *For service can be utterly spoiled by the opposite attitude of superciliousness, condescension, lordliness.* Service may be flung to people as coins are flung to beggars. So Moses, about to bestow a blessing, cried: "Hear now, ye rebels; shall we bring you forth water out of this rock?" He was doing a gracious deed, but he was not doing it graciously. A good deal of intended usefulness is spoiled by this "flunkeyism of benevolence." We condescend to people, we stoop when we help, we are secretly puffed up by the superiority which our ability to serve makes evident. We have not, as Paul points out in the succeeding verses, "the mind of Christ."

O my God, enable me to thwart and utterly mortify my cursed vanity and pride, by giving me strength to hide all my good in this sense: not to speak to my nearest of good deeds done, but to do them cheerfully before Thee only, and to have the delight in making others happier and better. Let me please Thee, my Father, for I know Thou art so good as to be pleased with Thy children who by Thy grace are in any degree imbued with Thy goodness! Amen.—Norman Macleod (1812-1872).

Seventh Week, Third Day

And why beholdest thou the mote that is in thy brother's eye, but considerest not the beam that is in thine own eye? Or how wilt thou say to thy brother, Let me cast out the mote out of thine eye; and lo, the beam is in thine own eye? Thou hypocrite, cast out first the beam out of thine own eye; and then shalt thou see clearly to cast out the mote out of thy brother's eye.—Matt. 7:3-5.

The notable fact in this passage is the enthusiasm for service on the part of the man with a beam in his eye. He was zealous to be of use; he was positively officious about it; but the Master did not commend him. Sometimes it is easier to work up zeal for helping another than it is to handle well the problem of one's own life. So Charles Dickens, with clever strokes, drew the portrait of Mrs. Jellyby. To be of use was her ambition. So far from being deliberately selfish, she was resolutely unselfish. But her kind intentions all centered about Borrioboola-Gha in Africa. Her home disordered, her children neglected, her most obvious duties slatternly performed, she lavished her sentimental, long range interest upon a need thousands of miles away. She wished well, but she was useless. The beam in her own eye made negligible her strenuous ministries to the Africans.

O Lord, our heavenly Father, by whose Providence the duties of men are variously ordered, grant to us all such a spirit that we may labour heartily to do our work in our several stations, as serving one Master and looking for one reward. Teach us to put to good account whatever talents Thou has lent to us, and enable us to redeem our time by patience and zeal; through Jesus Christ Thy Son. Amen.—Bishop Westcott (1825-1901).

Seventh Week, Fourth Day

For I say, through the grace that was given me, to every man that is among you, not to think of himself more highly than he ought to think; but so to think as to think soberly, according as God hath dealt to each man a measure of faith. For even as we have many members in one body, and all the members have not the same office: so we, who are many, are one body in Christ, and severally members one of another.—Rom. 12:3-5.

Bear ye one another's burdens, and so fulfil the law of Christ. For if a man thinketh himself to be something when he is nothing, he deceiveth himself.—Gal. 6:2, 3.

This is a characteristic note in Paul's epistles. In both these passages the apostle is speaking about service, and in each he is anxious lest intended helpfulness should be spoiled by *self-conceit.* Many folk are earnestly desirous to be of use, but they are so self-confident about their own aims and methods, so intolerantly cocksure about social remedies, that they do their cause more harm than good. They lack the grace to see that at least occasionally they may be mistaken. One of the most familiar forms of such self-conceit among us is found in the man or woman, who having lighted upon some notion, likely to be of use to the world, at once erects it into the one panacea for which all the ages have been waiting. He becomes a crank. All other ideas save his seem negligible; all folk who do not appreciate his notion or assist him in it he marks down for fools; he rides the hobby of his special cure-all tirelessly. The pathos of the situation often dies in the man's self-renouncing devotion. But the devotion is so heavily cumbered with conceit, intolerance, dogmatism, and extravagant claims of unique importance, that a spectator finds it easier to stomach the original sin of selfishness than such a highly developed perversion of self-sacrifice.

O God, who hast promised to hear the prayers of Thy people, give me, I beseech Thee, the spirit of wisdom and understanding, of counsel and knowledge: keep me from folly and rashness: when I am right do Thou confirm me, when I am wrong do Thou correct me, and so give me, O Thou wisdom of God, a right judgment in all things, that I be not barren nor unfruitful in the knowledge of Thee and in the service of my fellowmen. Amen.—"A Book of Prayers for Students."

Seventh Week, Fifth Day

Now when Jesus saw great multitudes about him, he gave commandment to depart unto the other side. And there came a scribe, and said unto him, Teacher, I will follow thee whithersoever thou goest. And Jesus saith unto him, The foxes have holes, and the birds of the heaven have nests; but the Son of man hath not where to lay his head.—Matt. 8:18-20.

In spite of the brevity of the record the scene is not difficult to imagine. The popularity of the Master is at its height, the multitudes throng about him, association with him is fashionable, and a sentimental scribe is swept off his feet and proposes to join his company. But Jesus pricks the bubble of his effervescent feeling. He pictures the reality of hardship and self-denial. Today service has gained remarkable vogue. It is good form to be engaged in philanthropic work. People take up organized charity or settlement work or "slumming" as they do golf or bridge. A few such interests are to be expected in a well-furnished life. Philanthropy has become a fad. Many sentimental folk are emotionally ready, like the scribe, to follow Jesus in service. But they do not go far. They are caricatures of his real disciples, and often they bring into contempt the causes with which they dally. When folk are cruelly in need they are not thankful for the service of those who make a fashionable game of helping them. One cannot easily imagine any character more likely to receive the scathing rebuke of the Master than the one who tried to make a fad of service to "the least of these," his brethren.

Give us, O Lord, a mind after Thine own heart, that we may delight to do Thy will, O our God; and let Thy Law be written on our hearts. Give us courage and resolution to do our duty, and a heart to be spent in Thy service, and in doing all the good that possibly we can the few remaining days of our pilgrimage here on earth. Grant this, we humbly beseech Thee, for the sake of Jesus Christ Thy Son our Lord. Amen.—John Tillotson (1630-1694).

Seventh Week, Sixth Day

And as these went their way, Jesus began to say unto the multitudes concerning John, What went ye out into the wilderness to behold? a reed shaken with the wind? But what went ye out to see? a man clothed in soft raiment? Behold, they that wear soft raiment are in kings' houses. But wherefore went ye out? to see a prophet? Yea, I say unto you, and much more than a prophet. This is he, of whom it is written,

Behold, I send my messenger before thy face,
Who shall prepare thy way before thee.
Verily I say unto you, Among them that are born of women there hath not arisen a greater than John the Baptist: yet he that is but little in the kingdom of heaven is greater than he.—Matt. 11:7-11.

Of all the perversions of service none makes it more distasteful than *sentimental softness*. Some, endeavoring to live by love and to express love in usefulness, succeed only in achieving an oily, obsequious imitation of the splendidly rugged and vigorous ministry of Jesus. For Jesus approved folk like John the Baptist, where the stern, masculine qualities were prominent. He himself could serve by fearless words, audacious deeds, fierce denunciation, and unbending endurance as well as by tenderness. Scientists tell us that if there be health in the body when disease enters, the white corpuscles go out into the blood like warriors to attack the evil. A healthy body has capacity to resent the intrusion of destructive things; it has capacious power to repel invaders and to cast them out; and if any body lacks that protective force it dies. What is true of the body is true of the person. The power of repulsion against evil, of swift and eager indignation against cruelty and hypocrisy, is indispensable to any soul. General Booth said, "Go on hating, night and day, in every place, under all circumstances. Bring this side of your nature well into play." Nor is it easy to see how one can be in any worthy sense a disciple of Jesus, if he has not harnessed his combative faculties to the service of human weal. Of all misadventures in the imitation of Jesus, none can be farther from the mark than a pallid, pulseless, sentimental man.

Grant, O Lord, as Thou hast cast my lot in a fair ground, that I may show forth contentment by rejoicing in the privileges with which Thou hast strewn my path, and by using to the full my opportunities for service.

In hours of hardship, preserve me from self-pity and endow me with the warrior's mind, that even in the heat of battle I may be inspired with the sense of vocation and win the peace of the victor; through Jesus Christ our Lord. Amen.—Bishop Charles H. Brent.

Seventh Week, Seventh Day

Then came to him the mother of the sons of Zebedee with her sons, worshipping him, and asking a certain thing of him. And he said unto her, What wouldest thou? She saith unto him, Command that these my two sons may sit, one on thy right hand, and one on thy left hand, in thy kingdom. But Jesus answered and said, Ye know not what ye ask. Are ye able to drink the cup that I am about to drink? They say unto him, We are able. He saith unto them, My cup indeed ye shall drink: but to sit on my right hand, and on my left hand, is not mine to give; but it is for them for whom it hath been prepared of my Father. And when the ten heard it, they were moved with indignation concerning the two brethren. But Jesus called them unto him, and said, Ye know that the rulers of the Gentiles lord it over them, and their great ones exercise authority over them. Not so shall it be among you: but whosoever would become great among you shall be your minister; and whosoever would be first among you shall be your servant: even as the Son of man came not to be ministered unto, but to minister, and to give his life a ransom for many.—Matt. 20:20-28.

To seek notoriety and prominence even in the circle of Jesus' disciples, is a common perversion of service. We give ourselves to a sacrificial life, as James and John did, but we twist the meaning of our very sacrifice until we are thinking of the gains in fame and

121

popularity and power which may accrue to us. How few St. Francis
Xaviers there are, of whom it can be said that he "would like to
reform the world without his own existence being known." Old
John Donne put such self-effacement at the summit of spiritual
achievement:

> "I have done one braver thing
>   Than all the worthies did;
> And yet a braver thence doth spring,
>   Which is, to keep that hid."

Such are a few of the familier perversions of service: we become
meddlesome, we condescend, we make officious care for others a
substitute for the cleansing of ourselves, we become fanatics,
faddists, sentimentalists, or seekers after notoriety. When we
cannot be driven from the desire to be useful, we may yet be drawn
into some caricature of usefulness.

*I have been careless, cowardly, mutinous. Punishment I have
deserved, I deny it not; yet have mercy on me for the sake of the truth
I long to learn, and of the good which I long to do. Take the will for
the deed, good Lord. Accept the partial self-sacrifice which Thou
didst inspire, for the sake of the one perfect self-sacrifice which Thou
didst fulfil upon the Cross. Pardon my faults, out of Thine own
boundless pity for human weakness. Strike not my unworthy name
off the roll call of the noble and victorious army, which is the blessed
company of all faithful people; and let me, too, be found written in
the Book of Life, even though I stand the lowest and last upon its
list.*—Charles Kingsley.

COMMENT FOR THE WEEK

I

Hitherto we have been thinking of a generously useful life
against the background of thoroughgoing selfishness, ungracious
and unjust. While it is true, however, that the blatant enemy of
serviceableness is selfishness, it is also true that not often do men
deliberately set themselves to live self-centered lives. Selfishness,
like any other sin, is not often seen dressed in full uniform and
advertising candidly her true designs. Her ways are subtle; she
disguises herself in winsome forms; her ample box of tricks

supplies many such subterfuges as making proposed service unlovely by tactlessness or twisting an unselfish intention into a useless result.

Some characters, to be sure, have been and doubtless are avowedly and colossally selfish. To their ambition for aggrandizement they have deliberately handed the reins of their lives. They have concluded like Napoleon, "I am not an ordinary man, I am an extraordinary man, and ordinary rules do not apply to me," and in their unabashed self-seeking they have ridden roughshod across all considerations of justice and mercy. But probably such folk are few. Even Napoleon, doubtless deceiving himself as well as others, clothed his insatiable personal ambition in the plausible desires to spread the ideals of French liberty. One must turn to the imagined characters of literature to be sure that he has found utter selfishness, deliberate and unashamed. There, like Milton's Satan, some do indeed say, "Better to reign in hell than serve in heaven."

The uselessness of most of us, however, springs from meaner causes than such deliberate self-inflation. On the slope of Long's Peak in Colorado lies the ruin of a forest giant. The naturalist tells us that the tree had stood for four hundred years; that it was a seedling when Columbus landed on San Salvador; that it had been struck by lightning fourteen times; that the avalanches and storms of four centuries had thundered past it. In the end, however, beetles killed the tree. A giant that age had not withered nor lightnings blasted nor storms subdued fell at last before insects that a man could crush between his forefinger and his thumb. So human characters collapse into futile uselessness not only through "presumptuous sins" but more frequently through "secret faults." And nowhere is this subtle cause of ruined character more obvious than in the destructive work of the small enemies of usefulness.

II

The best intentions to live a serviceable life may evaporate for no other reason than the *habitual substitution of well-wishing for well-doing.* Superficially to wish people well is a habit easily acquired. In church under the spell of worship, or alone stirred by meditation or by a book, a man can warmly wish well to all humanity. So in an old jingle a captain brought to his crew the map of a shoreless sea:

He brought them a map representing the sea,
Without the least vestige of land;

And the crew were all glad when they found it to be
A map they could all understand.
What's the use of Mercators, North Pole and equators,
Tropics, zones, and meridian lines?
So the captain would cry, and the men would reply,
They are only conventional signs.

On such a zoneless, shoreless sea of well-wishing how many folk congenially are sailing! Their lives are not storm-tossed with hate nor wrecked by tempests of selfish ambition. Rather the breeze of a mild good will fills their sails, their skies are benignantly blue, and underneath is the gentle heave of kindly feeling. But they never *land.* The sea of their well-wishing has no shore. They arrive nowhere. They mean well but they mean well feebly. To no concrete deed of service, to no practical assumption of responsibility, to no costly and efficient expenditure of time, thought energy, and money in useful work, do they ever come.

The peculiar peril of such well-wishing lies in the complacent opinion of oneself which it induces. Good intentions and kindly emotions are the most efficient opiates for an uneasy conscience. We hear an address on the need of China or the sufferings of the Armenians and we are deeply stirred. We wish well to all the yellow race, to all oppressed and stricken people everywhere, to Australian bushmen, the hill tribes of the Himalayas, the barbarians of Timbuctoo, to Asia, Africa, and the islands of the sea! In our swelling and inclusive sympathy—and that, too, without the need of stirring from the pew—we may gather up all the sick, afflicted, and despised on earth, feeling in secret that so compassionate a spirit must argue an admirable life. When a rapacious man revels in cruelty, or a truculent man seeks vengeance, or a miser worships mammon, one easily can see that they are wrong. But kindly wishing, such as rises in a man of humane and generous emotions, quiets the accusing conscience and, like a vampire, lulls the victim while it sucks his blood. For well-wishers, while often in appearance the most sensitive, kindly, sympathetic, responsive folk one meets, still deserve the scathing rebuke of James, the Lord's brother: "If a brother or sister be naked and in lack of daily food, and one of you say unto them, Go in peace, be ye warmed and filled; and yet ye give them not the things needful to the body; what doth it profit? (James 2:15, 16).

There comes a time in certain experiments in chemistry when the fluid in solution awaits the decisive jar of the operator's finger to make it crystallize. So does many a well-intentioned spirit await the resolute act of will which will precipitate his kindly feelings into practical deeds. A large part of true religion is fulfilled when a man takes himself deliberatey in hand and walks himself up to tasks undone, concerning which he long has been wishing well. Sign that check; write that letter; pay that call; seek that interview; bear that testimony; accept that office; assume that responsibility—such crisp imperatives are indispensable, if well-wishing is not to prove the ruin of a serviceable life.

III

Another enemy of usefulness whose alluring disguise makes the peril greater is *the substitution of pleasing people for serving them.* One who sets himself to the task can soon become an adept at making himself agreeable. Consider these smooth and plausible folk who like human chameleons crawl across life, taking a new color from every person whom they meet! What infinite adaptability! Vain people enjoy flattery; they purr like kittens when their favorite vanities are stroked; and the specialist in pleasing folk knows how to touch each vain man's favorite nerve, until it tingles with delight. Weak people want pity; they are in minor mood and they wish all who meet them to wail, like dogs at a sad tune upon a violin; and the adept in agreeableness can wail to the satisfaction of the most self-pitying. Proud folk wish deference; when it shines upon them, they preen their feathers like peacocks in the sunlight; and your specialist in congeniality is positively radiant with deference when proud folk are near. Optimists enjoy the company of hopeful spirits who agree that the world is at the dawning of a great new day; and the adept in giving pleasure can affirm that hope with an enthusiatic assurance that puts new color into the roseate visions of the most optimistic. Pessimists love to see heads shaken over the world's lamentable state, and to hear sad affirmations that things will be much worse before they are better; and the specialist in adapatability can do both with an abandoned lugubriousness which makes the most pessimistic sure that conditions are even worse than he had hitherto supposed.

So Hamlet and Polonius in the drama talked together. Says Hamlet, "Do you see yonder cloud that's almost in shape of a camel?" "By the mass," says Polonius, "and 'tis like a camel, indeed." "Methinks," says Hamlet, "it is like a weasel." "It is backed like a weasel," agrees Polonius. "Or like a whale?" says

Hamlet. And Polonius consents, "Very like a whale." After a day so spent in being agreeable, the congenial man comes home well satisfied. Has he not pleased people? Has he not made the world happier? Is he not a useful character?

It should be obvious that so far from being thus identical, pleasing folk and serving them are often opposite. Ex-President Eliot of Harvard University once was asked to name the fundamental quality essential to a successful college president. After thinking a moment he replied, "The capacity to inflict pain." No serious mind can miss his meaning. Without that stern capacity no great leadership, friendship, or parenthood is imaginable. For lack of it lives that might have been useful now are fallen into soft futility. Parents to please their children relax all discipline and allow perilous indulgences; preachers to please their congregations prophesy smooth things; legislators to please their constituencies deny their own most assured convictions; husbands and wives to please each other give up their own most cherished principles. How frequently agreeableness is the enemy of usefulness! A serviceable man is congenial when he can be, but for the sake of leaving folk temporarily pleased he will not leave them permanently worse. Service sometimes shines as pleasantly as the sun in June, and sometimes it bursts like a thunder storm and clears the air. Now it is as delicate and refreshing as dew; and again it is as brisk and hearty as a winter day. For service and softness are two different things, and deeply to help folk sometimes involves displeasing them.

IV

Another familiar enemy of usefulness is discouragement over *the humdrum and monotony of commonplace living* to which the large and glowing ideals of service seem so little applicable. The principles of the self-sacrificial life, finding its fullness in its outpouring, are alluring when set in fitting words, and those self-denying lives, the remembrance of which is the glory of history, are stimulating when we read of them. But when from the contemplation of the great ideals of service and their supreme embodiments we turn to the narrow horizons, the petty tasks, the tiresome drudgery, the limited opportunities of our ordinary days, the vision often fades the examples seem inapplicable.

The fact is that, save in a small proportion of cases, service does not involve any dramatic surrender of life at all, but rather the faithful, painstaking use of life in ordinary tasks. One wonders which of the two is harder. It is said that thirty-seven flashes of lightning would be needed to keep one common incandescent lamp burning for a single hour. So the assumption of commonplace responsibilities, carried with constancy and fortitude through many years, may be far harder than one supreme adventurous deed of self-sacrifice that puts a name forever into manhood's memory. Thousands of soldiers in France would gladly have gone to the first line trenches that they might thereby escape the monotony of service in the camps.

One wonders also which of the two, the flaming deed of self-sacrifice or the obscure humdrum practice of it, is in the end more useful. There are two ways of saving folk at sea. Grace Darling's way is startling, unforgettable. All honor to her for that one wild night when with her father she risked her life to save the shipwrecked mariners on Longstone Ledge! There is, however, the blacksmith's way of saving mariners. A few old-fashioned smithies still are left where one may see the links of an anchor chain forged by hand with conscientious thoroughness. In the workers' imagination, for all the commonplaceness of his task, there well may be the picture of a mad night upon the ocean, when only that chain will stand between rocks and foundering ship. He will not be there to achieve a rescue that will make his name rememberable in the annals of the sea. But for all that, by conscientious work in the smoke of the smithy, he can save that ship. He who loses the ideal of a serviceable life because he cannot serve in Grace Darling's way lacks vision. Only a few are called to that. It is more fundamental to forge strong anchor chains than to rescue the victims of broken ones; it is more basic to build fireproof buildings than to save the occupants when buildings burn; the most important business in the world is the undergirding of home, and neighborhood, and nation with

> "Plain devotedness to duty
> Steadfast and still, nor paid with mortal praise,
> But finding amplest recompense
> For life's ungarlanded expense
> In work done squarely and unwasted days.

An American soldier in the first World War won the Croix de Guerre but refused to wear it, and this is his explanation: "I was no good back home. I let my sister and my widowed mother support me. I was a dead beat. And now they have given me the Croix de Guerre for something I did at the front. I am not going to put it on. I am going back home first. I am going to win out there. I am going to show my mother that I can make good at home. Then I will put on the Croix de Guerre." He is not the only one who has discovered that being heroic in a crisis is sometimes easier than being useful at home.

V

Kindred with what we just have said is this further fact: many people lose the ideal of usefulness because they are discouraged not about the commonplaceness of their tasks, but about their own *meanly endowed or severely handicapped lives*. Exhortation to usefulness so far from inspiring them, sickens them. They would count it their crown and joy to be useful, but what can they do?

By how may roads does Selfishness contrive to offer an escape from service! Some folk are *not* humbly dismayed about themselves. They are too conceited to be of use. They will not work on committees except as chairmen, nor in societies except as presidents. They are always seeking vainly for opportunities ample enough to be worthy of the exercise of their exalted powers. They are habitually aggrieved because, being eagles, folk expect them to hatch eggs on humming-birds' nests. Their professed desire to be of use is extraordinary, but the conditions which they insist on as indispensable are dictated by pride. They have not learned that effective service is the child of humility; they do not see that the real way to get things done is not to care who gets the credit for doing them.

When, however, Selfishness cannot so contrive to make pride a stumbling-block to usefulness, but finds instead a deeply humble soul, he is too experienced and wily a foe to be discouraged. Humility, if it be skillfully handled, will do quite as well as self-conceit to make life useless. Let a humble man's self-depreciation become exaggerated; let him meditate morbidly upon his poorly endowed life, his meagerness of mind, his crippled health, his slender store of strength, his little reputation; let him handle his one talent in disheartened comparison with the larger gifts of other men! He will soon be ready to lay what power he was away in a napkin; he will soon be as useless through false humility as Selfishness ever could have made him through false pride. It is a clever foe who knows how to persuade his victim to fall on his own sword. But so Selfishness uses a man's humility to his own undoing.

The fact is, however, that one thing in human life of which ill-fortune and crippling handicap never can deprive an earnest man is the privilege of being useful. One door which no man and no circumstance can shut is the opportunity to serve. Paul at liberty can give himself to splendid tasks. Paul in prison is deprived of many privileges which he had loved; but Paul in prison is not deprived of the privilege of being useful. Even the men to whom he is chained present a chance to preach the Gospel to an audience which cannot escape, and enforced leisure he can use for the writing of letters which thrill and burn in the Christian churches yet. When a man is earnestly set on being useful, he is in a country where he can dig anywhere and strike water.

Indeed, the indispensableness of all sorts of people, from the genius to the most meanly endowed, was clearly illustrated during the Great War. Everybody counted. In the saving of food, in the raising of crops, in the disposal of bonds, the fidelity of all the populaion was needed, and the children were mobilized in the schools for work as were the armies in the field. There was no one too small in ability to share in the campaign. Great handles to the burden there were which needed great hands to lift them, but all around the task were little handles also on which the smallest fingers could obtain a hold. Even the blind, whose hearing by nature's compensation is keener than ordinary men's, were set to the task of listening for the hostile airplanes on the English coast. Each person found some gift, however small which could be contributed to the general fund.

It were a pity to forget in peace a truth which shone so clearly in the War. Life seldom gives to any man so barren a day that chances to help somebody are not plentiful. To be cheerful under difficulties, by fortitude and patience making even sick rooms holy lands; to appreciate some fine unadvertised endeavor of an unnoticed man; to display that rare virtue, magnanimity to an unfriendly person; to speak a stout word for a good cause; to be kind to the humiliated and gracious to the hurt; to touch some youth with new confidence in human goodness and with fresh resolve to live life for noble ends—such opportunities are as free as air to breathe. The chance to serve is the great democrat. He comes to all doors. He lodges in all houses. To any who will take he gives

That best portion of a good man's life,
His little, nameless, unremembered acts
Of kindness and of love.

It is not lack of opportunity or of endowment that makes us useless. It is lack of insight, thoughtfulness, sympathy, imagination, and love.

Moreover, no trouble need keep any man from the joys of service. Some forms of work strong folk must do, but for those deeper ministries to the souls of men—the inbreathing of new hope, the conquest of disillusionment and doubt, the inspiration of fresh faith in the reality of the spiritual world—the most useless man is one who has had no trouble. What can *he* do for us? In all the deeper needs of life, we turn not to the fortunate, the popular, the merry and unhurt, but to One "despised and rejected of men, a man of sorrows and acquainted with grief." His troubles did not prevent his usefulness; they are the chief instruments of his service. His incomparable influence on human hearts would have been impossible, if men had not known that he was "touched with the feeling of our infirmities." His Cross was not an interruption of his usefulness but the climax of it. For when anyone gives himself wholeheartedly to helping men, any experience of life, glad or sorrowful, transfiguration or crucifixion, can be used in ministry. When life digs pickaxes into us, this indeed is the deepest comfort—that new springs of understanding, sympathy, and service may be opened up.

Ask who most of all have influenced your life for good, and to what unlikely places does the trail of the answer lead! Folk whose outward eyes have been long blinded but whose inward eyes have been opened wide to things invisible; shutins whose patient, unembittered faith re-creates in the young and strong a new confidence that spirit alone is real; men who live in unbreakable companionship with pain, but whose courage is not broken nor their spirits crushed; martyrs of the home, whose failing health is the evidence of unfailing preference of other's welfare to their own; the aged, grown beautifully old, whose increasing frailty of flesh the better lets the light of the eternal through—such people are not shut out from service. They are often the most efficient ministers to some of man's profoundest needs. Many an admired warrior for the common good whose resounding blows are everywhere applauded draws his secret inspiration from some upper room where, like the light in a lighthouse, a life is shut in but still is luminous.

To all folk discouraged about crippled lives, this then is the message: The world is in trouble and none can help more than hearts by trouble touched to understanding. Where millions are in adversity, serviceable men taught by hardship are deeply needed. So when John Bright sat mourning in his widowed home, Cobden came to comfort him: "Bright," he said, "there are thousands of homes in England at this moment, where wives, mothers, and children are dying of hunger. When the first paroxysm of your grief is past, I would advise you to come with me and we will never rest until the Corn Laws are repealed." That is real comfort, to know that one's trouble can be capitalized into usefulness. As "the Lady of the Decoration" said, "The most miserable, pitiful, smashed-up life could blossom again if it would only blossom for others."

The substitution of well-wishing for well-doing, of pleasing people for serving them, disheartenment over small opportunities, self-conceit, and humility overdone—such beetles gnaw at the pith of our usefulness. Our prayer against colossal selfishness are often wide of the mark. We are not deliberately unselfish. We are driven from a useful life, like travelers from the woods, not by lions but by midgets. We need to pray not, "O God, save me from the brutal self-seeking of Milton's Satan!" but rather, "Who can understand his errors? Cleanse Thou me from secret faults!"

CHAPTER VIII

COOPERATION

Daily Readings

We need to recognize, before we go further in our thought of service, how much of our helpfulness must be extended, not individually from one person to another, but through the medium of cooperative organizations. Unless one sees the necessity of this, understands its principles, and practically accepts it in his program of usefulness, he will inevitably be robbed of a large part of his possible service.

Eighth Week, First Day

And they were bringing unto him little children, that he should touch them: and the disciples rebuked them. But when Jesus saw it, he was moved with indignation, and said unto them, Suffer the little children to come unto me; forbid them not; for to such belongeth the kingdom of God. Verily I saw unto you, Whosoever shall not receive the kingdom of God as a little child, he shall in no wise enter therein. And he took them in his arms, and blessed them, laying his hands upon them.—Mark 10:13-16.

Service for children, personally rendered, lies within reach of most of us. But consider in any community what numbers of children may be beyond the reach of casual individual good will. Christian people have no right to avoid such questions as these: Do we need a day nursery or a home for the care of orphaned and destitute children? Are our boys and girls being supplied with such organized help as the Christian Associations or the Boy Scouts or the Camp Fire Girls could supply? Does the community face the problem of children in industry, and is the problem being rightly and thoroughly handled? Are decent opportunities for play and recreation being provided for the young? Are the day schools what they ought to be? Are the Sunday schools effective? The time has gone by when personal service, individually rendered, can suffice in any form. "Nowadays the water main is my well, the trolley car my carriage, the banker's safe my old stocking, the policeman's billy my fist." *Service cannot refuse to face the necessities and to use the instruments which the new age has brought.*

O Heavenly Father, whose unveiled face the angels of little children do always behold, look with love and pity, we beseech thee, upon the children of the streets. Where men, in their busy and careless lives, have made a highway, these children of thine have made a home and a school, and are learning the bad lessons of our selfishness and our folly. Save them, and save us, O Lord. Save them from ignorance and brutality, from the shamelessness of lust, the hardness of greed, and the besotting of drink; and save us from the greater guilt of those that offend thy little ones, and from the hypocrisy of those that say they see and see not, whose sin remaineth. Amen.—Walter Rauschenbusch.

Eighth Week, Second Day

And when he was come down from the mountain, great multitudes followed him. And behold, there came to him a leper and worshipped him, saying, Lord, if thou wilt, thou canst make me clean. And he stretched forth his hand, and touched him, saying, I will; be thou made clean. And straightway his leprosy was cleansed. And Jesus saith unto him, See thou tell no man; but go, show thyself to the priest, and offer the gift that Moses commanded, for a testimony unto them.—Matt. 8:1-4.

All of us at times have the privilege of ministering directly to the comfort and recovery of the sick. *But no Christian who uses his imagination can be content with those opportunities which chance throws in his way.* The sick who most need care are often outside the range of individual ministry. Has your community a hospital property equipped to minister to the whole community? Are there visiting nurses to be summoned in case of need? Is there a health department in your community which is cleaning up unsanitary districts, removing the cause of disease, and preventing its spread?

Is there need of a convalescent home, a fresh air program, a special physician's superintendence of school children? No wordy profession of Christian care about the sick amounts to much in a modern community, save as such questions are answered. What multitudes of Christians need a baptism of public-mindedness!

Lord, have mercy on all miserable bodies; those that are ready to famish for want, feed them; those that are bound to beds of pain, loose them; those that are in prison and bonds, release them; those that are under the fury of persecution, and cry under the yoke of oppression, relieve them; those that lie smarting in their pains and wounds, cure them; those that are distracted in their thoughts and wits, settle them; those that are in perils of their estates and lives, preserve them. Wherever they are, and whosoever they be, what help I would pray for myself from Thee, or comfort from men, in their condition, I beseech Thee, the God of all help and comfort, to give it to them; take them to Thy care and tend them; supply them, and succour them; have compassion on them and heal them. Amen.—Dr. Brough.

Eighth Week, Third Day

Then shall the King say unto them on his right hand, Come, ye blessed of my Father, inherit the kingdom prepared for you from the foundation of the world: for I was hungry, and ye gave me to eat; I was thirsty, and ye gave me drink; I was a stranger, and ye took me in; naked, and ye clothed me; I was sick, and ye visited me; I was in prison, and ye came unto me. Then shall the righteous answer him, saying, Lord, when saw we thee hungry, and fed thee? or athirst, and gave thee drink? And when saw we thee a stranger, and took thee in? or naked, and clothed thee? And when saw we thee sick, or in prison, and came unto thee? And the King shall answer and say unto them, Verily I say unto you, Inasmuch as ye did it unto one of these my brethren, even these least, ye did it unto me.—Matt. 25:34-40.

It is the commonplace of Christian teaching that we should care for the poor, afflicted, destitute. And most of us, touched by special instances of need, are ready to give help. *But how many fail either to see need or to feel obligation beyond those particular cases that come under their individual observance!* It stands to reason, however, that the most hopeless, abject want will be found in precisely those places where our casual observation does not fall. It stands to reason, also, that the most self-respecting poor, to whom beggary is agony and who would almost rather die than ask alms, are the very ones whose cries for help will never reach our ears. A modern community, therefore, of any size, which has not organized its philanthropy, mapped out the districts where poverty is frequent, studied scientifically its problem of destitution, examined the reasons for all cases of habitual want, and provided systematic measures for relief and constructive help, is not really caring for the poor at all. No words, no kindly feelings, no prayers, no individual beneficence, ever can make up for lack of cooperative organization in relief of want.

O Thou, who art Love, and who seest all the suffering, injustice, and misery which reign in this world, have pity, we implore Thee, on the work of Thy hands. Look mercifully upon the poor, the oppressed, and all who are heavy laden with error, labour, and sorrow. Fill our hearts with deep compassion for those who suffer, and hasten the coming of Thy kingdom of justice and truth; for the sake of Jesus Christ our Lord.—Eugéne Bersier.

Eighth Week, Fourth Day

Now all the publicans and sinners were drawing near unto him to hear him. And both the Pharisees and the scribes murmured, saying, This man receiveth sinners, and eateth with them.

And he spake unto them this parable, saying, What man of you, having a hundred sheep, and having lost one of them, doth not leave the ninety and nine in the wilderness, and go after that which is lost, until he find it? And when he hath found it, he layeth it on his shoulders, rejoicing. And when he cometh home, he calleth together his friends and his neighbors, saying unto them, Rejoice with me, for I have found my sheep which was lost. I say unto you, that even so there shall be joy in heaven over one sinner that repenteth, more than over ninety and nine righteous persons, who need no repentance.—Luke 15:1-7.

No one would doubt the Christian's duty to work for reclamation of character. Many chances for personal service to tempted and beaten men come to any Christian who is looking for them. But even here no Christian ought to content himself with individual service alone. Have the Christians of your community ever faced together the moral conditions of your town? Do you know whether organized vice has invaded your city, whether the police are in cahoots with evil or are honestly about their business, whether vile plays that could be stopped are being given and vile resorts are debauching the town's youth? A few spoonfuls of reclaimed humanity are dipped up in churches; but often the full stream of moral filth pours into the community, unnoticed by any collective Christian attention, unopposed by any Christian public-mindedness. There is hardly a neighborhood in Christendom which the Christian people could not cleanse, putting the fear of God into corrupt officials, and driving out blatantly vicious influences, if they earnestly chose.

O Lord, who doest not willingly afflict the sons of men, behold from Thy holy habitation the multitude of miserable souls and lives among us, and have mercy upon them.

Have mercy upon all ignorant souls, and instruct them; upon all deluded minds, and enlighten them; on all seducing and seduced spirits, and convert them.

Have mercy upon all broken hearts, and heal them; on all struggling temptation, and rescue them; on all languishing in spiritual desertion, and revive them.

Have mercy on all who stagger in faith, and establish them; that are fallen from Thee, and raise them; that stand with Thee, and confirm them.

Have mercy on all who groan under their sins, and ease them; that go on their wickedness, and curb them.

O Blessed Jesus, who didst shed Thy Blood for our souls to save them; shed Thy Holy Spirit upon all and heal them, for Thy mercy's sake. Amen.—Dr. Brough.

Eighth Week, Fifth Day

We have been saying that Christians ought to take collective responsibility for such communal affairs as the care of children and of the sick, the relief of the poor and the cleaning up of moral conditions. This collective responsibility, however, ought to be extended far beyond the individual community. Our worst sins are no longer merely individual or communal; they are organized on a national scale. We have now "the man who picks pockets with a railway rebate, murders with an adulterant instead of a bludgeon, burglarizes with a 'rake-off' instead of a jimmy, cheats with a company prospectus instead of a deck of cards, or scuttles his town instead of his ship." Nothing can handle such forms of iniquity except public-mindedness. If a man hates sin, but hates it only in its individual forms, how far short has he fallen from his full share of service! To be a public-minded citizen, to make citizenship an agency of Christian usefulness, to understand public needs, public sins, public remedies—such cooperative ministry is indispensable to a full-sized Christian life. What would the world become if all Christians felt for their countries what the prophet felt for Zion?

For Zion's sake will I not hold my peace, and for Jerusalem's sake I will not rest, until her righteousness go forth as brightness, and her salvation as a lamp that burneth. And the nations shall see thy righteousness, and all kings thy glory; and thou shalt be called by a new name, which the mouth of Jehovah shall name. Thou shalt also be a crown of beauty in the hand of Jehovah, and a royal diadem in the hand of thy God. Thou shalt no more be termed Forsaken; neither shall thy land any more be termed Desolate: but thou shalt be called Hephzi-bah, and thy land Beulah; for Jehovah delighth in thee, and thy land shall be married. For as a young man marrieth a virgin, so shall thy sons marry thee; and as the bridegroom rejoiceth over the bride, so shall thy God rejoice over thee.—Isa. 62:1-5.

O God, whose Kingdom is an everlasting kingdom and whose dominion endureth from generation to generation, abase our pride and shatter our complacency. Open our eyes to see the vanity of this world's riches and renown; make us to understand that there is no wealth but life, that living men are Thy glory and our life is the vision of Thee. Keep us from being terrorized by wealth and influence, or beguiled by pleas of custom and expediency, or distracted by the glamor of prosperity and aggrandizement; keep us securely in Thy way of righteousness and truth. Amen.— "Prayers for the City of God."

Eighth Week, Sixth Day

And it shall come to pass in the latter days, that the mountain of Jehovah's house shall be established on the top of the mountains, and shall be exalted above the hills; and all nations shall flow unto it. And many peoples shall go and say, Come ye, and let us go up to the mountain of Jehovah, to the house of the God of Jacob; and he will teach us of his ways, and we will walk in his paths; for out of Zion shall go forth the law, and the word of Jehovah from

Jerusalem. And he will judge between the nations, and will decide concerning many peoples; and they shall beat their swords into plowshares, and their spears into pruning-hooks; nation shall not lift up sword against nation, neither shall they learn war any more.—Isa. 2:2-4.

Cooperative responsibility must overpass national lines, if this hope of the prophet is to be fulfilled. The old age still lifts up its voice to cry, War is inevitable; the new age cries, War is no more inevitable than slavery! The old age still insists, The State has no obligation but power; the new age answers, The State can be as Christian as a man. The old age urges, All nations must be armed against each other; the new age replies, All nations must cooperate for the world's peace. In this choice between Christ and Satan, Christians have an enormous stake. War in its origins, motives, methods, and issues is the most powerful anti-Christian influence on earth. But individual service alone cannot handle the problem. The cooperative organization of all the international good will there is, is indispensable. What an expanded, steady, wise, and ardent public-mindedness will be necessary to make such cooperation win the day!

Almighty God, who art the Father of all men upon the earth, most heartily we pray that Thou wilt keep Thy children from the cruelties of war, and lead the nations in the way of peace. Teach us to put away all bitterness and misunderstanding, both in Church and State; that we, with all the brethren of the Son of Man, may draw together as one comity of peoples, and dwell evermore in the fellowship of that Prince of Peace, who liveth and reigneth with Thee in the unity of the Holy Spirit, now and ever.—Percy Dearmer.

Eighth Week, Seventh Day

Consider this paragraph from the Edinburgh Conference Report:
"The evangelization of Africa means something more than the introduction of the Gospel into existing forms of social life. It means the introduction of education and letters, of agriculture and industries, of Christian marriage and due recognition of the sanctity of human life and property. The problem before the Church is the creation of an African civilization."

That is to say, Christianity cannot content itself with the cure of evil already done; it must seek, in the reconstruction of social life, the prevention of the evil at its source. Here lies the ultimate necessity of cooperation as contrasted with individual service. Our personal usefulness may occasionally cure, but only collective effort can finally prevent the ravages of sin, sickness, poverty, and social wrong. To relieve famine sufferers in India is good; to teach them collectively to practice irrigation and scientific agriculture, so that there will be no famines, is better. In how far are you, through influence and gift, supporting the great cooperative endeavors to reach the social roots of man's ills in community, nation, and the world?

And the word of Jehovah came unto me, saying, Son of man, prophesy against the shepherds of Israel, prophesy, and say unto them, even to the shepherds, Thus saith the Lord Jehovah: Woe unto the shepherds of Israel that do feed themselves! should not the shepherds feed the sheep? Ye eat the fat, and ye clothe you with the wool, ye kill the fatlings; but ye feed not the sheep. The diseased have ye not strengthened, neither have ye healed that which was sick, neither have ye bound up that which was broken, neither have ye brought back that which was driven away, neither have ye sought that which was lost; but with force and with rigor have ye ruled over them. And they were scattered, because there was no shepherd; and they became food to all the beasts of the field, and were scattered. My sheep wandered through all the mountains, and upon every high hill; yea, my sheep were scattered upon all the face of the earth; and there was none that did search or seek after them.

Therefore, ye shepherds, hear the word of Jehovah: As I live, saith the Lord Jehovah, surely forasmuch as my sheep became a prey, and my sheep became food to all the beasts of the field, because there was no shepherd, neither did my shepherds search for my sheep, but the shepherds fed themselves, and fed not my sheep; therefore, ye shepherds, hear the word of Jehovah: Thus saith the Lord Jehovah, Behold, I am against the shepherds; and I will require my sheep at their hand, and cause them to cease from feeding the sheep; neither shall the shepherds feed themselves any more; and I will deliver my sheep from their mouth, that they may not be food for them.—Ezek. 34:1-10.

O God, we praise Thee for the dream of the golden city of peace and righteousness which has ever haunted the prophets of humanity, and we rejoice with joy unspeakable that at last the people have

*conquered the freedom and knowledge and power which may avail
to turn into reality the vision that so long has beckoned in vain. We
pray Thee to revive in us the hardy spirit of our forefathers, that we
may establish and complete their work, building on the basis of
their democracy the firm edifice of a cooperative commonwealth, in
which both government and industry shall be of the people, by the
people, and for the people. May we, who now live, see the oncoming of
the great day of God, when all men shall stand side by side in equal
worth and real freedom, all toiling and all reaping, masters of
nature but brothers of men, exultant in the tide of the common life,
and jubilant in the adoration of Thee, the source of their blessings,
and the Father of all. Amen.*—Walter Rauschenbusch.

COMMENT FOR THE WEEK

I

Hitherto our thought of service has largely concerned itself with
one individual's usefulness to another. But the finest forms of
serviceable living are reached not when I give some helpful
ministry to you, but when we in mutual fellowship work out our
welfare together. The most gracious and the most useful ministries
are found in cooperation. So a mother long blind complimented her
son: "It is not so much that he does things for me, as that he so
arranges matters that we can do things together."

In the mutual loyalties which such partnerships involve most of
us find our richest satisfaction. To be sure, some men are made to
work in solitude. Newton forbade the publication of his name in
connection with his solution of the problem of the moon. "It would
perhaps increase my acquaintance," he wrote, "the thing which I
chiefly study to decline." Such solitary living, however, is reserved
for geniuses. Most of us were made for comradeship, and we are
bereft without it. Said a very young and lonely lad, "Mother, I wish
that I were two little puppies, so that I could play together." Why,
from the time our primitive forefathers communicated with one
another by grunt and gesture because they had no other speech,
has man so tirelessly worked out his elaborate languages, until
now in the marvel and mystery of words we have so facile an
instrument? The motive behind the development of language is
men's irresistible desire to break over the isolating barriers that
separate individuals and to achieve their proper destiny in
thinking together and working together for common ends.
Self-preservation may be the strongest instinct in men, but close

alongside is the companion instinct for comradeship. "Only mankind together is the true man," said Goethe, "and the individual can be joyous and happy only when he feels himself in the whole."

So deeply is this need for cooperation wrought into all life that it reveals itself long before man arrives. The lowest orders of animals do indeed appear to talk like this: There is barely enough food to go around. What I gain you lose and what I lose you gain. We are natural enemies; there is between us an unavoidable hostility. But one rises only a little way in the scale of animal life before he hears a different tone: It may be that we were mistaken, they seem to say. It may be that our mutual antagonisms are superficial, our mutual interests profound. It may be that if you and I were blended into we, we would do more for both of us than either you or I could do for either of us. So the bees hive and the birds flock and the wolves hunt in packs.

As the creeper that girdles the tree-trunk the law runneth forward
    and back—
For the strength of the Pack is the Wolf, and the strength of the
    Wolf is the Pack.

What begins thus among animals continues among men. The story of advancing civilization is mainly the record of mankind's enlarging capacity to cooperate. From the days when humanity began, not with a solitary individual, but with a unit of three—father, mother, and child—to the days when internationalism becomes a live issue and increasing numbers of people think in planetary terms, we can mark the major changes that have passed over human life in terms of cooperation, its enlargements and lapses, its victories and failures. In our time the whole structure of human life is so intricately interrelated, men, no matter how various their colors, customs, or habitats, are so inextricably interdependent, that the problem of cooperation has become supremely the critical question of the world.

No kind of help, therefore, that individuals can give each other exhausts the meaning of service. For all the fine spirit manifest, it is vain for one man to lug water in a bucket from a spring to give drink to the thirsty of a modern town. He must serve in another way. He must call a town meeting and arouse the citizens to build a water system in cooperative effort for the good of all. However admirable in intention it may be, it is of negligible import for one man to sweeten the bitterness of war by maintaning personal friendship with one enemy citizen. The problem must be met in another way. The people as a whole must be aroused to see the immedicable evils of war, to hate it with a blazing hatred, to purpose its abolishment with all their hearts, and mutually to seek those covenants that will achieve their end. From the smallest enterprises to the greatest, the direst human need is far beyond the reach of individual usefulness.

II

This basic problem in human relationships received its classic Christian treatment in the twelfth and thirteenth chapters of Paul's first letter to the Corinthians. The twelfth chapter pictures the cooperative unity of human life, ideally presented in the Church, as one body with many members. Not like loose shot in a bag, isolated and unrelated, does Paul see human kind, but like eyes, ears, hands, feet, in one body, vitally joined and mutually interdependent. Having presented this unforgettable picture of a human society where cooperation is indispensable, he swings out into the thirteenth chapter in praise of that most excellent and necessary of all gifts, love. The thirteenth chapter did not by accident follow the twelfth. It is the fine flower that grows up out of the roots of the twelfth. Paul saw a basic fact about life, that we are cooperating members one of another; then he declares that only one quality of relationship can keep such members from catastrophe. Love in Paul's thirteenth chapter is the necessary principle of conduct in life, based upon the major fact about life which his twelfth chapter has presented.

Thoroughly to grasp the fact, therefore, that we are vitally related members of one social body, to see it vividly, to feel it convincingly, is the first step toward understanding the meaning of Christian love. Two sets of forces continually play upon us like centrifugal and centripetal forces among the planets. One set pulls us apart, disentangles us from each other, sets us over against each other, sharply individual and competitive. The other set of forces weaves us together, places the solitary in families, welds us into friendships, braids us into neighborhoods, nations, and mankind. Both these sets of forces are present in life and both are needful, but one of them is primary and the other is secondary. We are not first of all isolated individuals, says Paul; first of all we are members of the social body and have no true life apart from it.

Therefore, the primary law of life is not selfishness; the primary law is love.

A man can assure himself that this is true by many tests. Let him look back to the source out of which his life has sprung. If from the day of birth he had been cast upon a desert island and like some Romulus had been suckled by a wolf, and then had grown, utterly cut off from the whole heritage of mankind's past, its national traditions, its social accumulations, its intellectual gains, its religious faiths, would he be himself? Rather he would not be anybody. He would be an animal, highly organized, it may be, but lacking all the characteristic qualities of human life. A person so abstracted from his social background is no person at all.

Let a man look in and, granting all the gains of past inheritance, let him consider the contributions of social relationships that immediately surround him! If he goes down into the thing he calls his self and rummages through its contents as one searches an old chest, how little he will find that is not social! His wife and children are there, his neighborhood and nation, the recreations he enjoys, the causes that he loves. So far from being isolatedly individual, he is like a tree in a forest, whose trunk indeed stands separate, but whose branches are twined and whose roots are woven into an inextricable network with all the other trees, and whose source is the seeds of forests that reach back into the past.

Or let a man look out into the world about him, and endeavor to picture a life independent of the society from which he came and to which he belongs! Such an isolated self is as difficult to imagine as the grin on the face of the cat in *Alice in Wonderland* that stayed after the cat had gone. Ex-Presiednt Harris of Amherst College has drawn for us the details of one small area of a man's unescapable membership in human kind: "When he rises, a sponge is placed in his hand by a Pacific Islander, a cake of soap by a Frenchman, a rough towel by a Turk. His merino underwear he takes from the hand of a Spaniard, his linen from a Belfast manufacturer, his outer garments from a Birmingham weaver, his scarf from a French silk-grower, his shoes from a Brazilian grazier. At breakfast his cup of coffee is poured by natives of Java and Arabia, his rolls are passed by a Kansas farmer, his beefsteak by a Texan ranchman, his orange by a Florida Negro."

Let a man look back, or in, or out, he sees one primary fact. We are members one of another. Out of society we came, to it we belong, from it we are not separable. God made us what we are, in and through our fellows. "We are told that our body is a little condensed air living in the air," says Gabriel de Tarde. "Might we not say that our soul is a little bit of society incarnate, living in society? Born of society, it lives by means of it."

But if the principle of the twelfth chapter of First Corinthians is true, the thirteenth chapter is inevitable. Nothing can solve the problems of human life, so constituted, except cooperative love. "Is it true," some one asked, "that all the people in the world could get into the state of Texas?" "Yes," was the answer, "if they were friends." So always, increase of contacts demands access of friendliness. Love is not a luxury. It is the profoundest practical need of mankind. On no other terms can human life sustain the mutual relationships into which by its very nature it is increasingly compressed.

III

It is a great day for a Christian when he sees that the gospel of love is founded on the rock of fact. Many people think of love as an ideal sentiment, a gracious irridescent quality, which gives a touch of radiant color to life's solid structure, otherwise complete. "Upon the top of the pillars was lilywork": runs an Old Testament verse, "so was the work of the pillars finished." Such floral decoration upon the substantial column of man's life does love appear to be. Ask a man what makes life strong and he thinks of self-seeking power; ask him what makes life winsome and he thinks of love. He changes gear from business to sentiment when he picks up the thirteenth chapter of First Corinthians. But that chapter is not sentiment. It is the plain statement of the way of living which alone corresponds with the facts of life. On no other basis can humanity, constituted as it is, live decently and fortunately upon the earth.

The solid grounding which the gospel of cooperative love has in the facts of life is clear when one considers history. Whatever real progress mankind has made has lain in the redemption of new areas of life from the regime of violence to the regime of good will. The family used to be founded upon force. Men did not woo their wives, they captured them by violence and held them by constraint. Parents were not bound to love their children. Infants were exposed at birth if the parents chose, and fathers held the absolute power of life and death over their growing offspring. Moreover, this regime of violence was counted on in theory as well as fact as necessary to sustain the home. Could anyone from a modern Christian family have entered such a household and explained the constitution of a home where marriage is an affair of mutual love and mutual consent, where the children from their earliest childhood are cooperating members of the family, not driven by violence but won by love, and where so far from having power to kill their children, parents administer the simplest corporal punishment only as a last resort, the visitor would have been met with utter incredulity. He would have seemed an arrant sentimentalist to suppose that a family could so be run by love instead of violence. The fact is, however, that family life over wide areas has actually been thus redeemed. Only when such redemption is wrought does a family come to its true nature, and no one who knows what a family can thus become, would propose relapse into the old barbarism.

So, too, the school used to be founded upon force. An unwhipped child was a lost opportunity. Of the Rev. James Boyer, an English schoolmaster, it was said that "it was lucky the cherubim who took him to heaven were nothing but wings and faces, or he infallibly would have flogged them by the way." The stories of cruel punishment pitilessly inflicted as a matter of principle upon unwary children are almost incredible to a modern mind. But they are not so incredible as would have been the description of a modern school to one of the old schoolmasters. To have a school the children deeply love, around which their thoughts of play center as well as their thoughts of work, in which they are cooperating members, and from which violence has been excluded as a needless intruder—that would have left an ancient pedagogue utterly incredulous. The man who proposed it would have seemed impossibly sentimental. But the taunted dreamers have turned out to be right. The facts were too much for the old educators, who, like the Sadducees, cried, "My right arm is my god." No one who knows the truth supposes that in a school cooperative good will will not work. It is the only thing that will work.

Religion also used to be under the domain of force. Let a man come into the Church willingly, if he would, but if he willfully refused, then violence was the swift and terrible resort. The Christian centuries are sick with cruelties born of the endeavor to make terror a motive for the Christian life, and violence an effective minister of the Christian Church. One does not wonder at accounts of black-haired priests going into torture chambers to force the recantation of disapproved beliefs and coming out white-haired with the horror of their own performances. It seemed incredible that the Church could be made a matter of voluntary cooperation. To tolerate in other men beliefs you did not hold yourself seemed as much as denying your convictions. Cried Thomas Edwards: "Could the devil effect a toleration, he would think he had gained well by the Reformation, and make a good exchange of the hierarchy to have a toleration for it." Said the saintly Baxter: "I abhor unlimited liberty and toleration of all, and think myself easily able to prove the wickedness of it." The Long Parliament in 1648 made death the penalty for eight errors in doctrine and indefinite imprisonment the penalty for sixteen others. But the facts were too much for these blind champions of forced religion. Human life is fundamentally built to be voluntarily cooperative, and the highest area of human life, religion, never came to its own until it was redeemed from the regime of force.

All progress moves thus to the rescuing of some new area of life from violence to the domain of cooperative good will. Already we have gone a long way on that road in local government. Once family feuds were matters of course. How else could one sustain the honor of his clan? But wherever that old barbarism still maintains its belated sway, it is the butt of general contempt and ridicule. Yet there was a time when the whole idea of settled local government, with ordered justice strong enough to make armed residences needless and family feuds a shame, seemed as Utopian as a warless world. From the city of Florence in the fourteenth century to the city of Florence in the twentieth century is as long a step as from the Europe of 1914 to the Europe of the internationalist's dream.

Moreover, what has been done in the government of neighborhoods has become indispensable in the larger government of nations. Once all sovereignty was assumed to rest on power. But one day mankind turned a corner and came face to face with a prodigious and revolutionary thought: all the people can be trusted in cooperative fellowship to establish laws which then all the people together will obey. That idea seemed incredible to multitudes. That the great mass of men could be trusted loyally to say our government—for that is the gist of democracy—was Utopian beyond belief. But the facts were all on the side of the new hope, for human life is essentially built to be cooperative and cooperation is the only way of life that in the end will work.

In family, school, church, neighborhood, state, all progress has consisted in this substitution of cooperative good will for violence. This is the essence of the redemption by which the social life of humanity is saved. And when in our generation the hopes of increasing multitudes begin to center around a cooperative industrial system instead of a continuance of disorder and violence, and around a cooperative internationalism instead of a continuance of world-wide chaos and anarchy, the facts of life are all on the side of the new hopes. Many experiments will have to be tried; blunders and excesses may mark the trail of the advance; obstacles at times may well appear to faint-hearted folk to be insuperable; and always there are some—the belated, the obstinate, the criminally-minded—who refuse to move up into the spirit of the new regime, upon whom force must still be used. But the general mass of human kind are capable of enlarging cooperation, and already mankind has gone too far on the road from force toward fellowship to turn back.

IV

Tolerance, patience, selflessness, faith, courage, fairness, tact, magnanimity—what fineness and strength of character are required by anyone who undertakes to be a cooperator! Many a man finds it far easier to be individually useful. He enjoys the flattering sense of his own munificence, when he as one individual gives service to another. Charles Lamb once said that the happiest sensation in the world is to do a good deed in secret and to have it found out by accident. So does a superior's helpfulness to an inferior prove one of the most personally gratifying experiences which the superior enjoys. It increases his consciousness of superiority. But to be a good cooperator means the abnegation of pride, the esteeming of others better than oneself, the willingness to take a lowly place in the fellowship of common enterprise, the loss of anxious self-seeking in collective enthusiasm. To be a good cooperator involves the possession of a love that suffers long and is kind, envies not, vaunts not itself, it not puffed up, does not behave itself unseemly, is not easily provoked, keeps no record of injuries, bears, hopes, believes, and endures all things.

Even in individual service this spirit of cooperation is indispensable to real effectiveness. A great industrial leader is said to have called to his office a young man in his employ who was going wrong with drink. The employee with shaking knees went up to his chief, expecting his discharge. The end of an hour's conversation ran like this: "My boy," said the chief, "we are not going to drink any more, are we?" "No, sir," said the youth, "we're

THE MEANING OF SERVICE

not!" "And we are going to send each week so much money home to the wife and kiddies, aren't we?" "By heaven, sir!" said the youth, "we will!" To serve folk not only by doing service for them, but working with them, is the very essence of the finest helpfulness.

When one's thought moves out from such individual relationships to the problems of philanthropy, the same truth stands clear. Charles Kingsley once told Huxley the story of two mullahs who came to a heathen khan in Tartary to win his allegiance to their gods. The first mullah argued, "O Khan, worship my god, he is so wise that he made all things!" The second mullah argued, "O Khan, worship my god, he is so wise that he makes all things make themselves!" For an obvious and sufficient reason the second god won out. For, whether with God or man, to work upon another from without is not half so serviceable as to work with another from within. Parental dictatorship in a family is easier than comradeship, but it is correspondingly valueless. Welfare work in a factory, handed down from above, is easier than cooperative industrial democracy, but it is correspondingly ineffective. Munificent largess to a ne'er-do-well is easier than cooperative measures to encourage him in self-support, but only the latter amounts to much. No normal person wishes to be serve by condecension; any normal person welcomes service by cooperation. "If I bestow all my goods to feed the poor," said Paul, "and have not love, it profiteth me nothing."

If the spirit of cooperation is so essential to the finest usefulness in individual relationships, and in family, factory, and philanthropy, how deep is the need of it and how searching its demands if one is to serve the coming of world-wide human brotherhood! No small, provincial soul can ever understand the hopes of international fraternity. The cooperative mind at its largest and its best is needed here. What holds back the coming of human brotherhood is not basic impossibility in achieving a world where reason and fraternity have taken the place of violence and exploitation; it is the provincial mind. All false pride of caste and class and rank, of race and nation, is provincialism, and provincialism is simply self-inflation in one of its most deadly forms. The Hottentots call themselves "the men of men"; the Eskimos call themselves "the complete people," but their neighbors the Indians "are louse-eggs"; the Haytian aborigines believed their island was the first of all created things, that the sun and moon issued from one of its caves and men from another; to the Japanese Nippon was the middle point of the world, and the Shah of Persia yet retains the title "The

Center of the Universe." That is provincialism. When Americans or British or Frenchmen or Germans talk in the same spirit, it is provincialism still, a wretched survival of belated racial egoism—one of the deadliest forms of selfishness known to men.

This does not mean that a man should not love his own people best of all. A man should love his own people, as his own mother, with a unique devotion. Ties of nature are there which it is folly to deny. A man can mean to his own mother and she can mean to him what no other man's mother can mean to him or he can mean to any other man's mother. What is true of mothers is true of motherlands. We are bone of their bone, blood of their blood, bred in their traditions, and suckled at their breasts. We can do for our own people and they can do for us, what no other people can give to us or claim from us. Unique relationships are sacred because they offer the opportunity for unique service.

One primary effect, however, of such devotion to one's own mother should be the making of all motherhood everywhere infinitely sacred. He is a poor son who's sonship does not make him desire to serve all men's mothers. He is a poor patriot whose patriotism does not enable him to understand how all men everywhere feel about their altars and their hearthstones, their flags and their fatherland. Local patriotism should not hold back from but lead to internationalism. He who thinks that loyalty to his family means dislike of his village is a fool. A good family and a good village are fulfilled in each other; so are a good nationalism and a good internationalism the complement one of the other. But it requires a conquest of self-inflation by the cooperative spirit to perceive it. Such a victory over his own provincialism is one of the first necessities for the man who seeks to be useful to his generation's deepest need and greatest task. He must rise above inveterate racial prejudices and animosities, above the scorn that embitters the color line, above the petty pride that is contemptuous of strange customs, strange clothes, strange speech, above the jingoism of perverted patriots. He must learn to say our in friendship and family, in factory and philanthropy, in world-wide sympathy and good will, or else he ought forever to forgo the Lord's Prayer, "Our Father who art in heaven."

CHAPTER IX

NEW FORMS OF SERVICE

Daily Readings

"Truth is compar'd in Scripture to a streaming fountain," wrote Milton. "If her waters flow not in perpetual progression, they sick'n into a muddy pool of conformity and tradition." What is true of man's ideas is true also of their practical expressions. Methods of work change. To print from Gutenberg's movable wooden type would be misdirected energy. Methods of service also change, or, refusing to progress, may harden into set forms which a new generation will find inadequate. In this week's study let us see the application of this general truth to our own generation's problems.

Ninth Week, First Day

Pure religion and undefiled before our God and Father is this, to visit the fatherless and widows in their affliction, and to keep oneself unspotted from the world.—James 1:27.

But whoso hath the world's goods, and beholdeth his brother in need, and shutteth up his compassion from him, how doth the love of God abide in him? My little children, let us not love in word, neither with the tongue; but in deed and truth.—I John 3:17, 18.

Some people still need to see with unmistakable clearness that Christian service is not simply a spiritual ministry to men's souls. A certain type of mind always is tempted to conceive this present life as a short, narrow-gauge railroad, whose one objective is the junction of death where the through express of immortality is met. All questions of comfort, health, and wholesome circumstance upon this present shuttle-train seem negligible. We shall not be here long. To achieve a fortunate immortality is the one absorbing and exclusive aim of religion. But long since it has become evident that the spiritual interests of men are powerfully affected by outward circumstance. "Here then is Africa's challenge to its missionaries," writes Dan Crawford in *Thinking Black:* "Will they allow a whole continent to live like beasts in hovels, millions of negroes cribbed, cabined, and confined in dens of disease? No doubt it is our diurnal duty to preach that the soul of all improvement is the improvement of the soul. But God's equilateral triangle of body, soul, and spirit must never be ignored. Is not the body wholly ensouled, and is not the soul wholly embodied? . . . In other words, in Africa the only true fulfilling of your heavenly calling is the doing of earthly things in a heavenly manner." In view of the plain insistence of the New Testament, is there any other way of fulfilling our heavenly calling in Britain or America?

Pour into our hearts the spirit of unselfishness, so that, when our cup overflows, we may seek to share our happiness with our brethren. O Thou God of Love, who makest Thy sun to rise on the evil and on the good, and sendest rain on the just and on the unjust, grant that we may become more and more Thy true children, by receiving into our souls more of Thine own spirit of ungrudging and unwearying kindness; which we ask in the name of Jesus Christ. Amen.—John Hunter.

Ninth Week, Second Day

I planted, Apollos watered; but God gave the increase. So then neither is he that planteth anything, neither he that watereth; but God that giveth the increase. Now he that planteth and he that watereth are one: but each shall receive his own reward according to his own labor. For we are God's fellow-workers: ye are God's husbandry, God's building.—I Cor. 3:6-9.

Many folk need to achieve in a modern way *this happy blending of dependence on God with energetic work*. For many are still living in the pre-scientific age before the law-abiding forces of the word were so largely delivered into man's hands, and they are tempted to trust God to do *for* them what he is waiting to do *through* them. Before medical science came, a plague was the occasion of public penitence in the churches. Men knew no other help for a pestilence than dependence on God. Now, however, we know that God has put into our hands the means by which, if we will, age-long plagues can be driven from the earth. He is waiting to do through man, by means of the wise and devoted use of law-abiding forces, more than our fathers ever dared ask him to do for man. A plague now ought indeed to drive us to our knees, but in penitence that we have used to so little purpose the powers intrusted to us. A pestilence ought indeed to make us cry to God, but for help to be more faithful in letting him use our dedicated knowledge for the saving of the race from its inveterate ills. A new and massive meaning has come into the old truth, "We are God's fellow-workers." Dependence on God does not mean sitting still: it means in part letting God use us to put at man's disposal all the potential service which is still folded in our new knowledge of natural law.

O God, we rejoice in the tireless daring with which some are now tracking the great slayers of mankind by the white light of science. Grant that under their teaching we may grapple with the sins which have ever dealt death to the race, and that we may so order the life of our communities that none may be doomed to an untimely death for lack of the simple gifts which Thou hast given in abundance. Make Thou our doctors the prophets and soldiers of Thy kingdom, which is the reign of cleanliness and self-restraint and the dominion of health and joyous life. Amen.—Walter Rauschenbusch.

Ninth Week, Third Day

When a man recognizes thus his Christian responsibility to minister to *all* the needs of men, and his further obligation to use in that ministry *all* the powers available, he finds himself faced in our modern world with four new conditions which somehow he handled in the interests of service.

First, the modern Christian faces the *new powers conferred by science*. Whether man is going to wreck himself with these or with them rebuild a fairer world is one of the crucial questions of the coming centuries. Saloman Reinach, looking foward to the Peace Conference at Versailles, wrote:

"At the future Congress, among the seats reserved for the delegates of the great Powers, one seat should remain vacant, as reserved to the greatest, the most redoubtable, though youngest of Powers: science in scarlet robes. That is the new fact; that is what diplomacy should not ignore, if that imminent and execrable scandal is to be averted—the whole of civilization falling a victim to science, her dearest daughter, brought forth and nurtured by her, now ready to deal her the death-blow. The all-important question is the muzzling of the mad dog. Science, as subservient to the will to destroy, must be put in chains; science must be exclusively adapted to the works of peace."

How prodigious a problem is this which the servants of man must somehow succeed in solving, if we are not to be lost! For if we cannot harness science to service, all our vaunted knowledge will come to no better issue than that long ago reported by a disillusioned naturalist:

I the Preacher was king over Israel in Jerusalem. And I applied my heart to seek and to search out by wisdom concerning all that is done under heaven: it is a sore travail that God hath given to the sons of men to be exercised therewith. I have seen all the works that are done under the sun; and, behold, all is vanity and a striving after wind. That which is crooked cannot be made straight; and that which is wanting cannot be numbered. I communed with mine own heart, saying, Lo, I have gotten me great wisdom above all that were before me in Jerusalem; yea, my heart hath had great experience of wisdom and knowledge. And I applied my heart to know wisdom, and to know madness and folly: I perceived that this also was a striving after wind. For in much wisdom is much grief; and he that increaseth knowledge increaseth sorrow.—Eccl. 1:12-18.

We praise Thee, O Lord, for that mysterious spark of thy light within us, the intellect of man, for Thou hast kindled it in the beginning and by the breath of Thy spirit it has grown to flaming power in our race.

We rejoice in the men of genius and intellectual vision who discern the undiscovered applications of Thy laws and dig the deeper springs through which the hidden forces of Thy world may well up to the light of day. We claim them as our own in Thee, as members with us in the common body of humanity, of which Thou art the all-pervading life and inspirer. Grant them, we pray Thee, the divine humility of Thine elect souls, to realize that they are sent of Thee as brothers and helpers of men and that the powers within them are but part of the vast equipment of humanity, entrusted to them for the common use. May they bow to the law of Christ and live, not to be served, but to give their abilities for the emancipation of the higher life of man. Amen.—Walter Rauschenbusch.

Ninth Week, Fourth Day

The second factor with which the modern Christian must deal is *new contacts between races and people.*

When the proposal to evangelize the heathen was brought before the Assembly of the Scotch Church in 1796, it was met by a resolution, that "to spread abroad the knowledge of the Gospel amongst barbarous and heathen nations seems to be highly preposterous, in so far as philosophy and learning must in the nature of things take the precedence, and that while there remains at home a single individual every year without the means of religious knowledge, to propagate it abroad would be improper and absurd." And then Dr. Erskine called to the Moderator, "Rax me that Bible," and he read the words of the great commission in a voice which burst upon them like a clap of thunder. Such a policy of aloofness as that proposed by the Scotch Assembly now would be impossible whether to churches or to states. The world is webbed into one fabric; we cannot longer live apart. In the new contacts lie possibilities of organized fraternity such as mankind never before possessed; in the same contacts lie terrific possibilities of friction, strife, and endless war. In what new and unexplored regions must the old spirit of service in our day become a pioneer!

So, in his smaller world, long centuries ago, Isaiah dreamed:

In that day shall there be a highway out of Egypt to Assyria, and the Assyrian shall come into Egypt, and the Egyptian into Assyria; and the Egyptians shall worship with the Assyrians.

In that day shall Israel be the third with Egypt and with Assyria, a blessing in the midst of the earth; for that Jehovah of hosts hath blessed them, saying, Blessed be Egypt my people, and Assyria the work of my hands, and Israel mine inheritance.—Isa. 19:23-25.

Almighty God, Ruler of the nations . . . quicken our consciences that we may feel the sin and shame of war. Inspire us with courage and faith that we may lift up our voices against private greed, social injustice, the aggression of the strong on the weak, and whatsoever else works enmity between man and man, class and class, nation and nation. Create within us a passion for the reign of righteousness, the spread of brotherhood and good will among the nations, so that we may hasten the fulfiment of Thine ancient word, "Nation shall not lift up sword against nation, neither shall they learn war any more." Amen.—Samuel McComb.

Ninth Week, Fifth Day

The third factor with which the modern Christian must deal is *new wealth*. There never has been so much wealth in the world. We are right in our indignation against injustice in its making and in its distribution, but the fact remains that history offers no parallel to the increase of wealth which the last few generations have created. Nor has the comparative centralization of that wealth in a few hands prevented widespread increase in the general comfort of living for the majority of the people. An average laboring man takes for granted luxuries of which a medieval princeling never dreamed. Now wealth is a potential servant or destroyer of manhood, with almost magical powers. To harness money for usefulness, to create the sense of stewardship in those who possess it, to educate all the people in the ministries to which it can be put, to redeem money from sordidness and to baptize it into the service of God and his children, this is one of the great tasks of the modern age.

Moreover, brethren, we make known to you the grace of God which hath been given in the churches of Macedonia; how that in much proof of affliction the abundance of their joy and their deep poverty abounded unto the riches of their liberality. For according to their power, I bear witness, yea and beyond their power, they gave of their own accord, beseeching us with much entreaty in regard of this race and the fellowship in the ministering to the saints: and this, not as we had hoped, but first they gave their own selves to the Lord, and to us through the will of God.—II Cor. 8:1-5.

Lord of all things in heaven and earth, the land and the sea and all that therein is; take from us, we humbly implore Thee, the spirit of gain and covetousness; give us the spirit of service, so that none may want, but each according to his need may share in Thy bountiful liberality; for the love of Thine only Son Jesus Christ our Lord. Amen.

Ninth Week, Sixth Day

The fourth factor with which modern Christian service must deal is the *new personal equipment of educated folk*. Widespread popular education is a comparatively new thing in Christendom. Not until 1832 did England recognize any national responsibility for popular education or impose on parents any legal contraint to see that their children were taught. Sixty-five years ago in the United States it was still an open question whether state-supported education was wise. We are dealing now with a problem which no previous ages ever faced: a large majority of the people possessed of the privileges and powers of education. And we face in consequence the peril which Froude described, "Where all are selfish, the sage is no better than the fool, and only rather more dangerous." We face the tragedy of unguided and undedicated personal ability. We face the opportunity of harnessing to the cause of service a mass and force of trained skill such as the world never before had at its disposal.

Let not sin therefore reign in your mortal body, that ye should obey the lusts thereof: neither present your members unto sin as instruments of unrighteousness; but present yourselves unto God, as alive from the dead, and your members as instruments of righteousness unto God.—Rom. 6:12, 13.

Thou knowest, O heavenly Father, the duties that lie before me this day, the dangers that may confront me, the sins that most beset me. Guide me, strengthen me, protect me.

Give me Thy life in such abundance that I may this day hold my soul in Thy pure delight. Give me Thy power, that I may become a power for righteousness among my fellows. Give me Thy love, that all lesser things may have no attraction for me; that selfishness, impurity, and falseness may drop away as dead desires, holding no meaning for me. Let me find Thy power, Thy love, Thy life, in all mankind, and in the secret places of my own soul. Amen.—"A Book of Prayers for Students."

Ninth Week, Seventh Day

Such, then, is a modern Christian servant. He knows that the Master would serve *all* the needs of men, with *all* the resources available. He is challenged to new forms of ministry by the new powers conferred by science, the new contacts which make all people one in interest, the new wealth at the world's disposal, and the new equipment of trained personal ability. Finally, into all these he tries to pour the old spirit of self-renouncing love.

Brethren, I count not myself yet to have laid hold: but one thing I do, forgetting the things which are behind, and stretching forward

to the things which are before, I press on toward the goal unto the prize of the high calling of God in Christ Jesus. Let us therefore, as many as are perfect, be thus minded: and if in anything ye are otherwise minded, this also shall God reveal unto you: only, whereunto we have attained, by that same rule let us walk.

Brethren, be ye imitators together of me, and mark them that so walk even as ye have us for an ensample. For many walk, of whom I told you often, and now tell you even weeping, that they are the enemies of the cross of Christ: whose end is perdition, whose god is the belly, and whose glory is in their shame, who mind earthly things.—Phil. 3:13-19.

So Paul presses forward in service, and at the same time harks back to the Cross of Christ, to the love which it reveals and to the self-sacrifice which it demands. Laurence Oliphant has said that our great need is a "spiritually minded man of the world." Have we not this week been pleading for such a character? Alive to the needs of his time and the movements of his generation, as keen as the Athenians not to miss any new thing worth knowing, seeking ever for more efficient methods, as canny and alert in service as a merchant keeping pace with the requirements of business, and through it all shedding the radiance of that eternal spirit of love, most ancient yet ever new, which shone in the Master's ministry—may we all be such spiritually minded men of the world!

O God, the Enlightener of men, who of all graces givest the most abundant blessing upon heavenly love, we beseech Thee to cleanse us from selfishness, and grant us, for Thy love, so to love our brethren that we may be Thy children upon earth; and thereby, walking in Thy Truth, attain to Thy unspeakable joy, who art the Giver of life to all who truly love Thee. Grant this prayer, O Lord, for Jesus Christ's sake. Amen.—Rowland Williams.

COMMENT FOR THE WEEK

I

While the spirit of unselfishness remains constant through passing generations, the forms of its expression continually change. *One of the most fatal enemies of effective service, therefore, is the belated mind,* which while it feels unselfishly has not caught up with new ways in which efficient usefulness must work. Many people of sincere good will are spoiled in their service because they are behind the times; they lack intelligent grasp on present human needs and on present means available for meeting them. To pole a neighbor's stranded rowboat off a shoal is useful service; but to try to pole an ocean liner off a reef, while the effort may reveal the same good intention, is distinctly not useful. A modern ocean liner cannot be gotten off a reef that way, and no amount of willingness to help can make up for lack of knowledge as to how it should be done.

This peril of a belated mind to efficiency of service is grounded in the deeper truth, that much of man's most ruinous sin consists in being behind the times. It is a most disturbing fact that God is not dead but alive. We love to settle down in customary ways; we put our minds to bed and tuck them in. But the forward moving purposes of the living God are forever disturbing our repose and forcing us to move. Humanity settled down on a flat and stationary earth, with the vault of heaven a few miles above, and to that cosmology scaled all its thinking, but of a sudden the flat earth rounded out into a sphere and went spinning through space. God tipped the minds of all the world out of bed that day and cried "move on!" Humanity settled down in a universe large in space but limited in time, created by fiat a few thousand years before Christ, but of a sudden the years gave way to aeons and men saw the long leisureliness of the Eternal unfolding a growing world. God tumbled the minds of men out of their beds that day and forced a forward march.

What the living God does with our minds he does with our *morals.* Polygamy once practiced by the Hebrew patriarchs whose names still are precious in our memory. Paul's phrase about idolatry is true of polygamy as well: "The times of this ignorance God winked at" (Acts 17:30). But neither God nor man winks at polygamy now, and those who live as the Hebrew patriarchs did are put in jail. Slavery was taken for granted in the ancient world; without a word against it as an institution, the Bible in law, precept, and parable, assumes its presence. But the day came when God commanded all men everywhere to repent of it. Under old aristocracy, commercial monopolies given by royal grant to individuals and families were accounted most sacred property, desecration of which was robbery, but now what once was an hereditary right would be looked upon as scandalous graft. Drunkenness once was taken for granted, and with no diminution of public standing or personal respect was practiced by laymen and clergymen alike. But now neither God nor man allows it any more.

A thousand things once thought to be right men now repent of in dust and ashes. What God once semed to condone, we now know that he condemns.

In wide areas of its worst exhibition, therefore, sin means living in the present age upon the ideals and standards of an age gone by. "It was said unto you of old time," the Master repeatedly insists "but I say unto you." The commandments which thus he supersedes are not precepts obviously bad; they are allowances of conduct that in the times of men's ignorance God winked at. "Thou shalt not kill," as a sufficient law of brotherliness; "Thou shalt not commit adultery," as a sufficient law of purity; "Thou shalt love thy neighbor and hate thine enemy," as a sufficient law of mercy; "An eye for an eye, and a tooth for a tooth," as a sufficient law of justice—these old standards and ideals, now overpassed, Jesus discards. One way to be a sinner in his eyes is to live in his new day as though the old day still were here. Everywhere in the New Testament the characteristic sinners are men who thus refused to go forward with Jesus' living truth, who refused to move on with Paul's universal Gospel. They were men of the closed mind and the backward look. How many folk there are who deserve Proudhon's comment on Metternich! "If he had been present when God began to bring order out of chaos, Metternich would have prayed fervently, 'O God, preserve chaos!' " The pith and marrow of such sin is this: *men lack the insight to perceive and the willingness to follow the forward movement of the living God.*

The practical consequence is clear. If, being in fact a member of a moving humanity with a living God, a man acts as though he were a member of a stationary humanity with a dead God, he inevitably falls out of the forward march of man's moral life. What else were the atrocities of the late war? The burning of Louvain was shameful. Yet consider this story from Joshua: "Joshua drew not back his hand . . . until he had utterly destroyed all the inhabitants of Ai. . . . Behold the smoke of the city ascended up to heaven and they had no power to flee this way or that way. . . . So Joshua burnt Ai, and made it a heap forever, even a desolation" (Josh. 8:26, 20). The needless destruction of the fruit trees of France aroused universal indignation. Consider then this Old Testament record: "They beat down the cities . . . they stopped all the fountains of water, and felled all the good trees; until in Kir-hareseth only they left the stones thereof" (II Kings 3:25). Personal atrocities seemed intolerably barbarous. Yet listen to this story of David: "He brought forth the people that were therein, and put them under saws, and under harrows of iron and under axes of iron, and made them pass through the brickkiln; and thus did he unto all the cities of the children of Ammon" (II Sam. 12:31). How horrible was deliberate cruelty to enemy children! Yet the Hebrew psalmist sings: "Happy shall he be, that taketh and dasheth thy little ones against the rock (Ps. 137:9). If, then, we indignantly protest against the atrocious conduct of men in modern war, it is becasue this is twenty centuries after Christ. Conduct which one was thought to be divinely allowed, we now know to be intolerably cruel and devlish.

So does the living God continually force new truths and new ideals upon his children. As General Booth remarked, "You can keep company with God only by running at full speed." Being up to date too often means cheap compliance with a passing fad. It even means refusal to obey truths that being old are ever new, because they never fail. But the perversions of so important a matter as being abreast of the times ought never to cause a Christian to surrender the virtue of it. Imagine a soldier in the trenches who at zero hour decides not to stir. The forward movement has begun but he sits still. Is it, then, so heinous a deed merely to sit still? They *shoot* men for that. So one who stays where he is when the living God has ordered an advance falls under the condemnation of the New Testament. The New Testament throbs with new truths, new hopes, new enterprises, and it called men to its cause who had eyes to see and courage to follow unblazed trails. The true successors of the first apostles have been men of Livingstone's spirit: "I will go anywhere provided it be forward."

II

What the living God does with our minds and our morals he does with our methods of service. The spirit and motive of unselfish living abide, but the machinery of their expression changes. When selfishness fails to conquer a man's generous sentiments, it still may spoil his usefulness by a belated mind. A soldier at Verdun with bow and arrows, however brave he be, is about as valuable as no soldier at all.

The urgency of this fact is evident as soon as one remembers the amazing new powers that modern science has given to men. The gambler, the murderer, the thief, and the Christian alike have new tools to work with which make old methods as obsolete as winnowing by wind. Science has put into the hands of the race such power as the ancient world never dreamed of; what the race will do with it is the question on whose answer the hopes of human kind depend. The one solution of this crucial problem which can relieve the race from the certainty of ruin is that this new power should be used for man's service, not for man's destruction.

How perilous the situation is the last terrific years have unmistakably revealed. Once science was widely hailed as the savior of the world. It is reported, however, that Sir Oliver Lodge, lecturing in his classroom, called the attention of his pupils to the fact that hitherto science has dealt largely with molecular forces, like steam and electricity, but that now science has its finger tips upon atomic forces, such as radium. There is enough atomic force, he said, in a mass of matter no larger than a man's fist to lift the German fleet fom the bottom of the sea and put it on the hill behind Manchester. Then he paused in his enthusiasm. God forbid, he said, that science now should cast its harness over the atomic forces! We are not fit to handle them. Put such a prodigious power into our possession in our present state and with it we would damn the race.

Such a shift of emphasis from confidence in science to deadly fear of it is not unjustified. Science has made liquid fire and poison gas, the submarine and the tank. Science has made guns that at seventy miles can blast to pieces undefended towns. Science has threatened to use bacteriology, at first intended to halt epiemics, to cause them instead. Science has made it possible for war that started with the crack of an assassin's pistol at Serajevo to spread over all the world and to comprehend humanity in colossal ruin. Science has opened the door to financial systems by which nations, waging war to the point of exhaustion, can pledge the credit of many generations yet unborn. Nobel the inventor gave the world dynamite with one hand, and then with the other, Nobel the philanthropist gave the Peace Prize to help save the world from the appalling consequence of the use in war of his invention. The incident is a true parable of our situation. Modern science presents us with a world headed for perdition unless the spirit of service can take possession of the new powers which science has conferred.

III

At first this task seems too immense to lay special responsibility upon the little powers of ordinary folk. But like all large tasks it is soon reduced to fractions, and every worker for the good of men can handle part of it. A serviceable man will indeed catch the vision of a new world in which the increasing powers conferred by science are set to useful, not destructive tasks. But he will also catch the vision of his own life mastered by the same spirit. From teaching a Sunday school class to managing an industry, from tending children in the home to conducting a missionary enterprise, he will seek to belt new knowledge into his usefulness. He will look on inefficiency as sin. He will regard with the same abhorrence visited on all iniquity any willingness to do a good task in less than the best way. He will hate with perfect hatred the slipshod spirit—

All along o'doing' things rather-more-or-less."

In home and school, in church and business, in court and legislature, this is a fact upon the recognition of which great issues hang: usefulness is not a matter of heart alone but of head, not of kind intention but of efficient skill; slovenliness is wickedness and escapable ineptitude is treachery; no man's benevolent feeling can cover from condemnation his avoidable fumbling of a noble task. So says the Book of Proverbs: "He that is slack in his work is brother to him that is a destroyer."

One subtle temptation continually assails all Christian service. Folks suppose that the good will which motives it and the good ends for which it works will somehow assure its victory. The children of light, as Jesus said, are tempted to be less wise in their generation than the children of darkness. Outworn methods that we would scorn in business we employ in church. We use the aptest tools, the latest knowledge to make money; we give it away with spasmodic carelessness, as though it were not one of life's most difficult tasks to give money wisely to the help of need. We know efficiency is necessary in self-seeking; we often act as though service were so beautiful in spirit that efficiency could be dispensed with. But God is no friend of fools. We can no more successfully serve him with obsolete ecclesiastical machinery and methods long outgrown than we can carry on modern commerce with dug-out canoes or clothe the world from family spinning wheels. We can no more heal the sick and feed the hungry by institutions appropriate to our grandfathers' tasks than we could use oxcarts for locomotives.

Neighborly alms were sufficient in the simple life of a Palestinian village. But he who now restricts his ministry to the poor of a modern city to such haphazard giving as may be called out by his personal discovery of need, is behind the times. Organized philanthropy is indispensable and systematic support of it is a duty. To visit the sick and minister to their healing was a sufficient expression of Christian good will at first, but a man without imagination to see the necessity of hospitals and board of health and education in hygiene in modern society has a belated mind. To be friendly with fellow-workmen and apprentices in a home shop was adequate brotherliness in days before our modern factories came. But now that employers and employes do not know each other, often have never met each other, live far apart from each other in sympathy and circumstances, and bitterness grows rampant out of the sundered brotherhood, one who does not see the necessity of establishing on a wide scale new methods of democratic cooperation in industry has a mind like Rip Van Winkle's, a generation behind the times. Sectarian Protestantism was once the servant of liberty and men worked through it for great gains, but he who does not see now the necessity for cooperation and unity among Christians, in the face of the world's present needs and tasks, belongs to a past age and is alive after his time. Kindly feeling alone cannot gird a modern man for usefulness. Alert and disciplined intelligence is indispensable to the largest service. To desire to do good is positively dangerous unless one knows what it is good to do.

No one of us can escape the application of this truth to his own service in any realm, however limited. To "take" a Sunday school class is one thing, to teach it is another. To give money is one thing, to help people by giving it is another. To have friends is one thing, to be a master of effective friendliness is another. To be a father or mother, intrusted with a child, is one thing, to be fit to be one is another. In particular, however, our truth is a challenge to all men and women to whom God has given special gifts of leadership. Blessings forever on that youth, endowed with an alert and able mind, who uses his skill to guide bewildered folk, eager to serve but not knowing how, into wise uses of some new power that mankind possesses!

If mankind's intelligence is once deliberately set to this task of using the powers of the new era for serviceable ends, the vistas are as bright with hope as otherwise they are dark with dread. Men thought the age of miracles had passed, but through the knowledge of law a greater age is here. Possibilities that to older generations seemed Utopian now are practicable hopes: humanity can be saved from illiteracy and poverty, war can be abolished, industry can be democratized, and physical and moral scourges that have afflicted the race through all its history can be eliminated. Yellow fever for ages has been the bane and dread of men. Today the five localities on the planet where yellow fever breeds have been plotted out and now are being stalked by scientists as a hunter stalks his game. Surgeon-General Gorgas said that in the end we could make the yellow fever germ as obsolete as the woolly rhinoceros. Hookworm has been sapping the vigor, destroying the ambition, ruining the characters and homes of men for generations. It is a secret, insidious, debilitating disease, whose consequence is listlessness of mind, body, and spirit. One agency took up the problem; found a simple and absolute remedy; proved its case in experimental localities; and today the leading nations of the world are cooperatively attacking and in time can completely overcome an evil that now makes a belt of needless feebleness around the world. Famines, periodic and overwhelming, concerning which no attitude seemed possible save pious resignation, now are known to be utterly needless. Engineering can reclaim useless lands by irrigation; chemistry can save useless soil by fertilization; scientific agriculture can multiply output; means of communication can make one country's products available everywhere on earth.

Nor are the new agencies less useful to the higher ranges of man's life. Better education more widely given, better philanthropy more effectively administered, better government more ably managed, better churches more splendidly useful—such things are within the grasp of our hands if we will take them. And as for the world-wide Christian cause, Mr. J. Brierley was right: "George Stephenson has as little to do as most men with theology. But his railway locomotive in making the evangelist free, on easy terms with the whole world, has enlarged the religious frontier more than the united labors of shiploads of D.D.'s."

"The moral equivalent of war" has been sought for as though it were difficult to find. Surely not only the moral equivalent of any supposed benefit of war, but the moral cure of war's undoubted horrors and spiritual debaucheries is at hand. To discover and harness for useful tasks the immense powers of our world, to build here in the face of appalling obstacles a decent home for the family of God, is the most arousing task that mankind ever faced. If mankind will but face it in genuine earnest, the stimulus of war will not be missed.

When that leading figure in American philanthropy, Samuel Gridley Howe, left the army of Greece where he had fought for Greek independence and threw himself into a lifelong war against the hardships that oppressed the blind and the insane, he did not cease to be a "Sir Galahad and Good Samaritan" combined. It was this last fight that made Whittier sing of him:

> Knight of a better era,
> Without reproach or fear,
> Said I not well that Bayards
> And Sidneys still are here?

IV

In one special realm the perils of a belated mind can be clearly illustrated. Consider the *financial responsibilities* which in an early American settlement a Christian might be expected to assume! They were few and simple. To support his family, to pay taxes, to contribute to the local church, to help his neighbors in their need—whoever did these well was a good Christian and a generous man. If famine raged in India, he did not hear of it. If Turks massacred Armenians, no rumor of it reached his ears. Or if at last the news did come, of what benefit was that? No railroads, no steamship lines, no cables, no world-wide credit system that makes money fly faster than the wind, were at his service. No possibility of world-wide helpfulness was open to him, no responsibility for extensive generosity rested on him.

How many who call themselves Christians live in this new day as though the old day still were here! They, too, support their families, pay taxes, contribute to the local church, and on occasion give to the neediest cases in their town. That is the limit of their financial output. In this modern world they are anachronisms. They are as out of date as horse-cars on New York City's streets. At least a century has passed over their heads without their knowing it. For one of the miracles of our age is the power it puts into the hands of a man with a few dollars to join himself with other men who have a few dollars, and within a few hours to put the pooled resources of all at work anywhere on earth from the center of China to the heart of the Congo. One marvel of this new era is the romance of stewardship.

When an appeal for money is made in church or town or nation, it commonly is regarded as a necessity to be endured or a nuisance to be avoided. Nor is there any wonder that such distaste is associated with financial campaigns, when one considers the frequent tone of their appeal. You *ought* to give; you *ought* to be generous; it is your *duty*—how commonly are we assailed by such injunctions! yet modern opportunities for money's use are more marvelous and enticing than "Arabian Nights" and more romantic than the folklore of any people. A Christian missionary, Armenian by birth, American by education, was slain by the Kurds on his sickbed in the presence of his wife. His family escaped. Once, no matter how dearly his American friends had loved him, no matter how ardently they had wished for his sake to help his children, they could have done nothing. But in this marvelous era they at once reduce a little of themselves to monetary form, the most portable shape into which human personality can precipitate itself, and in that form they go straightway overseas to Persia and bring back their friend's wife and children to a safe home and a liberal education. One who can see in such an opportunity nothing but duty is blind. Who would not love to play with this new white magic by which a man can put himself at work around the world?

Once in an isolated settlement of the old world of slow communications, a man could hear of cruel need in the antipodes and could go home with nothing but sympathy to offer. Let no man in this modern world express sympathy with any need anywhere on earth unless he *means* it! The acid test can straightway be applied. For we can *do something,* no matter where the need may be. The agencies of human helpfulness now reach in an encompassing network over all the earth. The avenues are open down which our pennies, our dollars, or our millions can walk together in an accumulating multitude to the succor of all mankind. Each of us can take some of his own nerve and sinew reduced in wages to the form of money, and through money, which is a naturalized citizen of all lands and which speaks all languages, can be at work wherever the sunshines. It is a privilege which no one knew before our modern age. It is one of the miracles of science, mastered by the spirit of service, that a man busy at his daily tasks at home can yet be preaching the Gospel in Alaska, healing the sick in Korea, teaching in the school of Persia, feeding the hungry in India, and building a new civilization at the head waters of the Nile. Consider, then, the shame of one who in such an era is still a spiritual inhabitant of an age gone by! Only a man who with generous, systematic stewardship is taking advantage of the new opportunities is fully abreast of his times.

What is true of opportunity for financial service is true of many new agencies for usefulness which the modern world has given us. Once our fathers living under absolutism could not control at all the processes of government; now a democratic state offers new chances of usefulness through citizenship and new obligations to employ them well. Once our fathers, never having dreamed of such an invention as movable type, had neither chance nor responsibility to use the printed page; now the printing press offers a supremely powerful agency of education and evangelization. Once nations, lacking all vital contacts with one another, could become international neither in their spirit nor in their political arrangements; now nations are woven by countless vital relationships into each other's lives and these accumulating contacts offer the supreme opportunity to all history to bring in the day of international cooperation. On every side new powers and new possibilties are put into our hands. The best hopes of mankind cannot be realized save as these new powers are converted, baptized, Christianized, and harnessed for ministry to human weal. A belated mind, therefore, is fatal to large usefulness:

New occasions teach new duties; Time makes ancient good They
    must upward still, and onward, who would keep abreast of
    Truth;
Lo, before us gleam her camp-fires! we ourselves must Pilgrims be,
Launch our Mayflower, and steer boldly through the desperate
    winter sea,
Nor attempt the Future's portal with the Past's bloodrusted key.

CHAPTER X

THE GREAT OBSTACLE

Daily Readings

We are to consider this week the difficulties which the Christian spirit of service faces when it encounters the economic motives and practices common in industry and commerce. There is a strange prejudice in some quarters that Christianity ought not to concern itself with economic questions at all. One would suppose that any system of faith and conduct, if it is to be good for anything, must concern itself with the most absorbing portion of man's life, his toil for sustenance. It certainly is clear that Jesus had more to say about money, its making and its spending, its perils and its uses, than about any other subject whatsoever. Let us inquire, therefore, in our daily readings, what the enormous stakes are which Christianity has in the economic problem.

Tenth Week, First Day

But they that are minded to be rich fall into a temptation and a snare and many foolish and hurtful lusts, such as drown men in destruction and perdition. For the love of money is the root of all kinds of evil: which some reaching after have been led astray from the faith, and have pierced themselves through with many sorrows.

But thou, O man of God, flee these things; and follow after righteousness, godliness, faith, love, patience, meekness.—I Tim. 6:9-11.

No one would deny that Christianity is chiefly interested in the conquest of sin. But sin does not exist in general, it exists in concrete, particular forms, and when one traces to their origin the iniquities that are most familiarly ruinous, one discovers how correctly this passage from First Timothy locates their source. "The master iniquities of our time," says Professor E. A. Ross, "are connected with money-making." It is fultile, therefore, for the Christian individual or the Christian Church to deal in general with a vague, diffused, undefined idea of sin, while all the time the concrete sins of the economic life are ruining men. And it is also futile to attack the merely personal transgressions of equity in business and avoid dealing with the organization of business itself which so often is the occasion of them. Consider this passage from St. Augustine's "City of God":

That was an apt and true reply which was given to Alexander the Great by a pirate whom he seized. For when that King had asked the man how he durst so molest the sea, he answered with bold pride: "How darest thou molest the whole world? But because I do it with a little ship I am called a robber, whilst thou who dost it with a great fleet art styled Emperor."

Surely the Christian cannot so lend himself to discrimination against minor economic sins in favor of great ones. Whoever sets himself seriously to be a Christian and to labor for a Christian world, therefore, must deal with the economic problem, in both its individual and social aspects.

O Thou, whose commandment is life eternal, we confess that we have broken Thy Law, in that we have sought our own gain and good rather than Thy gracious Will, who willest good unto all men. We have sinned by class injustice, by indifference to the sufferings of the poor, by want of patriotism, by hyprocrisy and secret self-seeking. But do Thou in Thy mercy hear us. Turn Thou our hearts that we may truly repent, and utterly abhor the great and manifold evils which our sins have brought upon the nation. Break down our idols of pride and wealth. Shatter our self-love. Open our eyes to know in daily life, in public work, that Thou alone art God. Thee only let us worship, Thee only let us serve, for His sake, who sought not His own will but Thine alone.—M.P.G.E.

Tenth Week, Second Day

Come now, ye rich, weep and howl for your miseries that are coming upon you. Your riches are corrupted, and your garments are moth-eaten. Your gold and your silver are rusted; and their rust shall be for a testimony against you, and shall eat your flesh as fire. Ye have laid up your treasure in the last days. Behold, the hire of the laborers who mowed your fields, which is of you kept back by fraud, crieth out: and the cries of them that reaped have entered into the ears of the Lord of Sabaoth. Ye have lived delicately on the earth, and taken your plasure; ye have nourished your hearts in a day of slaughter.—Jas. 5:1-5.

One has only to read such passages as Matt. 19:24, Luke 6:24, Luke 12:15 f, Luke 16:13 f, to see that James, the brother of our Lord, was true to the tradition which Jesus left, when he spoke these words. One reason why the Christian cannot avoid the economic application of the Gospel is because he is sincerely interested in character; and wealth, acquired as it often is, is ruinous to the characters of those who win it. Two per cent of the people in the United States own sixty per cent of the wealth. If by the poor we mean those whose possession consists only of clothing, furniture, and personal belongings to the value of $400 each, then one man in the United States owns as much as 2,500,000 of his fellow-citizens. That is perilous to the commonwealth but it is also perilous to the rich. When we see a wealthy man, who, honorably fortunate, is as simple in his life and as sensitive in his conscience as when he was a boy, as amiable, approachable, democratic, fraternal, and generous as when his business life began, we have seen one of the most difficult and admirable spiritual victories that a man can win. But consider Henry Ward Beecher's vivid and precise description of the other type, which James also had in mind.

There are men of wealth in New York, honored, because prosperous, who heap up riches, and hoard them, and live in a magnificent selfishness. They use the whole of society as a cluster to be squeezed into their cup. They are neither active in any enterprise of good, except for their own prosperity, nor generous to their fellows. They build palaces, and fill them sumptuously; but the poor starve and freeze around about them. No struggling creature of the army of the weak ever blesses them. And yet their names are heralded. They walk in specious and spectacular honor. Men flatter them, and fawn upon them. Dying, the newspapers, like so many trumpets in procession, go blaring after them to that grave over which should be inscribed the text of Scripture, "The name of the wicked shall rot."

We pray for our land. Let us not be left unrich in manhood. Destroy our ships; destroy our dwellings; but grant that poverty may not come upon manhood in this nation. Raise up nobler men—men that shall scorn bribes; men that shall not run greedily to ambition; men that shall not be devoured by selfishness; men that shall fear God and love man; men that shall love this nation with a pure and disinterested love. And so we beseech of Thee that our peace may stand firm upon integrity, and that righteousness may everywhere prevail. Amen.—Henry Ward Beecher.

Tenth Week, Third Day

Thus said Jehovah: For three transgressions of Israel, yea, for four, I will not turn away the punishment thereof; because they have sold the righteous for silver, and the needy for a pair of shoes—they that pant after the dust of the earth on the head of the poor, and turn aside the way of the meek: and a man and his father go unto the same maiden, to profane my holy name: and they lay themselves down beside every altar upon clothes taken in pledge; and in the house of their God they drink the wine of such as have been fined.—Amos 2:6-8.

Jehovah will enter into judgment with the elders of his people, and the princes thereof: It is ye that have eaten up the vineyard; the spoil of the poor is in your houses: what mean ye that ye crush my people, and grind the face of the poor? said the Lord, Jehovah of hosts.—Isa. 3:14, 15.

The people of the land have used oppression, and exercised robbery; yea, they have vexed the poor and needy, and have oppressed the sojourner wrongfully.—Ezek. 22:29.

How can one say that the prophets of God were not dealing with their business when they were dealing with the problem of poverty? Poverty is not alone a matter of dollars; it translates itself into *sickness, ruined family life, wayward and untended children, cramped opportunity, blasted character.* Consider the portentous meaning in terms of human life of such simple facts as these: in Chicago, in 1914, one person in every twenty-eight was given relief; of every ten persons who die in New York City, one is buried at public expense in the Potter's Field; upward of thirty per cent of the city and town population in England live in extreme poverty; some 10,000,000 people in the United States are habitually below the poverty line. Add also the fact that in Great Britain and the United States the cases of destitution due to misfortune outnumber two to one the cases due to misconduct. Can the

Church pass by on the other side of such a situation?[1] Can the Church content itself with giving alms to alleviate poverty when the conditions which cause it are still at work? Theodore Roosevelt once said: "This country will not be a good place for any of us to live in unless we make it a good place for all of us to live in."

We pray for our own Nation, and for all whom we ourselves have set in authority, and for all true social reformers therein, that crying evils may be abolished, and that peace and happiness, truth and justice, true religion and piety may be established in the land for all generations.—W. B. Graham.

Tenth Week, Fourth Day

Whence come wars and whence come fightings among you? come they not hence, even of your pleasures that war in your members? Ye lust, and have not: ye kill, and covet, and cannot obtain: ye fight and war; ye have not, because ye ask not. Ye ask, and receive not, because ye ask amiss, that ye may spend it in your pleasures.—Jas.4:1-3.

Surely there is no more central interest in Christianity than *the winning of human life to the principle of love and brotherhood.* How, then, can the Christian avoid the economic problem? For the seams and cracks and open ruptures that rend class from class today, and plunge us into endless turmoil and fratricidal strife, all run along economic lines. James is right when he ascribes wars and fightings to covetousness. The very crux of the whole problem of fraternal living lies not in home and church and neighborhood but in the class-conscious strife of employers and employees, in the rivalry of competitive industry, in the avarice of nations for economic advantage. To talk of brotherhood without reference to these crucial questions is to beat the air. Must not the Church, then, take to heart such words as these from Bishop Gore? "This is the first great claim that we make upon the Church, then, take to heart such words as these from Bishop Gore? "This is the first great claim that we make upon the Church today; that it should make a tremendous act of penitence for having failed so long and on so wide a scale to behave as the champion of the oppressed and the weak; for having tolerated what it ought not to have tolerated; for having so often been on the wrong side. And the penitence must

---

[1]Warner, "American Charities," revised edition, 1908, pp. 50-53.

lead to reparation while there is yet time, ere the well-merited judgments of God take all weapons of social influence out of our hands."

O God, the Father, Origin of Divinity, good beyond all that is good, fair beyond all that is fair, in whom is calmness, peace, and concord; do Thou make up the dissensions which divide us from each other, and bring us back into an unity of love, which may bear some likeness to Thy sublime Nature. Amen.—Jacobite Liturgy of St. Dionysius.

Tenth Week, Fifth Day

My brethren, hold not the faith of our Lord Jesus Christ, the Lord of glory, with respect of persons. For if there come into your synagogue a man with a gold ring, in fine clothing, and there come in also a poor man in vile clothing; and ye have regard to him that weareth the fine clothing, and say, Sit thou here in a good place; and ye say to the poor man, Stand thou there, or sit under my footstool; do ye not make distinctions among yourselves, and become judges with evil thoughts? Hearken, my beloved brethren; did not God choose them that are poor as to the world to be rich in faith, and heirs of the kingdom which he promised to them that love him? But ye have dishonored the poor man. Do not the rich oppress you, and themselves drag you before the judgment-seats? Do not they blaspheme the honorable name by which ye are called? Howbeit if ye fulfil the royal law, according to the scripture, Thou shalt love thy neighbor as thyself, ye do well: but if ye have respect of persons, ye commit sin, being convicted by the law as transgressors.—Jas. 2:1-9.

With all the failures of which organized Christianity has been guilty, something of this accent of human equality before God has been retained. Where today do we find the acutest economic unrest? In the non-Christian world? Rather in Christendom, and often in those very parts of Christendom where wisespread privilege has been greatest. Our economic restlessness does not come because conditions are worse, but because, in general, they are better. We cannot educate the people, build schools, erect libraries, print newspapers, and make as widespread as possible the gains of civilization without awakening such ambition for more education, more comfort, more leisure, more equality, in the whole mass of the people as never stirred men in history before. Edwin Markham's "Man with a Hoe" causes no industrial unrest.

> Bowed by the weight of centuries he leans
> Upon his hoe and gazes on the ground,
> The emptiness of ages in his face,
> And on his back the burden of the world.

But awaken in his sluggish, sullen breast even the dim suspicion that seeds are slumbering there which, sunned by fairer economic opportunity, would blossom into education, privilege, comfort, equality, and power for him and for his children, and then industrial unrest will come. Spencer was right: "The more things improve, the louder become the exclamations about their badness." Our very economic problem, therefore, is in large part the child of Christianity's desire and hope. It springs from just such vehement championship of the poor as the Lord's brother felt. And multitudes of Christian business men share that spirit and are trying to work it out in industry and commerce. Christianity cannot evade her responsibility. *The problem which she helped to create, she must help to solve.*

> *Merciful Father, to whom all sons of men are dear, we pray for all that sit in darkness and in the shadow of death, that the Dayspring from on high may visit them; for the poor and oppressed, for those that dwell amid ugliness and squalor, far from loveliness and purity, and for whom the fire-gemmed heavens shine in vain; for those who toil beyond their strength and beyond Thine ordinance, without pleasure in the work of their hands, and without hope of rest; for those who sink back to the beast, and seek to drown all thought and feeling, and for all who are trampled under foot by men. Raise up deliverance for the peoples. Amen.*—"A Book of Prayers for Students."

Tenth Week, Sixth Day

Ye are the salt of the earth: but if the salt have lost its savor, wherewith shall it be salted? it is henceforth good for nothing, but to be cast out and trodden under foot of men. Ye are the light of the world. A city set on a hill cannot be hid. Neither do men light a lamp, and put it under the bushel, but on the stand; and it shineth unto all that are in the house. Even so let your light shine before men; that they may see your good works, and glorify your Father who is in heaven.—Matt. 5:13-16.

These words, usually applied to individuals, have today an unmistakable application to Christendom as a whole. Is she letting her light shine that the non-Christian world may see her good works? *Rather the whole program of foreign missions is inextricably tied up with the present economic and international situation in Christendom,* and our evil deeds often speak louder than any words our missionaries can say. The church's stake in the economic question is immediate and vital. The most critical point in her missionary program lies here: the non-Christian world suspects our civilization of colossal failure and has reason to. The barriers are all down. Calcutta and Peking know us through and through; the islands of the sea understand our miserable failure to be brotherly in business and in statecraft. So an Oriental speaks: "You wonder why Christianity makes such slow progress among us. I will tell you why. It is because you are not like your Christ." Until we can make brotherhood work in industry and international relations we leave a great barrier across the path of all the heralds of the Cross.

We beseech Thee to hear us, O God, for all who profess and call themselves Christians, that they may be led to the right understanding and practice of their holy faith; for all who preach the Gospel of Jesus Christ; for all missionaries, evangelists, and teachers, and for all who are seeking and striving in other ways to bless their fellows, and to build up the Kingdom of God in the world, that they may be steadfast and faithful, and that their labour may not be in vain; through Jesus Christ Thy Son our Lord. Amen.—John Hunter.

Tenth Week, Seventh Day

After this manner therefore pray ye: Our Father who art in heaven, Hallowed be thy name. Thy kingdom come. Thy will be done, as in heaven, so on earth. Give us this day our daily bread. And forgive us our debts, as we also have forgiven our debtors. And bring us not into temptation, but deliver us from the evil one.—Matt. 6:9-13.

How often we say that prayer without praying it! At its very beginning the Master put the dominant desire of his life—the

Kingdom. And he defined what he meant—no superhuman realm of disembodied spirits, but God's will done here on earth. But that transformed earth cannot come without changes. To save the world without altering it is absurd. Wherever Christianity goes, it transforms conditions; it becomes in any land where its disciples carry it a "standard of revolution." Would anybody expect polygamy, human sacrifice, infanticide, cannibalism, to persist where Christian missions go? How then can conditions at home which hurt the children of God be tamely allowed, undisturbed by the antagonism of the Christian people? *Christianity denies its own nature when it keeps its hands off any situation which cripples personality.*

Such is the stake which Christianity has in the economic question. The sins it fights are often born of the economic struggle; the characters it tries to save are often spoiled by excessive wealth or crushed by excessive poverty; the brotherhood it endeavors to further is prevented by economic strife; the very industrial unrest which must be dealt with, Christianity itself somehow helped to cause; its world-wide evangel is hampered by our lamentable economic chaos; and the hope of the Kingdom is a perpetual challenge to discontent with conditions which deny it.

We beseech of Thee that Thou wilt forgive us our selfishness, and our pride, and our sordidness, and our abandonment of things spiritual, and our inordinate attachment to things carnal and temporal. Forgive, we beseech of Thee, our unkindness one to another. Forgive us that in honor we have sought our own selves first, and not others; that we have not borne one another's burdens, and fulfilled the law of God. Forgive us that we have made ourselves unlovely by our evil carriage. Forgive us that we have failed to discharge those obligations of love and gratitude which thy sufferings and thy death and Thy resurrection have laid every one of us under. Open the way of the future for us, that we may walk without stumbling; that we may live with a higher purpose and better accomplishment; that we may not only be forgiven for past sin, but be cured of sin, and of those infirmities out of which so many transgressions spring. Amen.—Henry Ward Beecher.

COMMENT FOR THE WEEK

I

The *giving* of money clearly is involved in effective modern service, but the *making* of money is even more closely interlaced with the problem of a serviceable life. In what sharp contrast with our acquisitive spirit in business, where men compete for profit and where one's success so often means another's failure, does our talk of service stand! We are told to love each other, to desire each the other's good as though it were his own, to let sympathy, magnanimity, generosity, control our thought and conduct. Then we go out into the scramble of our commercial life. Just how can the ideal of service be naturalized in so alien a land as this industrial system of competing individuals, corporations, economic groups, and greedy nations, all struggling for profit?

Two Christians may meet in brotherly love in family and neighborhood and wish each other every good. But if one opens a grocery in their little town next door to the grocery which the other long has kept, how shall they pray for each other when each man's gain means the other's loss? "O God"—will the older merchant pray?—"bless his business; give him customers; open the hearts of our citizens more and more to desire his wares; may each year enlarge his boundaries and increase his patrons and his profits!" One suspects that if Saint Francis of Assisi himself, instead of leaving the world to be a monk, had been a grocer—a much more difficult enterprise—he could not with earnest zeal have prayed like that. "Thou shalt not covet," sounds well in the abstract, but it becomes perplexing when one adds, "Thou shalt not covet they neighbor's customers."

From so simple a situation through the whole *melée* of our industrial life, how much of our business is a constant and terrific temptation to selfishness! Men are tempted to hire laborers as cheaply as possible, regardless of the living conditions imposed by the wages paid, and laborers are tempted to give as slack work as they can manage for as large pay as they can get. Men are tempted to sell goods as dearly as possible, regardless of families thrust below the poverty line by the increasing cost of life's necessities. "I think it is fair to get out of the consumers all you can, consistent with the business proposition"—so testified the head of a great American corporation supplying an article of food without which men cannot live. Men are tempted to knead chalk, alum, and plaster into bread, to make children's candy with terra alba, to put cocaine into popular drinks and chloroform into children's remedies, to preserve milk with formalin, and to sell dried peas and cocoa shells for coffee. And they *do* it, so that in 1906 before the Pure Food Bill was passed the American Secretary of Agriculture reported that thirty per cent of all money paid for food in the

United States was paid for adulterated and misbranded goods.

What appalling selfishness is engendered by our competitive struggle after profits! For money's sake men defraud the poor, so that in a single three months in New York City 3,906 falsely adjusted scales and measures were confiscated by inspectors. For money's sake men make life-preservers that will not float; they practice jerry-building to the jeopardy of all subsequent occupants; they fill our business life with petty pilfering and small graft; they gamble in securities in an organized endeavor to get something for nothing; they make journalism yellow with tales of crime and appeals to sex; they take profiteering advantage of war and coin into cash the bloody sacrifices of the world's best youth; they play on the appetite for drugs and stimulants and make commercial gain from the purposed degradation of manhood; they traffic in the bodies of women; they prostitute the drama to ignoble uses and seek eagerly for plays that, as a producer recently declared with appalling candor, "appeal from the waist down." The meanest, most cynical and unscrupulous selfishness that stops at no cruelty and that feels no shame is the fruit of the economic struggle. The New Testament is right: "The love of money is a root of all kinds of evil" (I Tim. 6:10).

We have spoken in these studies of sacrificial conflicts against inveterate abuses, such as political absolutism, legal monopolies, slave systems, the liquor traffic. What, then, is the sinister power which has made these conflicts for a better world so difficult and has made so laggard and uncertain the final victory? Always the selfishness of vested interests has stood across the path of progress. In New York City a northern merchant called out Mr. May, the philanthropist, from an antislavery meeting and said to him: "Mr. May, we are not such fools as not to know that slavery is a great evil; a great wrong. But it was consented to by the founders of our Republic. It was provided for in the Constitution of our Union. A great portion of the property of the Southerners is invested under its sanction; and the business of the North, as well as the South, has become adjusted to it. There are millions upon millions of dollars due from Southerners to the merchants and mechanics of this city alone, the payment of which would be jeopardized by any rupture between the North and the South. We cannot afford, sir, to let you and your associates succeed in your endeavor to overthrow slavery. It is not a matter of principle with us. It is a matter of business necessity. We cannot afford to let you succeed. I have called you out to let you know, and to let your fellow-laborers know, that we do not mean to allow you to succeed. We mean, sir," he said, with increased emphasis—"we mean, sir, to put you Abolitionists down—by fair means if we can, by foul means if we must."

When the interests of property have been imperiled by humane reforms, that tone of voice has been one of the most familiar sounds in history. Why do so many children still work in the shops and factories of rich America? Why is it so bitterly difficult to pass legislation for their relief, or to assure safety appliances in factories, or to gain decent conditions for women in industry? What was the organized source of power that for years bribed legislators, bought up electorates, debauched the judiciary, and exhausted every sinister method known to human ingenuity to stave off all encroachments on the liquor traffic's exploitation of the people? Macaulay said that if the multiplication table had interfered with any vested interests, some people would not have believed it yet.

Nor is this hardness and selfishness of our economic struggle altogether a matter of personal ill will. Men of generous good will are caught in it, and do not know how to extricate themselves. How can a merchant easily pay high wages and give shorter hours to the girls who serve him, when his rival pays low wages and works his laborers long hours? How can a manufacturer in one state welcome legislation that saddles him with the expense of safety appliances, shorter hours, and high wages, when in a neighboring state his rivals are under no restrictions? Just what shall an honest and serviceable business do when it is held up by a legislature with ruinous bills plainly intended for blackmail? What shall an employer do if, when wages increase, shiftless laborers work only half as many days and live as they did before? What shall laborers do if, working faithfully, they find themselves out of employment half the year? *Whether he be employer or employee, the most colossal difficulty which many a man faces when he sets himself to live unselfishly, is presented by the ingrained selfishness of the economic struggle.*

II

All this, in principle, is familiar to anyone who knows the gospels. The preeminent enemy which the Master faced as he proclaimed his evangel of good will was Mammon. He, too, saw rich young men not far from the Kingdom, held back from whole-hearted service by the love of money (Mark 10:17 f). He, too, saw

Dives lulled into selfish indolence by great possessions (Luke 16:19 f); saw brotherhood cut asunder by covetous desires (Luke 12:13 f); saw grafters even in the temple courts (Mark 11:15). He, too, found his message met by the sneers of "Pharisees, who were lovers of money" (Luke 16:14), and in the circle of his friends he was betrayed by a man with an itching palm.

The Master was not the sponsor of any economic theory. No social panacea may rightly claim the sanction of his name. But he was the teacher and exemplar of the spirit of service, and he found in the economic struggle for money his chief antagonist. He wanted men to possess the heavenly treasures of the Spirit, and they sought with absorbed concern treasures where moth and rust corrupt and thieves break through and steal (Matt. 6:19). He sowed the seed of the Gospel, looking for fruitage in serviceble lives, and the "deceitfulness of riches" choked it (Matt. 13:22). He saw life as a marvelously rich experience, but his passion to share his life with others was balked in those who sordidly thought that their lives consisted in the abundance of the things which they possessed (Luke 12:15). Everywhere he found the issue joined between economic acquisitiveness and useful living, and he stated the issue in clear-cut, uncompromising words: "No servant can serve two masters: for either he will hate the one and love the other; or else he will hold to one, and despise the other. Ye cannot serve God and mammon" (Luke 16:13).

The situation since the Master's day has not in essence greatly changed. What tragedies today befall the characters of our young men and women! Youth is naturally idealistic; it responds to the appeal of chivalry; if rightly trained, it feels the lure of knighthood and desires to ride abroad redressing human wrongs. With such a spirit of service our best youth go out from our schools and colleges, and the saddest sight that eyes can see is their gradual disillusionment, their loss of knightly thoughts, their subjugation to mercenary motives, and at last in how many cases the utter triumph in them of sordid ambitions!

Many of them long maintain the struggle between the ideals of sacrificial usefulness and the actualities of business. They live a bifurcated life. They read the Master's teaching with an approval which they cannot deny; they see in the economic conflict necessities which they cannot evade; and the two do not agree. Finally, however, the balance dips one way or the other. Some deliberately throw over the Christian ethic and become confessedly selfish; some consciously apply one set of ideals to home and friends, to church and neighborhood, and another to business, changing gear between the two, and losing all unity and wholeness from their lives; some become morally blinded by the continual impact of the economic struggle, until they seriously think that our merciless competitive conflict after profits is not unchristian in the least. The last estate is the most helpless. So Bishop Gore cries: "What I am complaining of is—not that commercial and social selfishness exists in the world, or even that it appears to dominate in society; but that its profound antagonism to the spirit of Christ is not recognized—that there is not among us anything that can be called an adequate conception of what Christian morality means."

III

In his relationship with the making of money, therefore, lies for many a man the nub of the problem of a serviceable life. Let it be frankly said that the problem is fundamentally social; that no man alone can satisfactorily solve it in his own life until society as a whole makes economic relationships more decent than they are. In the meantime, however, some obvious duties are enjoined upon the individual by Christian principles.

For one thing, *let a man take both his investments and his personal work away from any business that in its main intention is not useful to the community!* That business and service ever should conflict is the more pathetic, because the basic idea of all good business is to serve the people. A fair bargain is far better than charity, for charity involves one man in want served by a superior, while a fair bargain involves two men on an equality, the exchange of whose goods is a mutual benefit. So Ruskin, summing up the functions of the five great intellectual professions which have existed in every civilized country, says: "The Soldier's profession is to defend it; the Pastor's to teach it; the Physician's to keep it in health' the Lawyer's to enforce justice in it; the Merchant's to provide for it." Service is the primary intention of commerce. And the tragedy of our economic conflict lies here: *the very purpose of business is perverted when service which should be first is put last or is lost sight of altogether.* In war we have seen how indispensable to the common weal are farm and shop and factory, railroad and steamship line; in war we appealed for industrial help not alone to avarice but to loyalty, not alone to greed but to patriotism. Has that appeal no standing ground in time of peace? What traitors are in an army, what hypocrites are in the ministry, what shysters are in the law, what quacks are in medicine—perversions and caricatures of their profession's main intention—so are men in business who have lost sight of their function as loyal servants of the common weal in providing for the needs of men. The first duty of a Christian, therefore, is to desert, with his money and his labor, any parasitic, useless business, any traffic that seeks something for nothing, or that makes profit from demoralizing men. A Christian must at least be conscious that he is in a business upon whose presence in some form the happy maintenance of human society depends.

Again, *a Christian must never in any business be a consenting party to the sacrifice of manhood and womanhood for profit.* When Ruskin had exalted the five professions, with the merchant as the climax of them all, he turned to define their obligation to society: "The duty of all these men is, on due occasion, to die for it. 'On due occasion' namely: the Soldier, rather than leave his post in battle; the Physician, rather than leave his post in plague; the Pastor, rather than teach falsehood; the Lawyer, rather than countenance injustice; the Merchant—what is *his* 'due occasion' of death? It is the main question for the Merchant." That question is not difficult for a Christian to answer. The merchant should die rather than willingly make profit that involves the degradation of manhood and womanhood.

Lord Shaftesury, the great Christian philanthropist, and his allies worked fourteen years to secure a ten-hour bill in England. How widely was he helped by Christian business men, who knew as well as he did that in Lancashire alone, for example, 35,000 children from five to thirteen years of age were working fourteen and fifteen hours a day in the factories to pile up profits for them? Let Lord Shaftesbury's diary answer: "Prepared as I am, I am oftentimes distressed and puzzled by the strange contrasts I find; support from infidels and non-professors; opposition or coldness from religionists or declaimers." "I find that evangelical religionists are not those on whom I can rely. The factory, and every question for what is called 'humanity' receive as much support from the men of the world as from church men, who say they will have nothing to do with it." "Last night pushed the bill through the committee; a feeble and discreditable opposition! 'Sinners' were with me; 'saints' were against me—strange contradiction in human nature." "The clergy here (Manchester) as usual are cowed by capital and power. I find none who cry aloud and spare not; but so it is everywhere." Such records are the disgrace of the Church.

No money can be so spent in charity as to atone for such a satanic spirit in its making. A disciple of Jesus must be free from such willing consent to take profit out of human degradation. This does not mean that he must throw away securities in every business whose policies he disapproves; it does mean that, however his private fortune may be affected, he must by every means in his power fight those policies and that he must always be on the side of any movement which promises more decent living to men and women. To put profits before personality is the swiftest and completest way of denying everything that Jesus ever said. Let a man be a pagan and say so, if he so chooses; but let him not call himself a follower of Jesus, while he forgets the spirit of Jesus: "It were well for him if a millstone were hanged about his neck, and he were thrown into the sea, rather than that he should cause one of these little ones to stumble" (Luke 17:2).

IV

To be engaged in a useful business and to be seeking to make the processes of that business contribute not to profits alone but to human welfare, are the simplest elementals of the Christian spirit in industry. The full flower of even these elemental qualities, however, is plainly impossible without putting the idea of service at the very center of one's business life. Consider what that would mean!

The essence of selfishness is to face any human relationship with the main intent of seeing what can be gotten out of it for oneself. What, then, shall we say of the common attitude toward business? That is one human relationship which multitudes of men confessedly face with the major purpose of making profit from it for themselves. Business as often conceived is the driving of a bargain with intent to win.

Another attitude toward life, however, is perfectly familiar, and in certain areas of human enterprise it is expected from all honorable men. Schubert sold his priceless songs for tenpence apiece. But he did not *write* them for tenpence apiece. He wrote them for the love of music and the joy and pride of fine workmanship. Milton sold "Paradise Lost" for ten pounds. But he did not write it for ten pounds. He wrote it for the easing of his spirit, for the love of poetry, and the delight of excellent craftsmanship. Such men take pay for work; but they do not work for pay. Their life is not a bargain but a vocation; it is not a trade but an art. They would say with a great teacher: "Harvard University pays me for doing what I would gladly pay for the privilege of doing if I could only afford it." They feel about their chosen tasks what Stradivari felt about his violins: God

> Could not make
> Antonio Stradivari's violins
> Without Antonio.

No man's life is fully redeemed to the spirit of Jesus until he has come over into this attitude toward his work. In the Master's figure he must cease being a hireling working for pay and must become a shepherd with a passion for service (John 10:11 f). Note that the shepherd was no musician or poet, no teacher, or builder of exquisite violins. He was doing the hardest of manual work, exposed to all weathers, so humble a toiler that the scribes counted him outside the orthodox pale, since he could not in his occupation keep all the law. Yet this toiler is the Master's figure of a man who glorifies his life work as a vocation and an art, who puts the passion of service into it, who scorns to be a hireling with his eye on payday, skimping his labor and seeking only cash. "You make pretty good hammers here," said a visitor to a workman in a factory. "No, sir," came the swift answer. "We make the best hammers that can be made." There is a man who has caught the spirit of the Master's shepherd. His life is not consumed in driving bargains; he has achieved the professional attitude; he has made a common task into a fine art.

It is evident that in no realm whatsoever is the best work ever done without this spirit. One may write hack music for money, but when Handel in a passion of tears and prayer writes the Hallelujah Chorus, money is forgotten. A soldier may conceivably join the army for pay, but when at Verdun men endure for their country what they never would endure for themselves, something more than money has motivated them. Caiaphas might well be High Priest for pay, but the Master's saviorhood had no such motive. How much money do we think would *buy* Luther to go to Worms; or *buy* John Knox to brave the wrath of Mary, Queen of Scots; or *buy* Washington to endure the winter at Valley Forge? Money can do some things; for the sake of it men have sometimes done good work; often they have done devilish work; but for the sake of it *no man ever did his best work.* Money never manned a lifeboat. Money never sent a preacher into this pulpit with declaration of unpopular but needed truth. Money never gave us railroads or steamships or telephones or telegraphs, for even such things could not have come if beyond the love of money had not risen joy and pride in scientific workmanship. Every discovery of new truth, every advance in social life, all basic industries introduced to supply the needs of men, rest back on lives that loved creative work for its own sake. Wherever one looks, man's life at its best has never been a trade. It has been a vocation.

This is the point of crisis which separates the secular from the sacred. When a minister in a pulpit preaches for pay, is that sacred? It is as secular a deed as the sun shines on. When a woman in the home or a man in business puts into daily life the professional spirit, facing the day's task with the major motive of putting service in rather than taking pay out, is that secular? It is as sacred a sight as God sees. For there are no secular *things;* there are only secular *people;* and secular people work for pay. How scathing is the comment that Gibbon passes on his tutor, who "remembered that he had a salary to receive and forgot that he had a duty to perform." This does not mean that the economic motive is unworthy. It may be one of the most valuable weapons in the human arsenal. Paul says that he who does not provide for his own family is worse than an infidel (I Tim. 5:8). But it does mean that when the economic motive becomes predominant, Christian living ceases. However hard the saying may at first appear, one surely cannot read the New Testament without perceiving that a physician who cares more for his patients' money than for their health; a lawyer who is more concerned to secure fees than to secure justice; a statesman whose first love is his purse and whose second is good government; a teacher who thinks of his salary before he thinks of his students; a minister who cannot sincerely say with Paul, "I desire not yours but you"; and a business man who in his desire for profits submerges his desire to serve the public, are none of them living Christian lives. The spirit of service cannot be given the freedom of all man's life except the quarantined area of his economic relationships. The spirit of service must comprehend and permeate that also. For this is the central heresy, which, so long as it maintains its hold, condemns our economic life to be unchristian, and involves us in industrial bitterness: *business is primarily a means of making wealth for individuals.* And this is the truth, whose recognition and enforcement alone can bring decency: *business primarily is an essential social service to the whole community.*

THE MEANING OF SERVICE

V

Under present circumstances, however, it is impossible to expect the general body of workers in our industries to put into their tasks the spirit of joyful and creative labor. Let a man put himself in their place and see. Workers at minutely subdivided tasks repeating a single process eight hours a day week in week out; workers who never rise above the poverty line no matter how hard they toil, but to whom life is a hopeless animal struggle to sustain a meager physical existence—these are at the bottom of our economic conflict. To expect such folk to put the professional spirit into their work is mockery.

Moreover, one fundamental fact in our present economic situation is the struggle between organized capital and organized labor, and in consequence the dominant note in our economic life is not service but conflict. Here is the description of a master tailor's shop before the modern machines came in: "His shop was upstairs in his home. Half a dozen journeymen and a couple of apprentices squatted cross-legged on tables plying the needle. The master worked with them and shared their talk. At noon all ate at his table, and he cut the bread and served the soup to them with due respect to seniority. When he said grace before and after meat all bowed their heads with him. Downstairs in a tiny store, like a hall bedroom, were a few bolts of stuff." Into this system of home manufacture came steam-driven machines, and in their wake great factories. Home manufacture was forced to the wall. The workers, in despair and hate, mobbed the first factories in England, and before their attacks were ended the legal penalty of death was affixed for destroying a machine. All production was centered then in the factory towns; no one could compete with them; all power was in the hands of the men to whom the machine belonged.

The years that followed are among the cruelest in human history. No one with squeamish sensibilities easily can read the records of the barbarous oppressions practiced on the workers before there was any organization among them for self-protection, or any laws to control wages, conditions of labor, or hours of toil. It is easy now to condemn the evils of organized labor. But if any group of our employers could themselves be put back into such conditions as the laborers faced before the days of labor unions, the first thing those employers would do would be to combine in leagues for mutual defense.

Our industrial life, therefore, has fallen inevitably into the two-group system: organized capital and organized labor. The old brotherhood of toil is broken. The employers and employees are far apart. However much individuals may feel good will, they find themselves arrayed against each other in economic groups from which they cannot extricate themselves. Our industry has become a tragic conflict, in which cooperation is swamped in class consciousness. And so much is human nature alike under all jackets that it is with difficulty that one can discern where the more selfihness lies, with capital or with labor, when either gains the power for self-aggrandizement.

In this intolerable situation only a blind man can recommend the endeavor to turn back the clock to the old days before laborers were oganized at all. Probably the most important movements now afoot in the economic world are experiments where employers and employes are trying out methods of democratic cooperation. *How, without impairing productiveness while the process of change is going on, can recognized channels be established in industry, by which the whole body of workers can have a fair and satisfying opportunity to help determine the conditions under which they live and work?*—that significant question must find reply. A hopeful fact is that scores of experiments are being tried in the endeavor to secure the answer. For the spirit of service cannot control industry, until from out this jungle of broken brotherhood the path is found that leads toward regularly established methods of industrial cooperation.

Moreover, behind these immediate and clamorous questions lie others more elemental still. Our present economic order is an organized denial of the spirit of service, because it involves the right of individuals to own and to exploit for private profit all the natural resources of the earth, and thereby to control the hate of multitudes of people, dependent on those natural resources for the means of their labor and the maintenance of their lives. The extension of private property to mean not simply the ownership of what we use, but the ownership of what other men must use or die, has given to a small group in the commonwealth more control over the destinies of their fellows than was often exercised by emperors in the ancient world. The Christianizing of our life involves the righteous solution of such critical problems at the basis of our economic order.

Until such questions are answered, even the *idea* of applying Jesus' principles of service to the conduct of industry will seem to some utterly unreal. When enforced religion is the established order, it is hard to think that voluntary religion will work; when feudalism is universally accepted, democracy looks Utopian; when judicial torture is agreed on by all as the motive for true testimony in the courts, truth obtained by voluntary evidence seems a dream; when the economic system is built on selfishness, to motive it by service seems sentimental. This, then, is the conclusion of the matter. The triumph of the spirit of Christian service in our economic relationships involves something more than the individual's desire to be in a useful business, to make industry help human welfare as well as create profit, and to put the professional spirit into his work. It involves profound changes in our economic system. Christians will differ, as other men will, about the nature of these changes and the methods by which they should be achieved. But that reforms are critically demanded to bring our industrial life under the sway of cooperative methods, he who takes in earnest Jesus Christ's rightful mastery of all man's life can hardly doubt. And such a man will seek, at any cost to his own profit, to bring those changes in.

CHAPTER XI

THE MOTIVE OF GRATITUDE

DAILY READINGS

Our study has concerned itself with the principles and methods of service which we ourselves are called upon to render. We have not yet faced the considerable fact that a great deal of serving was done before we were born; that our own lives are the children of sacrifice beyond our power to estimate or to repay. Let a man meditate upon the cost of all the blessings he enjoys, let him gratefully recall the burdens borne, the blood poured out for common benedictions which he shares, and he will be the readier to make repayment in service to the race. Consider in the daily readings the frequent experiences in which this backward look of gratitude would steady and strengthen us.

Eleventh Week, First Day

Say not ye, There are yet four months, and then cometh the harvest? behold, I say unto you, Lift up your eyes, and look on the fields, that they are white already unto harvest. He that reapeth receiveth wages, and gathereth fruit unto life eternal; that he that soweth and he that reapeth may rejoice together. For herein is the saying true, One soweth, and another reapeth. I sent you to reap that whereon ye have not labored: others have labored, and ye are entered into their labor.—John 4:35-38.

In service, as in every other activity, days come when monotony makes our tasks seem stale and tasteless. The bane of commonplaceness falls upon our work. Martineau wrote: "God has so arranged the chronometry of our spirits that there shall be a thousand silent moments between the striking hours." Many a useful life succumbs to fag, that never wuld have given in to opposition. Let a man, then, look back! What accumulated labor, obscure, patient, and wearisome, has made possible the privileges into the possession of which we were born! Civilization has grown like coral islands from the imperceptible contributions of innumerable sacrifices. In 1864, when Lee's army was invading Pennsylvania, a citizen of Philadelphia telegraphed General Halleck at Washington to know if he could be of any service. He received this grim reply: "We have five times as many generals as we want, but we are greatly in need of privates. Any one volunteering in that capacity will be thankfully received." We recall the names of the generals who have led the forward march of man. Think today of the privates, of the weariness of their marching, the monotony of their endurance, the patience of their obscure carrying on, to which we are illimitably indebted. Cannot we then add our quota of enduring labor for the common good?

Our Father, unto Thee, in the light of our Saviour's blessed life, we would lift our souls. We thank Thee for that true Light shining in our world with still increasing brightness. We thank Thee for all who have walked therein, and especially for those near to us and dear, in whose lives we have seen this excellent glory and beauty. Make us glad in all who have faithfully lived; make us glad in all who have peacefully died. Lift us into light, and love, and purity, and blessedness, and give us at last our portion with those who have trusted in Thee and sought, in small things as in great, in things temporal and things eternal, to do Thy holy Will. Amen.—Rufus Ellis.

Eleventh Week, Second Day

For it hath been signified unto me concerning you, my brethren, by them that are of the household of Chloe, that there are contentions among you. Now this I mean, that each one of you saith, I am of Paul; and I of Apollos; and I of Cephas; and I of Christ. Is Christ divided? was Paul crucified for you? or were ye baptized into the name of Paul? I thank God that I baptized none of you, save Crispus and Gaius; lest any man should say that ye were baptized into my name.—I Cor. 1:11-15.

Paul had poured out his labor on the Corinthian church, and here, in dissension, they were forgetting their indebtedness to him, were bestowing the credit of their founding and the loyalty of their allegiance on Cephas or Apollos. Let none suppose that this was easy for Paul to bear. He smarted under this lack of recognition. He knew that he was not being justly treated. Few servants of any cause can escape altogether such hours as Paul must have faced when Chloe told him the unhappy news from Corinth. We all like to be recognized and accorded due credit, and *we all are tempted to quit service when we are slighted.* Let a man, then, look back! What if all the unrecognized, unrewarded soldiers of the common good, whose beneficiaries we are, had left their posts because another received the credit that was their due? We ourselves are the offspring of that kind of devotion which Paul put into his work. He did not demand pay on Saturday night or ask for all the recognition he deserved. Cannot we, then, contribute our share of that self-forgetfulness without which the world could not go on?

O Almighty God, who hast knit together Thine elect in one communion and fellowship, in the mystical body of Thy Son, Christ our Lord: Grant us grace so to follow Thy blessed saints in all virtuous and godly living, that we may come to those unspeakable joys, which Thou hast prepared for them that unfeignedly love Thee; through Jesus Christ our Lord. Amen.—Book of Common Prayer, 1549.

Eleventh Week, Third Day

And what shall I more say? for the time will fail me if I tell of Gideon, Barak, Samson, Jephthah; of David and Samuel and the prophets: who through faith subdued kingdoms, wrought righteousness, obtained promises, stopped the mouths of lions, quenched the power of fire, escaped the edge of the sword, from weakness were made strong, waxed mighty in war, turned to flight armies of aliens. Women received their dead by a resurrection: and others were tortured, not accepting their deliverance; that they might obtain a better resurrection: and others had trial of mockings and scourgings, yea, moreover of bonds and imprisonment: they were stoned, they were sawn asunder, they were tempted, they were slain with the sword: they went about in sheepskins, in goatskins; being destitute, afflicted, ill-treated (of whom the world was not worthy), wandering in deserts and mountains and caves, and the holes of the earth.—Heb. 11:32-38.

Such a passage as this should always be read by those who *in their service are meeting with active opposition*. Many a servant of good causes in his community, who seriously proposes the abatement of some social nuisance or moral plague, is surprised at the hornets' nest of antagonism he arouses. Said General Booth in an impatient hour: "The day has gone when the priest and Levite are content to pass by the wounded man. They must needs stop now, turn back, and punch the head of any good Samaritan who dares to come to the rescue." If in such circumstances a man is tempted to be conquered by disgust, let him look back! Of what stuff have the men and women been, who refused to get on with the world but proposed to get the world on? The fire of their resolution was no flickering candle to be blown out by man's hostility; it was fanned rather to a stronger blaze by the antagonistic wind. Beneficiaries as we are of such courageous service, can we not render our share of it when the need comes? Moreover, "the memory of one good fight for freedom or justice gives a thrilling sense of worth for a lifetime."

Almighty and everlasting God, who adornest the sacred body of Thy Church by the confessions of holy Martyrs; grant us, we pray Thee, that both by their doctrines and their pious example, we may follow after what is pleasing in Thy sight; through Jesus Christ our Lord. Amen.—Leonine Sacramentary.

Eleventh Week, Fourth Day

For this cause left I thee in Crete, that thou shouldest set in order the things that were wanting, and appoint elders in every city, as I gave thee charge. . . . For there are many unruly men, vain talkers and deceivers, specially they of the circumcision, whose mouths must be stopped; men who overthrow whole houses, teaching things which they ought not, for filthy lucre's sake. One of themselves, a prophet of their own, said,
Cretans are always liars, evil beasts, idle gluttons.
This testimony is true.—Titus 1:5, 10-13.

What a remarkable reason for setting a man at work in Crete! The people there are bestial, idle liars—therefore work for them! They are gluttonous, sordid, scandalous—therefore, live among them! Surely, before he was through with Paul's commission, Titus must have faced the temptation to be thoroughly out of patience with the folk for whom he toiled. Nor can any serious servant of his fellows escape this trial. People are so often comtemptible; their sly deceits, their hard ingratitude, their characters as weak as rotted cloth that punctures at the touch, fill us with loathing. We are tempted to accept the motto which John Hay, with genial cynicism, has suggested, "Love your neighbor, but be careful of your neighborhood." Yet, before a man utterly surrenders to this easy doctrine, let him look back! If the Christian missionaries that evangelized our barbarous forefathers had lacked Titus's spirit when he went to Crete, where would our civilization now have been? The entire background of our lives from the Cross of Christ to our parents' patience with our wayward youth is compact with the *ministry of love to unloveliness*. Have we no gratitude that will lead us to repay a little on our immeasurable debt?

Almighty and everlasting God, who dost enkindle the flame of Thy love in the hearts of the Saints, grant to our minds the same faith and power of love; that as we rejoice in their triumphs, we may profit by their examples; through Jesus Christ our Lord. Amen.
—Gothic Missal.

Eleventh Week, Fifth Day

The godly man is perished out of the earth, and there is none upright among men: they all lie in wait for blood; they hunt every man his brother with a net. Their hands are upon that which is evil to do it diligently; the prince asketh, and the judge is ready for a reward; and the great man, he uttereth the evil desire of his soul: thus they weave it together. The best of them is as a brier; the most upright is worse than a thorn hedge; the day of thy watchmen, even thy visitation, is come; now shall be their perplexity. Trust ye not in a neighbor; put ye not confidence in a friend; keep the doors of thy mouth from her that lieth in thy bosom. For the son dishonoreth the father, the daughter riseth up against her mother, the daughter-in-law against her mother-in-law; a man's enemies are the men of his own house.

But as for me, I will look unto Jehovah; I will wait for the God of my salvation: my God will hear me.—Micah 7:2-7.

The Bible is not an optimist's paradise. The men of Scripture face black outlooks, meet discouraging situations, recognize frankly the appalling nature of human sin and its consequences. Nor can any servant of mankind in any age go on, wide-eyed to life's forbidding facts, without encountering the temptation to despondency.

> The time is out of joint: O cursed spite
> That ever I was born to set it right!

Yet, consider that all the great victories of the past have been won in the face of just such difficulties. Henry Ward Beecher said once in his pulpit: "Twenty years ago in my most extravagant mood, I could not have dared to say to Christ, 'Let me live to see slavery destroyed'; and yet I have lived to see it destroyed. One such coronation, one such epoch lived through, I should be indeed most unreasonable to ask to live through any more such victories. . . . I shall die before I see commerce and industry fairly regenerated. Some of you will live to see the beginnings of it. But I foresee it. I preach it. My word will not die when I am dead. The seed has sprouted and you cannot unsprout it." *Children as we are of such unconquerable faith and sacrifice, can we not pay our quota in to the world's salvation?*

From being satisfied with myself, save me, good Lord. Burn into me the sight of the Cities of Dreadful Night and the City of Righteousness. As I walk in mean streets, as I am importuned by beggars, as I talk with my friends, let impatience with the world make me patient to serve Thee in any way, however lowly; let discontent with modern life make me content to bear some part of the sorrows of the world. O Christ our Saviour, Man of Sorrows and King of Glory, ever leading us from darkness to light, from evil to goodness, ever calling us and recalling us from earth to heaven, let me count all things but loss that I may be found in Thee, and be numbered among those who follow Thee whithersoever Thou goest. Amen.—"Prayers for the City of God."

Eleventh Week, Sixth Day

But know this, that in the last days grievous times shall come. For men shall be lovers of self, lovers of money, boastful, haughty, railers, disobedient to parents, unthankful, unholy, without natural affection, implacable, slanderers, without self-control, fierce, no lovers of good, traitors, headstrong, puffed up, lovers of pleasure rather than lovers of God; holding a form of godliness, but having denied the power thereof: from these also turn away. For of these are they that creep into houses, and take captive silly women laden with sins, led away by divers lusts, ever learning, and never able to come to the knowledge of the truth. And even as Jannes and Jambres withstood Moses, so do these also withstand the truth; men corrupted in mind, reprobate concerning the faith. But they shall proceed no further: for their folly shall be evident unto all men, as theirs also came to be.—II Tim. 3:1-9.

The prevalence of selfishness oppresses the apostle's spirit. How familiar that mood is! The world seems to us, in our despondent moods, to be degenerating rapidly. We say in our haste that all men are not only liars, but are "lovers of pleasure rather than lovers of God." Professor Gilbert Murray of Oxford tells us that one of the oldest documents known to men—a cuneiform fragment from the lowest, most ancient stratum of the ruins of Babylon—begins with these words, "Alas! alas! times are not what they were!" When this familiar mood is on us, let us look back! What magnificent battles have been fought by folk whose service seemed swamped in the world's selfishness! Through what dismaying times, when all slick, swift schemes for tidying up the world went to pieces, have men, committed to unselfishness, gone on, depressed but not beaten! They ended even their dark visions of human sin on the major note of hope, as the Apostle does in our passage. They have said with Rupert Brooke,

> Now God be thanked,
> Who have matched us with His hour.

All our blessings have cost that indomitable spirit. Are we not under obligation to display our share of it in our own generation?

O Thou Lord of all worlds, we bless Thy Name for all those who have entered into their rest, and reached the Promised Land, where Thou art seen face to face. Give us grace to follow in their footsteps, as they followed in the footsteps of Thy Holy Son. Encourage our wavering hearts by their example, and help us to see in them the memorials of Thy redeeming grace, and pledges of the heavenly might in which the weak are made strong. Keep alive in us the memory of those dear to ourselves, whom Thou hast called out of this world, and make it powerful to subdue within us every vile and unworthy thought. Grant that every remembrance which turns our hearts from things seen to things unseen, may lead us always upwards to Thee, till we, too, come to the eternal rest which Thou hast prepared for Thy people; through Jesus Christ our Lord. Amen.—F. J. A. Hort.

Eleventh Week, Seventh Day

When a man looks back from any position of difficulty and stress in which his service lands him, he always sees behind him men who bore more of the same burden, suffered more of the same ill, overcame more of the same obstacle. He is unpayably indebted for his blessings, to sacrifices greater than any he can make.

Therefore let us also, seeing we are compassed about with so great a cloud of witnesses, lay aside every weight, and the sin which doth so easily beset us, and let us run with patience the race that is set before us, looking unto Jesus the author and perfecter of our faith, who for the joy that was set before him endured the cross, despising shame, and hath sat down at the right hand of the throne of God. For consider him that hath endured such gainsaying of sinners against himself, that ye wax not weary, fainting in your souls.—Heb. 12:1-3.

The fathers who have sacrificed before us may well surround us like a crowd of spectators to watch our contest, for we have in our hands the spoiling or the fulfilment of their hard-won gains. It is idle to suppose that civilization's gains cannot be lost. History is the narrative of one civilization after another that began with promise, rose to its climax, and, failing to learn the lessons of righteousness, fell on ruin. God does not guarantee the perpetuity of our blessings; "romantic belief in some ameliorative drift" is a fool's paradise. Only vigilance, devotion, self-sacrifice, righteousness, obedience to the law of God, can assure us the retention of present gains and the achievement of new advances. All that we have was bought and paid for by unselfishness. Can we not do for others, not simply as we would be done by, but as we have been done by?

O my God, O my Love, let Thy unwearied and tender love to me make my love unwearied and tender to my neighbour, and zealous to procure, promote, and preserve his health, and safety, and happiness, and life, that he may be the better able to serve and to love thee. Amen.—Bishop Ken.

COMMENT FOR THE WEEK

I

Behind the manifest differences between selfish and serviceable lives, there lies a contrast, deep though often hidden, between the ideas of life from which selfishness and service spring. Compare two contemporaries like Napoleon Bonaparte and William Wilberforce. While the colossus was busy bestriding the world, Wilberforce was busy killing the African slave trade. The story of his tireless labors against the villanous abomination is one of the most thrilling tales in history. Rich in fortune, frail in health, beset by bitter antagonism, he waged a philanthropic war that knew no truce and would accept no armistice. On the day when victory came and the slave trade of the British Empire finally was doomed, Sir Samuel Romilly, amid the cheers of the House of Commons, compared the thoughts of Wilberforce as he went to rest with the thoughts of Napoleon across the Channel, then at the climax of his power. The very tombs of the two still advertise the contrast: one symbolic of imperial pomp and pride, the other celebrating the life which "removed from England the guilt of the African slave trade." If one seeks the dominating ideas of life which controlled two such characters, how evident they are! Napoleon looked on life as an excellent place for self-aggrandizement; Wilberforce, as an excellent opportunity for self-bestowal. Napoleon assumed that the world owed him all that he could get; Wilberforce assumed that he owed the world all that he could give. Napoleon's principle was that humanity was under infinite obligation to him; Wilberforce's principle was that he was under infinite obligation to humanity.

Only this second motive is adequate to support such a life of service as we have been considering. But is it true? In what sense are we so under unpayable obligation to mankind that we should pour life out in sacrificial usefulness, and when we have done all, should say, "We are unprofitble servants, we have done that which it was our duty to do"?

II

Plenty of people plainly do not feel under any such indebtedness. They stroll into life and settle down in it, as though all its blessings had been dropped by accident and had cost nothing. They pick life up and spend it carelessly, as a tramp picks up a chance coin lost upon the street, with no gratitude to the one who earned it and with no sense of honorable obligation in its use. They take the liberties, the civic privileges, the cultural gains, the spiritual inheritance of the civilization in which at so late a date they have arrived, and they appropriate it all as though it were their own. They are like citizens who never have seen any flag except a bright new flag, unspoiled by battle. They lack the sobering effect that comes when a man sees a battle-flag, rent and torn by shot and shell and slit by saber strokes—a flag whose soiled dishevelment symbolizes the sacrifice which made the bright new flag a possibility.

How often one wishes that these flippant, easy-going batteners upon the privileges of their generation could be made seriously to face the sacrifices of their sires! While the first World War was on, Professor Gilbert Murray wrote: "As for me personally, there is one thought that is always with me—the thought that other men are dying for me, better men, younger, with more hope in their lives, many of whom I have taught and loved. The orthodox Christian will be familar with the thought of One who loved you, dying for you. I would like to say that now I seem to be familiar with the feeling that something innocent, something great, something that loved me, is dying and is dying daily for me." Shall men feel that once about their own contemporaries, and forget its constant truth about their sires? From the Stone Age until now, lives beyond our power to repay have been preparing for us physical comforts, civic security, spiritual enlightenment and liberty, cultural privilege and Christian faith. What do we suppose all this has cost? One of the most ennobling insights that can come to any man is the perception that no blessing's trail can be traced far back without running upon blood, that at the end of every road down which a benediction comes there stands a cross.

We take our *modern conveniences* for granted until we chance upon some comment like this from Roger Bacon, dreaming in the thirteenth century: "Machines for navigating are possible without rowers, so that great ships suited to rivers and oceans and guided by one man may be borne with greater speed than as if they were full of men rowing. Likewise cars might be made, so that without a draft animal they could be moved with incredible celerity. And flying machines are possible so that a man may sit in the middle turning some device by which artificial wings may beat the air in the manner of a flying bird." What a lavish expenditure of sacrificial thought and energy from that day to this, to give us the most commonplace conveniences of modern life!

We take our *educational systems* for granted, until we run by chance upon such a word as this from Governor Berkeley of the Colony of Virginia in 1670: "I thank God there are no free schools, nor printing, and I hope we shall not have them these hundred years; for learning has brought disobedience and heresy and sects into the world, and printing has divulged them and libels against the best government. God keep us from both!" Who can measure the sacrificial devotion that has been required from that day to this to give school to all the people?

We take for granted our *national security and our inherited ideals of civic life,* until some special anniversary like the Tercentenary of the Pilgrims reminds us of our unfathomable indebtedness. In 1607, thirteen years before the Mayflower came, a settlement of English commercial men was founded at Popham Beach in Maine. It lasted but a single winter. For one winter only did they bear the bitter cold, the loneliness of separation from their homes, the fear of hostile Indians. They had come for money, and all the money that they could get was not worth what they endured. but there was that other settlement that loneliness and bitter cold and hunger and fear of hostile savages could not dismay. Historians say that at Popham Beach they came for money and it was not worth while; but the Pilgrims and the Puritans remained, because they came for conscience's sake and God's. Consider those rememberable words of John Robinson and Elder Brewster: "We are knite togeather, as a body, in a most strict and sacred bond and covenante of the Lord, of the violation whereof we make great conscience, and by vertue whereof we do hould ourselves straitly tied to all care of each others good and of ye whole. . . . It is not with us as with other men; whom small things can discourage, and small discontentments cause to wish themselves at home again." Not a blessing does the Anglo-Saxon race enjoy today, that has not been baptized with the blood and tears of men like that.

How easily also do we take for granted the *innumerable blessings that have permeated our lives because the Christian Gospel has been for sixty generations at work among us!* The

English Book of Common Prayer can now be cheaply purchased, easily used, and peacefully enjoyed. We assume it as a possession of the Christian world, put freely at anyone's disposal. Dean Stanley, however, calls our attention to the strange tautologies which the book contains: "assemble and meet together," "acknowledge and confess," "humble and lowly," "goodness and mercy." Why this curious reduplication of ideas? Because "assemble," "confess," "humble," and "mercy" are Norman French, and "meet together," "acknowledge," "lowly," and "goodness" are Anglo-Saxon. Imbedded in the very structure of the book and strife two races were trying to live together on the Isle of Britain and one Church was striving to put her arms about them both. Here is a true parable of every Christian blessing that Christendom enjoys. The signs of sacrifice are on them all; their trail is red with blood; they come to us every one like Paul to the Corinthians, bearing in his body "the marks of the Lord Jesus." Common convenience, cultural opportunity, national inheritance, spiritual privilege—they are not to be taken for granted. They should awaken the depths of gratitude in every recipient. They have all been bought and paid for with other blood than ours, and with sacrificial toil that we never can repay.

III

Such a grateful consciousness of the cost which other generations and other men have paid for privileges which we commonly enjoy, cannot be left a passive sentiment expressed alone in words. For these men of olden times launched enterprises which they could not bring to a conclusion. They pushed as far as their finger tips could further them causes upon which they had set their hearts; but at the last they had to trust the generations which should come after them to bring those causes to successful culmination. *If we fail, they fail!* They fail as soldiers do who have fought well and fallen, but who have no successors now to press on over their dead bodies and complete the charge which they were making. they fail as builders do, who lay broad the foundations of their temple, but leave behind them children who forget their fathers' plans and neglect the shrine which the fathers had begun.

In Europe there are cathedrals that took as long as six centuries in building. What dreams dawned upon the minds of those who planned them at their start! What ideals may well have thronged the thoughts of those who, midway in their construction, wrought here a graceful spire or there a buttress! But at every stage in the building all the past depended upon the present. The generation then alive could leave to ruin and neglect, or bring to culmination, the things the fathers had conceived. Any sensitive man at work upon the structure during the six centuries of its building, may well have heard his forefathers pleading: Lo, how great a thing we planned! And now the responsibility for its furtherance falls on you; fail us not!

> Our fathers in a wondrous age,
> Ere yet the earth was small,
> Insured to us an heritage,
> And doubted not at all
> That we, the children of their heart,
> Which then did beat so high,
> In later time should play like part
> For our posterity. . . .
> Dear-bought and clear, a thousand year
> Our fathers' title runs.
> Make we likewise their sacrifice,
> Defrauding not our sons!

Sacrificial service, therefore, is not a matter of generosity alone; it is a matter of honor. To be selfish is to be an ingrate. The unserviceble man is taking with full hands blessings that cost toil and tears and blood, and is expending them all upon himself. His lack of generosity is fundamentally lack of gratitude.

IV

To this sentiment of gratitude the New Testament makes its characteristic appeal for service. The distinguishing quality of the Christian motive for unselfishness lies here: *we are expected to live sacrificial lives, because we ourselves already are the beneficiaries of sacrificial living beyond our power to equal or repay.* Now, gratitude, however homely its occasion or simple its expression, is in itself an engaging quality. Capacity to appreciate benefits received and thankfully to recall them is inseparable from fine-grained character. When races are discovered with no word to convey gratitude, no phrase for even the simple "Thank you," and with no apparent feeling that would call for such a phrase, we know that they are in the abysmal pit of human character. But both depth and delicacy of nature are revealed when in human relationships men are serviceably grateful to one another, or when they interpret their religious life as Benjamin Franklin did in his daily morning prayer: "Accept my kind offices to Thy other children as the only return in my power for Thy continual favors to me."

To this grace the New Testament makes its habitual appeal. We should love others because God first loved us (I John 4:19); we should forgive our enemies because we have been forgiven (Luke 6:36); we should lay down our lives for the brethren because Christ first laid down his life for us (I John 3:16); we should love even our enemies because God's impartial care has included us all, just and unjust, good and evil (Matt. 5:45); we should be kind one to another, tenderhearted, forgiving each other, even as God also in Christ forgave us (Eph. 4:32); the law of our life should be, "Freely ye have received, freely give" (Matt. 10:8). Continually in the New Testament one lifts his eyes from an appeal for generous service to see in the background prior service, still more generous, long since rendered us. The Gospel insists that we are under an unpayable debt of gratitude which all our self-denying service never can discharge.

Consider in terms of our personal experience how many things there are for which we never bargained and for which we cannot pay! They are not for sale. They belong to that area of life—the New Testament calls it "grace"—where we receive blessings which we did not earn, are given free gifts of which we must be as worthy as we can.

The beauty of nature is a free gift. We paid no intallment of service down, in return for which God so gloriously furnished the house in which we live. Sunrise and sunset, snowcapped mountains and the ancient sea, elm trees and fringed gentians, white birch trees against green backgrounds, the surf on a windy day, the grass.

> the handkerchief of the Lord,
> A scented gift and remembrancer designedly dropt,
> Bearing the owner's name someway in the corners,
> That we may see and remark, and say, *Whose?*

—all this is a free bestowal to be gratefully taken and worthily used.

The great spirits who have preceded us and through whom God has shined, like the sun through an eastern window, to our spiritual enlightenment, are a free gift. We can purchase the letter to the Ephesians for a few pence, but we cannot pay for Paul. A volume of Phillips Brooks's sermons is for sale, but nothing we can do could earn for us the presence in our world of such a soul as his. We can pay for the printing of Browning's poems, but what shall we give in exchange for the poems themselves or for the personal life from which they flow? A few dollars will buy a seat at the concert, but we can never pay for Bach's Passion music. Such blessings are not for sale; we cannot bargain for them; they are given us straightway when we are born, and we grow up, if we are wise, to be glad that they are in our world and to use them worthily.

Our most beautiful human relationships are a free gift. The first fact in our childhood was not service rendered but service received. We did not pay in advance for the motherhood that bore us and the love that nourished us; all this was poured out freely; we were the unconscious recipients of unselfish love that we had never earned. Home life is thus built on the honor system, where children are first of all served with uncalculating devotion and then are expected in return to live as gratitude will prompt. In some relationships we may work first and be paid afterward; in a home we are paid first with lavish love and afterward make our return in thankfulness. Moreover, all fine friendship and true love are free bestowals. One cannot buy them. They do not belong to the realm of the bargain counter; they belong to the realm of grace; and he who is blessed in possessing them, if he have an understanding heart, is humbly thankful for an unspeakable gift.

Whether we look, therefore, at the social life of man, with its large gains for which our sires poured out their sacrifice, or at our own personal experience, the whole background of our existence is compact with free bestowals for which we cannot pay. To be sure, life is not *all* grace; with other realms of experience differing from grace or conflicting with it our daily lives must deal. *Injustice* is here; we sometimes suffer ills that we do not deserve. *Just punishment* is here; fair retribution sometimes is meted out upon our ill deserts. *Just reward* is here; sometimes we are paid as we deserve for meritorious work. But around these other realms and interpenetrating them is the realm of grace, and the tone of a man's life depends largely upon where among these four realms his major emphasis falls. If he stresses life's injustice, he grows bitter. If he is too much impressed by life's stern punishments, he grows hard. If he relishes too much life's just rewards, he grows self-satisfied and proud. A man of fine quality is of another spirit altogether. He regards himself as the fortunate recipient of countless blessings which he never earned. He knows that he is in debt beyond his capacity to pay, and that therefore, so far from the world owing him a living, he owes the world a life. While some are greedily trying to get what they deserve, he is trying to deserve what already has been given him. He is gracious, because he sees his life in terms of grace.

V

If such a spirit is conceivable in one who is not consciously a Christian, what ought we to expect from one who has entered into saving fellowship with Jesus Christ? For the realm of grace belongs peculiarly to our Lord. He is its representative and master. Grace had been in the world before he came, but as a slender stream flows out at last into its main channel, deep and broad, and takes its name from the place of its debouching, so grace flowed out at last into human life through the ministry of Jesus, and from that day to this its name has been, "the grace of our Lord Jesus Christ."

He knew injustice; upon his brow the crown of thorns was pressed. Just punishment he understood, and warned men that the last farthing must be paid (Matt. 5:26). Just reward he believed in, and promised it to all who wrought righteousness. But the characteristic of his life which determines the flavor of his spirit is the constant presence in his thought of God's immeasurable grace. A love that surrounds us before we are born, broods over our unconsciousness, seeks us in our waywardness, and welcomes us home again as a father greets his long-lost son from a far country, is nothing which anyone can earn. A love which freely forgives when by the very nature of forgiveness the recipient does not deserve it, has no claim upon it, has merited its opposite, is pure grace. A love that opens before us vistas of expectation where

All we have willed or hoped or dreamed of good shall exist;
Not its semblance, but itself,

is clear grace. The Fourth Gospel describes him truly: He was "full of grace" (John 1:14).

Above all, his disciples poignantly have felt that the vicarious sacrifice of life and death, by which all his teaching was set afire in a conflagration that has lighted up the world, involves us in a debt which we can never pay. Sinners cannot themselves bear all the consequences of their own iniquity. Some consequences fall in punishment upon the evil-doers; some fall in unsought tragedy upon the innocent; some are voluntarily assumed by saviorhood when it seeks the reclamation of the sinners. This is the law of grace which runs through all of life, like the scarlet thread through the ropes of the British Navy which shows that they are the property of the Crown. This is the law that Christ exalted and made glorious, when for us men and our salvation he endured in life and death his Cross of vicarious saviorhood.

If, therefore, a man is indeed a Christian; if around his life he sees the generous bestowal of ancestral sacrifice, and in his daily experience feels the benediction of free gifts for which he never paid; and if still deeper he has been blessed by the love of God which Christ revealed, forgiven by his mercy, enlarged and liberated by his hopes, and so knows himself to be beyond computation the beneficiary of the Cross, honor demands of him nothing less than such a life of sacrificial service as the New Testament exalts. The essence of paganism is to see life as a huge grab bag, somehow mysteriously put here, from which the strongest hands may snatch the most. The heart of Christianity is to see life overshadowed by the Cross; to stand humble and grateful in the presence of immeasurable grace; to know that we have already been served beyond our possibility to make return. The inevitable consequence of such an outlook on life is tireless, self-denying usefulness, without condescension, for we are hopelessly in debt ourselves, without pride, for we have nothing to give which we did not first of all receive. Our spirit is Joyce Kilmer's when he went out to fight and to die in France:

> Lord, Thou didst suffer more for me
> Than all the hosts of land and sea.
> So let me render back again
> This millionth of Thy gift. Amen.

CHAPTER XII

VICTORIOUS PERSONALITY

Daily Readings

Granted that service to our fellows is both our obligation and privilege, what has religion to do with it? Might not a plea for service be made from which all mention of God had been elided, and in which alike the motive, exercise, and issue of helpfulness were confined to human relationships? Such questions are frequent in our generation. Mystical experience of fellowship with God and practical service to humankind do not seem to involve each other. According to temperament some are tempted to divorce service from a cherished religious experience, or to divorce religion from a zealous desire to serve.

Twelfth Week, First Day

We know that we have passed out of death into life, because we love the brethren. He that loveth not abideth in death. Whosoever hateth his brother is a murderer: and ye know that no murderer hath eternal life abiding in him. Hereby know we love, because he laid down his life for us: and we ought to lay down our lives for the brethren. But whoso hath the world's goods, and beholdeth his brother in need, and shutteth up his compassion from him, how doth the love of God abide in him? My little children, let us not love in word, neither with the tongue; but in deed and truth.—I John 3:14-18.

The love of God for us, our love for God, and our love for our brethren are in John's thought perfectly mingled. As old John Scotus Erigena put it: "We are not bidden to love God with one love, and our neighbour with another; neither are we instructed to cleave to the Creator with one part of our love, and to creation with another part; but in one and the same undivided love should we embrace both God and our neighbour." The difficulty which many folk have in seeing the need for God in a serviceable life is that they *miss utterly this vital idea of God as a present, permeating Spirit of Love*, the immediate source of all the love there is. Their God is an isolated individual a long way off; he is not a present Spirit in whom "we live and move and have our being." Say "God" to them, and their thought shoots up into the interstellar spaces; it leaps back into the pre-nebular aeons; it does not go down into the fertile places of the spirit, here and now, where, as Jesus said, living waters rise. We do actually deal daily with two kinds of existence: one material, the other spiritual. The central question of all life, then, is this: which of these two represents and expresses the eternal and creative Power? *To believe in God is to believe that our spirits, rather than our bodies, express Eternal Reality.* To believe in God is to believe that all that is best in us is the Eternal in us, and that when we deal with righteousness and love we are actually dealing with God, for "God *is* love."

God is ever ready, but we are ever unready; God is nigh to us, but we are far from Him; Go is within, we are without; God is at home, we are strangers. The prophet says: "God leadeth the righteous by a narrow path into a broad highway, till they come into a wide and open place"; that is, unto the true freedom of that spirit which hath become one spirit with God. God help us to follow Him, that He may bring us unto Himself. Amen.—John Tauler (1290-1361).

Twelfth Week, Second Day

Take heed, brethren, lest haply there shall be in any one of you an evil heart of unbelief, in falling away from the living God: but exhort one another day by day, so long as it is called To-day; lest any one of you be hardened by the deceitfulness of sin: for we are become partakers of Christ, if we hold fast the beginning of our confidence firm unto the end.—Heb. 3:12-14.

Evidently this writer did not think that faith in God or the lack of it was a small matter; clearly he felt the large concerns of Christian integrity and usefulness to be at stake. Nor has our modern naturalism with its insistence that our bodies, not our spirits, are the spokesmen of ultimate, creative power, done anything to mitigate the New Testament's serious estimate of unbelief. One naturalist has given us a candid picture of the universe in which he lives: "In the visible world the Milky Way is a tiny fragment. Within this fragment the solar system is an infinitesimal speck, and of this speck our planet is a miscroscopic dot. On this dot tiny lumps of impure carbon and water crawl about for a few years, until they dissolve into the elements of which they are compounded." On such a world-view, an individual, supported by the social and religious influences of his own and previous generations, may live a practically useful life. But suppose that all men at last shared this world-view, that no man held any other, that this was the universally accepted philosophy of life. *Just how much enduring, sacrificial service for men's salvation and the hope of social righteousness would persist on the earth?*

O Lord, our Light and our Salvation, banish the night of gloom and ignorance, and grant to those in doubt the illumination of truth and of knowledge; that their hope may be firmly set in Thee, and the assaults of malicious foes may be brought to naught. Establish their confidence upon a rock of stone, that, surely grounded in the faith of Christ, they may be built up in love to their highest perfection. Amen.—"A Book of Prayers for Students."

Twelfth Week, Third Day

Beloved, let us love one another: for love is of God; and everyone that loveth is begotten of God, and knoweth God. He that loveth not knoweth not God; for God is love. Herein was the love of God manifested in us, that God hath sent his only begotten Son into the world that we might live through him. Herein is love, not that we loved God, but that he loved us, and sent his Son to be the propitiation for our sins. Beloved, if God so loved us, we also ought to love one another. No man hath beheld God at any time: if we love one another, God abideth in us, and his love is perfected in us: hereby we know that we abide in him and he in us, because he hath given us of his Spirit.—I John 4:7-13.

John here expresses one of the immediate consequences of believing in God. He is assured that all the love in human life is begotten of God, that it has an eternal source and backing, that it is not thin, surface water which by chance has gathered in human lives but that it has behind it infinite reservoirs and ahead of it infinite destinies. So one of Cromwell's men said, *"It was a great instruction that the best courages are but beams of the Almighty."* Granted such a faith, the self-denying servant of his fellows is sustained, as a sentry is who knows that around his humble and often monotonous obedience are the encompassing movement of a great army and the supporting plan of a wise commander. A real Christian is not endeavoring somehow to save a world fundamentally unsavable. He is endeavoring to make his love an open channel down which the Love that is eternal may flow into human life.

Grant us, we beseech Thee, Almighty and most Merciful God, fervently to desire, wisely to search out, and perfectly to fulfil, all that is well-pleasing unto Thee this day. Order Thou our worldly condition to the glory of Thy Name; and, of all that Thou requirest us to do, grant us the knowledge, the desire, and the ability, that we may so fulfil it as we ought; and may our path to Thee, we pray, be safe, straightforward, and perfect to the end. Give us, O Lord, a steadfast heart, which no unworthy affection may drag downwards; give us an unconquered heart, which no tribulation can wear out; give us an upright heart, which no unworthy purpose may tempt aside. Bestow upon us also, O Lord our God, understanding to know Thee, diligence to seek Thee, wisdom to find Thee, and a faithfulness that may finally embrace thee; through Jesus Christ our Lord. Amen.—Thomas Aquinas (1225-1274).

Twelfth Week, Fourth Day

And Jesus answered and said, O faithless and perverse generation, how long shall I be with you? how long shall I bear with you? bring him hither to me. And Jesus rebuked him; and the demon went out of him: and the boy was cured from that hour.

Then came the disciples to Jesus apart, and said, Why could not we cast it out? And he saith unto them, Because of your little faith: for verily I say unto you, If ye have faith as a grain of mustard seed, ye shall say unto this mountain, Remove hence to yonder place; and it shall remove; and nothing shall be impossible unto you.—Matt. 17:17-20.

Faith in God is not simply, as we have said a high philosophy of life, a savior from the hopelessness of unbelief, and a sustaining motive for patient service. *It is also a source of power for positive achievement.* How often does the anxious servant of human weal face mountains that must be removed! Especially in mature years, when with unveiled eyes we long have looked on human life, its sin, its waywardness, its dull unwillingness even to wish a better day, its resurgent evils that ruinously flame up like dead volcanoes come to life again, it is not easy to believe in great possibilities for the race. But with faith in God this conviction always is involved: *what ought to be done, can be done.* If one believe really in God—not in a theoretical analysis of deity but in a basic Fact which makes the universe moral through and through—then he may be sure that *ought* and *can* are twins. To say that what ought to be done cannot be done is a brief but complete confession of atheism; a man who says that does not believe in God.

O Lord, in these difficult times, when there is a seeming opposition of knowledge and faith, and an accumulation of facts beyond the power of the human mind to conceive; and good men of all religions, more and more, meet in Thee; and the strife between classes in society, and between good and evil in our own souls, is not less than of old; and the love of pleasure and the desires of the flesh are always coming in between us and Thee; and we cannot rise above these things to see the light of Heaven, but are tossed upon a sea of troubles—we pray Thee be our guide and strength and light, that, looking up to Thee always, we may behold the rock on which we stand, and be confident in the word which Thou hast spoken. Amen.—Benjamin Jowett.

Twelfth Week, Fifth Day

Then cometh the end, when he shall deliver up the kingdom to God, even the Father; when he shall have abolished all rule and all authority and power. For he must reign, till he hath put all his enemies under his feet. The last enemy that shall be abolished is death. For, He put all things in subjection under his feet. But when he saith, All things are put in subjection, it is evident that he is excepted who did subject all things unto him. And when all things have been subjected unto him, then shall the Son also himself be subjected to him that did subject all things unto him, that God may be all in all.—I Cor. 15:24-28.

The need for a vital faith in God is further seen in such an expression of *hope in final victory* as Paul here presents. On the naturalistic basis alone there is neither hope nor possibility of any crowning triumph of righteousness. On the naturalistic basis alone generation after generation will pour out toil and sacrifice, until at last the sun will grow cold, and the vitality of the physical universe—which to the naturalist philosopher is the only universe there is—will fail. Like an ice-floe from the northern seas, drifting south and melting as it drifts, our habitable earth will shrink. And like polar bears upon the melting floe, hopelessly watching the wasting of their home, humanity will see its inevitable end approach, until it is finally engulfed and lost. That is the only expectation which naturalism can suggest or ever has suggested. But faith in God involves confidence in ultimate victory, in this world or in another or in both. What inspiration to service this means! Any sacrfice is worth while. "He is able to keep that which I have committed unto him against that day." (II Tim. 1:12).

O Eternal God, the Father of all mankind, in whom we live and move and have our being: Have mercy on the whole human race. Pity their ignorance, their foolishness, their weakness, their sin. Set up an ensign for the nations, O Lord, and bring them to Thy glorious rest. Let the earth be filled with the knowledge of the Lord as the waters cover the sea. Hasten Thy Kingdom, O Lord, and bring in everlasting righteousness, for the honor of Thy Son, our Lord and Saviour Jesus Christ. Amen.—"Prayers for the City of God."

Twelfth Week, Sixth Day

For ye, brethren, were called for freedom; only use not your freedom for an occasion to the flesh, but through love be servants one to another.—Gal. 5:13.

Let love be without hypocrisy. Abhor that which is evil; cleave to that which is good. In love of the brethren be tenderly affectioned one to another; in honor preferring one another.—Rom. 12:9, 10.

The Lord make you to increase and abound in love one toward another, and toward all men, even as we also do toward you.—I Thess. 3:12.

But concerning love of the brethren ye have no need that one write unto you: for ye yourselves are taught of God to love one another.—I Thess. 4:9.

Seeing ye have purified your souls in your obedience to the truth unto unfeigned love of the brethren, love one another from the heart fervently.—I Pet. 1:22.

He that loveth his brother abideth in the light, and there is no occasion of stumbling in him.—I John 2:10.

Consider how continuous is the emphasis on serviceable love in the New Testament! But no one can tear such verses loose from their entanglement with faith in God and immortality. These folk who love one another in that first century Church are all intent on strengthening one anothr's faith and deepening one another's spiritual experience. One reason for this indivisible relationship of love and faith is that to the writers of the New Testament the supreme service which love could render to another was the quickening and deepening of faith. People need bread, health, homes; a multitude of practical ministries the New Testament is concerned about; but *above all else people need God,* and to make him real, to illumine the path to him by godly living, to win to Christian trust and spiritual victory an unbelieving man—that, in the eyes of the New Testament, is the supreme service. The Master ministered to men by every avenue of need one could discover; but his supreme ministry lies in his revelation of God, for in that he met the deepest need of man. Men are hungry for this bestowal of faith and confidence upon their spiritual lives. Said Tennyson on his eightieth birthday: "I do not know what I have done that so many people should feel grateful to me, except that I have always kept my faith in immortality." To keep Christian faith, to be assured of its truth, to make it in life convincing and challenging, and to win people to see it and accept it—that is service at its climax.

O Thou God of infinite mercy and compassion, in whose hands are all the hearts of the sons of men, look, we beseech Thee, graciously upon the darkened souls of the multitudes who know not Thee. Enlighten them with the saving knowledge of the truth. Let the beams of Thy Gospel break forth upon them, and bring them to a sound belief in Thee, God manifested in flesh. Bring in the fulness of the Gentiles; gather together the outcasts of Israel, and make Thy Name known over all the earth. Grant this, through Jesus Christ. Amen.—Bishop Hall (1574-1656).

Twelfth Week, Seventh Day

What then shall we say to these things? If God is for us, who is against us? He that spared not his own Son, but delivered him up

for us all, how shall he not also with him freely give us all things? Who shall lay anything to the charge of God's elect? It is God that justifieth; who is he that condemneth? It is Christ Jesus that died, yea rather, that was raised from the dead, who is at the right hand of God, who also maketh intercession for us. Who shall separate us from the love of Christ? shall tribulation, or anguish, or persecution, or famine, or nakedness, or peril, or sword? Even as it is written,

> For thy sake we are killed all the day long;
> We were accounted as sheep for the slaughter.

Nay, in all the things we are more than conquerors through him that loved us. For I am persuaded, that neither death nor life, nor angels, nor principalities, nor things present, nor things to come, nor powers, nor height, nor depth, nor any other creature, shall be able to separate us from the love of God, which is in Christ Jesus our Lord.—Rom. 8:31-39.

What a triumphant personality Paul was! And what a source of triumphant personality have thousands like Paul found in the faith and fellowship of him who said: "Be of good cheer; I have overcome the world." When one asks what religion has to do with service, this answer is plain—*the most useful gift which anyone can bring to the world is a triumphant life,* and the sources of that lie deep in a spiritual experience of God. The fundamental failure of mankind is spiritual; the basic need of man is inward life, abundant, undiscourageable, victorious.

> It takes a soul
> To move a body: it takes a high-souled man,
> To move the masses—even to a cleaner style;
> It takes the ideal, to blow a hair's breadth off
> The dust of the actual.

To give people things may leave them much as they were before; but to have pesonality to bestow, radiant, triumphant, contagious—that not only changes circumstances, it changes *men.*

Religious faith supplies to service elements not easily dispensable: an idealistic interpretation of life, salvation from the deadening hopelessness of unbelief, a sustaining motive for patient service, dynamic power for achievement, reasonable basis for expecting victory, a spiritual message necessary to meet man's deepest need, and resources to make possible triumphant personality.

O Faithful Lord, grant to us, we pray Thee, faithful hearts devoted to Thee, and to the service of all men for Thy sake. Fill us with pure love of Thee, keep us steadfast in this love, give us faith that worketh by love, and preserve us faithful unto death; through Jesus Christ our Lord. Amen.—Christina G. Rossetti.

COMMENT FOR THE WEEK

I

Throughout our study we have been dealing with many ministries of practical helpfulness in which a Christian spirit ought rightfully to overflow. But the most serviceable gift which any man can give the world is a radiant and inwardly victorious personality. The long missionary journeys of Francis Xavier, his tireless labors, his inexhaustible devotion, his fearlessness of the face of mortal clay, have all been celebrated as they deserve to be. But one gains an insight into Xavier's quality which no record of outward ministry can give when he reads the words of a contemporay: "Sometimes it happened that if any of the brothers were sad, the way they took to become happy was to go and look at him." Such service, springing not so much from what a man does as from what he is, is the richest contribution which anyone can make to life.

This consideration at once gives pause to that glib and superficial readiness with which too many people propose for themselves a life of helpfulness. "Ach, man," they say in Goethe's words, "you need only blow on your hands!" Granted a little good will and energy, they think, and anyone who wishes can be useful. But not even such simple ministries as the Master named in his parable of the judgment (Matt. 25:31-46) can in such a spirit be well rendered. To feed the hungry, to clothe the naked, and to give drink to the thirsty are outward deeds, which by a thrust of will can be performed. But how deeply and permanently one will *help* people by these ministries depends on invisible accompaniments which are not to be had by blowing on one's hands. The same outward gift may leave the recipient in one case angry and humiliated, in another cold and thankless, in another comforted and inspired. "When I have attempted to give myself to others by services," said Emerson, "it proved an intellectual trick—no more. They eat your service like apples and leave you out. But love them and they feel *you*, and delight in you all the time." Not till the humblest ministry is thus made spiritually significant by the personality behind it, is full-orbed service rendered.

> Not what we give, but what we share,
> For the gift without the giver is bare;
> Who gives himself with his alms feeds three,
> Himself, his hungering neighbor, and me.

If this be true even of such external deeds as supplying food, drink, and clothing, what shall be said of the Master's next example of helpfulness? "I was sick and ye came unto me." Some strong, successful friend, with years of promising activity ahead of him, suddenly breaks down in health. His capacity to work is exhausted; his plans have crashed in ruin about his head; and you, aware of that, go up to help him "carry on." Is that a ministry to be lightly turned off? Rather you stand, humiliated and afraid, on your friend's door-sill. Yesterday you may have been self-compla-cent, but today you are miserable over your own weakness and futility. God in heaven, you pray, give me a stronger faith, a richer spirit! My friend needs me at my best and what have I to give?

Nothing so humbles a man, so reveals to him the poverty of his own spirit, so throws him back on God for a renewed and enriched life, as the serious attempt to be of use to other people. Christ introduces us to a life of service, and then in recoil a life of service sends us back to Christ and to the God whom he reveals for those full, spiritual reservoirs from which alone life-giving service flows. "Young man," said Tolstoi to an eager, youthful reformer, "you sweat too much blood for the world; sweat some for *yourself first*. . . . If you want to make the world better you have to *be* the best you can. . . . You cannot bring the Kingdom of God into the world until you bring it into your own heart first."

Anyone who is endeavoring to catch the spirit of the most serviceable life that ever ministered to men cannot avoid the fact that quality of personality is the supreme contribution which the world needs, without which any other gift is of minor worth. The Master's care for the poor and sick, his practical service to the physical needs of men, are examples not to be surpassed of tireless interest in the concrete, homely wants of man's daily life. But all these services have had permanent significance for mankind and the bestower of them has taken possession of the realm of service, as its acknowledged exemplar and master, just because all these concrete services flowed from a personality rich with those spiritual goods without which men cannot live.

The ultimate secret of the Master's greatness in service the Fourth Gospel gives us in an illuminating passage: "Jesus, knowing that the Father had given all things in his hands, and that he came forth from God, and goeth unto God, riseth from supper, and layeth aside his garments; and he took a towel and girded himself. Then he poureth water into the basin and began to wash the disciples' feet" (John 13:3-5). What an extraordinary preparation for a very humble act of service! Aware of illimitable spiritual wealth, he took basin and towel and like a household slave washed his disciples' feet. One's first impression is that an immense disparity exists between the Master's lofty consciousness and his lowly deed. One's second impression is that we recall that lowly deed these twenty centuries afterwards, see it still as a symbol of self-forgetful service, flooded with such rememberable dignity that we are always humbled and chastened by its recollection, just because of the lofty heights of personality from which it flowed. The two parts of that passage do belong together. It was the personality behind the deed that made the deed unforgettable. The window of that humble service was very small, but what a radiant sun was shining through it to make it glorious forever!

When, therefore, we have said all that may be said of the Christian's obligation to serve his fellows in every ministry that their most lowly needs require, we must stress this central service which lies behind and gives abiding value to all other ministries whatsoever. Above all else men need contact with personalities who infectiously re-create faith and courage, and inspire confidence in God and man. Above all else the disheartened spirits of ordinary folk, "laggard, fearsome, and thin-ranked," need the rallying impact of men whose vision and faith make them unafraid. A youth, now a professor at Harvard University, once sought Phillips Brooks for an interview on a problem that had long perplexed him. With careful thought he phrased his question that he might surely ask it right. When the long anticipated day arrived he spent a radiant hour with Phillips Brooks. He came out from it transfigured, life glorious again; until at last as he went up Beacon Street toward home, it dawned on him that he had clean forgotten to ask Phillips Brooks that question. "But," he says, "I did not care. I had found out that what I needed was not the solution of a special problem, but the contagion of a triumphant spirit." That is still the supreme need of the world. To supply that need is the richest gift that any man can bestow.

III

Not only does the ultimate significance of personal service thus depend upon quality of personality; the final efficiency of *social service* also springs from the same fountain. We have rightly emphasized the importance to the normal and wholesome life of man of social and economic readjustments. But such readjustments cannot in the first instance be obtained, nor once secured can they be preserved, unless they have their natural source in an inward, spiritual life, whose appropriate expressions they are. Of anything that happens in the social life of man, however vast its range or external its circumstance, the words of the prophet are true: "I will bring evil upon this people, even the fruit of their thoughts" (Jer. 6:19).

What, for example, is the ultimate source of the catastrophe from whose aftermath this generation cannot escape? Politicians will explain the trouble, doubtless with some truth, in diplomatic maladjustments. Economists will explain the War's source, doubtless truthfully, as due to economic maladjustments. But to prohetic insight such explanations are as incomplete as though a man in New Orleans should account for the Mississippi River by saying that it came from Memphis, or a man in Memphis should explain it by saying that St. Louis was its source. They speak truly enough so far as they go, but they have not traced the river back to its ultimate origin. It really rises from many springs far up in the Rockies. So, high up among the mountains of our human life, a prophetic spirit sees, innumerable and obscure, the inner thoughts of multitudes of folk, the quality of their spirits, the emhasis of their desires, from which, as from many fountains blending, flow down the resultant destinies of humankind. No matter how vast the public consequence with which he deals, he traces back the creative source of it to these springs in the habitual thinking of the people.

Behind this generation's cataclysm one sees clearly the group of old ideas, inveterately held, which brought on the dire disaster. That war is necessary, inextricably woven into the fabric of international relationships; that the ethic of good will and cooperation is applicable to individuals but not to states; that economic supremacy can be achieved by organized violence; that nations must always go on raising vast armies, building vast armaments, teaching all their youth to kill, and laying greedy hands on each new invention to make gregarious death more swift and horrible; that war is not only inevitable but desirable, a valuable tonic to man's moral life—such are the ideas out of which our catastrophe has come. And if repeatedly such disasters are not to fall upon the world, something more than new arrangements of diplomatic and economic affairs must be achieved. There must be a widespread, deep-seated, popular repentance of the old affairs as well as in personal character, out of the heart are the issues of life (Prov. 4:23).

So, to a man of insight, the noisy, angry busyness of the world, with its economic upheavals and its crashing armies, often seems illusion, through which as through a transparent veil on looks into the reality behind. And this is the reality: the minds of men and women like inward looms, where the tirelessly moving shuttles of our habitual thinking weave the texture of our human destinies.

The ultimate service, therefore, without which any other ministries are little worth, is spiritual. It consists in the spreading of information, in the teaching of truth, in the inspiration of faith, in the contagious bestowal of clean hearts and right spirits. Lacking such service, all confidence in the mere manipulation of outward circumstances is living in a fool's paradise. An American believes in democracy. Yet many nations, having constitutions like his own, still are the unstable victims of continual revolution. It is not so much the constitution that saves the country as it is the quality of manhood that makes the constitution work. An American believes in the abolition of the liquor traffic. Yet the Turks have lived under a regime where the liquor traffic is forbidden, from the days of the prophet until now, and by that fact alone have not been saved to greatness of personal and national character. An internationalist believes in a league of nations. But he should not forget that such a league will be the most extensive experiment in cooperation ever tried; that it will put an unprecedented strain upon tolerance, patience, good will, and faith; that such forty-story buildings cannot be erected safely on three-story foundations. An industrial reformer believes in more leisure for the workingmen. But he should recall that there has been leisure in plenty in the South Sea Islands for many generations, with little to do save to pluck fruit and to eat in the shade, but that no great consequence for human weal ever came from such spare time. Whether for employer or employe, it is one thing to achieve outward leisure; it is another thing to achieve that quality of character which will make good use of it. We may well be concerned lest, enthusiastic for outward reforms, we in the end achieve them—and get *nothing*. For outward reforms have permanence only when they proceed from, are sustained by, and issue in personality redeemed to wisdom and truth, to God and godliness.

Napleon, so the story runs, was once told that French letters were showing signs of decay under his regime, and that a renaissance of creative literature was needed. "So!" said the Emperor. "I will speak of the Minister of the Interior about it." Creative literature from a department of state! "King Lear," or the "Ode to the West Wind," or "Intimations of Immortality" by order of the Minister of the Interior! Yet one may as reasonably expect that, as to expect creative character from the mere manipulation of outward circumstance. Creative character comes from the deep fountains of spiritual life; changed circumstance gives it free room for utterance. The deepest service that one man can do for others, therefore, is to minister to the spiritual sources of life, inwardly to change their minds, to make great faiths real and great ideals convincing, to establish for them vital contacts with the spiritual world, to bring them into transforming fellowship with Jesus Christ.

IV

Not only are personal and social service thus dependent for their final efficiency upon the quality of man's inward life, but *the persistence of service itself*, in any form whatever, rests back at last upon that indispensable foundation. The streets are full of people who started out to be of use. They, too, had a youth when knighthood was in flower, but they have fallen now into disillusioned uselessness. Like automobiles with good self-starters they were off and away with fleet eagerness to serve the world, but they have petered out in a sandy stretch or have gone dead on a high hill. The Master's thumb-nail sketch in the parable of the Builder fits them exactly: "This man began to build but was not able to finish" (Luke 14:30).

This aspect of the problem of a serviceable life is one of the most serious that men face now, as it was when Jesus was on earth. He was not always met by callous selfishness, that grossly rebuffed his appeal and scorned his teaching. Plenty of people were swept off their feet by his presence, were stirred by swift and eager emotion at his words, but how much of this enthusiasm turned out to be bubbling effervescence! It had no substance in it, no abiding motives to give it permanence. Like seed in shallow soil, as he pictured it, "there was no deepness of root." So to this day the life of Jesus is too alluring, the ideals of Jesus too challenging, the first chivalrous endeavors in unselfishness too rewarding, not to lead many folk to accept gladly the life which he proposes. But the course of true service does not run smooth. People whom we try to help, turn out to be obstinate, ungrateful, incorrigible. They return evil for good. They cling to the very conditions from which we try to save them. The most gracious spirit is at times tempted to cry with Keats: "I admire human nature, but I do not like men." To one who has centered his hopes on social causes, how laggard their progress often seems, how round about and hard bestead is the wilderness journey to the Promised Land! It has been said of Alpine peaks that they pass through three stages: first, "absolutely inaccessible"; second, "a very dangerous climb"; third, "a pleasant summer excursion." But how long do the heights of social reformation have to wait before they thus are climbed and conquered!

The upshot of it is that of all who start to live lives of Christian service, one suspects that only a small proportion carry through. Launchings are a gala sight. Amid cheers and music the ship, gay with color, takes to the sea. But every old salt knows that launching is not the test of a ship. When northeasters howl and billows roll mast high, will she beat up against the tempest and make port when other ships go down? Such is the severe strain to which man's wickedness, ignorance, thanklessness, his sluggishness, blindness, apathy, subject a life of service. *The final resorce of a serviceable man must be his own inwardly victorious spirit, sustained by motives which wear well, but unsmothered faiths, and by hopes which refuse to grow dim.* Only a personality so equipped can easily see through to a triumphant close a life of sustained and sacrificial ministry.

V

With the ultimate efficiency and the abiding power of personal and social service thus depending upon inward spiritual resources, it is plain that not only does Christianity overflow in usefulness, but usefulness has need of all those sustaining and life-giving Christian faiths by which spiritual victory is gained in the souls of men. The final tragedy in human life is not physical poverty but whipped spirits, and whipped spirits are found on avenues as well as valleys, in palaces as well as hovels, in universities as well as barrooms. Men are beaten in spirit by the hugeness of the physical universe, until they think of it as a vast, pitiless machine, without spiritual origin, meaning, purpose, or destiny. Men are beaten by trouble until, maimed at the very center of their lives, they crawl through existence without God and without hope. Men are beaten in spirit by sin, and like dogs that return to lick the hand that flogged them, these bewitched souls come back again and again to the transgressions that are their ruin. Men are beaten in spirit by hopelessness, until they look out on the social life of man with no enthusiasm for any cause and with no expectation of any betterment.

Service to these victims of spiritual disillusionment, infidelity, and hopelessness cannot be rendered by man's fingers only. No *thing* that can be given greatly helps. Only spirits who are themselves victorious can minister to these deepest needs of men. Alice Freeman Palmer, second president of Wellesley College, was once reproved because she did not do more public lecturing; to which, out of her passion for personal service, she replied: "It is people that count. You want to put yourself into people; they touch other people; these, others still, and so you go on working forever." We easily applaud that program of service by personal contagion. But we may well inquire what richness of personality we possess that the world should greatly care whether or not we put our *selves* into people. How many who eagerly give themselves, have selves to give, so poor in quality, that for all their busyness the world is none the richer! The Master looked on service as too deep and inward an enterprise lightly to be undertaken. *"For their sakes,"* he said *"I sanctify myself."*

Sir Bartle Frere was coming to visit a Scotch home. The master of the household, sending a servant to meet him, sought for some description by which the visitor might easily be recognized. "When the train comes in," he said at last to the servant, "you will see *a tall gentleman, helping somebody.*" That, in parable, is the Christian ideal. Over these sixty generations one Figure has towered, from the fascination and dominance of whose pesonality mankind never can esape. Height and helpfulness in him were perfectly combined. And the world has come to recognize his spirit, living again on earth, whenever there appears spiritual altitude blending with lowly service—a tall gentleman, helping somebody.

The issue of this line of thought, however, is not a life which seeks *first* to be right and *then* to go out to serve. Victorious personality and practical service cannot be so chronologically arranged. They grow together, are mutually influential, are indispensable each to the other's health and wholeness. As one reads the New Testament he becoms aware that the Epistle to the Hebrews (6:4, 5) gives a true description of the fully Christian life of the first generation, and that the climax of this description is the gist of the matter: those first Christians had "tasted . . . the powers of the age to come." They believed in a new day of righteousness to appear upon the erth, when God's long-maturing plans would come to glorious fulfilment. That coming age they love, to its ideals they were devoted, for it they would die. They were patriots for a day not yet arrived.

One outstanding distinction, therefore, between Christians and non-Christians in the first generation lay here: like Demas, non-Christians "loved this present age" (II Tim. 4:10), with all its unconquered evil, while the followers of Jesus were working and waiting for the age to come. If one would be a Christian, then, he must in this sense be a revolutionist: he must have his heart set on a new order of humanity where godliness, righteousness, and brotherhood shall have superseded the reign of bitterness and wrath. He must believe in, pray for, and labor toward the coming of God's Kingdom in the world. This is the central passion of a fully Christian life, its guiding star, its regulating standard.

If that supreme patriotism for a better world, divinely ordered, "rooted and grounded in love," once does take intelligent possession of a human life, impressive consequences are certain: personal penitence for sin that hinders the Kingdom's coming, personal desire for inward life worthy of the Kingdom's ideals, personal entrance into secrets of spiritual power by which alone the Kingdom's coming is assured, personal devotion to every good cause by which the day of Christian triumph is hastened. Victorious personality is not the fruit of cloistered piety. It is the accompaniment of full devotion to God's Kingdom:

> I ask no heaven till earth be Thine;
> No glory crown while work of mine
> Remaineth here.

When earth shall shine among the stars,
Her sins wiped out, her captives free,
Her voice a music unto Thee,
For crown, more work give Thou to me.
Lord, here am I!